Shipwreck in the Early Modern Hispanic World

Campos Ibéricos
Bucknell Studies in Iberian Literatures and Cultures

Series Editors
Isabel Cuñado, Bucknell University
Jason McCloskey, Bucknell University

Campos Ibéricos is a series of monographs and edited volumes that focuses on the literary and cultural traditions of Spain in all of its rich historical, social, and linguistic diversity. The series provides a space for interdisciplinary and theoretical scholarship exploring the intersections between literature, culture, the arts, and media from medieval to contemporary Iberia. Studies on all authors, texts, and cultural phenomena are welcome and works on understudied writers and genres are specially sought.

Titles in the Series

Carrie L. Ruiz and Elena Rodríguez-Guridi, eds., *Shipwreck in the Early Modern Hispanic World*

Joan L. Brown, *Calila: The Later Novels of Carmen Martín Gaite*

Andrés Lema-Hincapié and Conxita Domènech, eds., *Indiscreet Fantasies: Iberian Queer Cinema*

Katie J. Vater, *Between Market and Myth: The Spanish Artist Novel in the Post-Transition, 1992–2014*

Shipwreck in the Early Modern Hispanic World

EDITED BY
CARRIE L. RUIZ
ELENA RODRÍGUEZ-GURIDI
Foreword by Josiah Blackmore

Bucknell UNIVERSITY | UNIVERSITY PRESS

LEWISBURG, PENNSYLVANIA

Library of Congress Cataloging-in-Publication Data

Names: Ruiz, Carrie L., editor. | Rodríguez-Guridi, Elena, editor. |
   Blackmore, Josiah, 1959– writer of foreword.
Title: Shipwreck in the early modern Hispanic world / edited by
   Carrie L. Ruiz and Elena Rodríguez-Guridi ; foreword by Josiah Blackmore.
Description: Lewisburg, Pennsylvania : Bucknell University Press, [2022] |
   Series: Campos ibéricos: Bucknell studies in Iberian literatures and cultures |
   Includes bibliographical references and index.
Identifiers: LCCN 2021017550 | ISBN 9781684483709 (paperback ; alk. paper) |
   ISBN 9781684483716 (hardback ; alk. paper) | ISBN 9781684483723 (epub) |
   ISBN 9781684483730 (mobi) | ISBN 9781684483747 (pdf)
Subjects: LCSH: Shipwrecks in literature. | Spanish literature—Classical period,
   1500–1700—History and criticism. | Spanish literature—Social aspects—
   16th century. | Spanish literature—Social aspects—17th century. |
   LCGFT: Literary criticism. | Essays.
Classification: LCC PQ6066 .S46 2022 | DDC 860.9/32162—dc23
LC record available at https://lccn.loc.gov/2021017550

A British Cataloging-in-Publication record for this book is available from the British Library.

www.bucknelluniversitypress.org

Distributed worldwide by Rutgers University Press

Manufactured in the United States of America

Contents

    and Decline in the Spanish Global Empire   109
    Ana M. Rodríguez-Rodríguez

8   The Shipwreck of the Manila Galleon *San Felipe*
    in Seventeenth-Century Histories and Accounts
    on Japan   122
    Noemí Martín Santo

    Bibliography   141
    Notes on Contributors   155
    Index   159

Foreword

Shipwrecks are restless. They have a habit of resurfacing: remnants of a ship or its cargo wash ashore years or centuries after the disaster, from which a story or a tentative explanation is pieced together. The story of a wreck, unlike the unfortunate vessel, never sinks, because to find ways of making sense of disaster is one way of attenuating the tragic loss inherent in calamity. In seafaring life, the wreck is always there; if not realized, then always *in potentia* along the route, in dangerous waters or in the next storm. To write a shipwreck tale is to confront the wreck, to interrogate it, to squeeze meaning out of it. The tale teller, in selecting which aspects of the wreck, its effects, or the circumstances of its occurrence to include in the narrative, participates in cultural values and perspectives that transcend the immediacy of the disaster.

In the history of nations with an established practice of oceanic voyaging—here, early modern Spain and the wider Hispanic world—shipwrecks are part of a collective imagination and infuse an array of literary, scientific, historical, and theological strains of thought and modes of textual expression. For a seafaring nation, shipwrecks are big semiotic business, and the value of their place in culture cannot be underestimated. Spain and Portugal are exemplary in this regard. Shipwreck is such a ubiquitous and polysemous component of Iberian (imperial) seafaring and the intellectual cultures that surround it that, as Elena Rodríguez-Guridi and Carrie L. Ruiz point out in their introduction to this volume, it is nothing less than "a central element in the epistemology of the era" and a reality informed by a "variety of ideological criteria." The rich variety of methodologies, intellectual traditions, contexts, critical approaches, and textual sources in the eight chapters in this collection amply demonstrate Rodríguez-Guridi's and Ruiz's assertion. The scholarly variety of these studies makes a telling statement about the hermeneutic appeal and flexibility of shipwreck, which is as vast and wide as the geographic expanses contained in the pages that follow—from Europe and the Atlantic Ocean to the Americas, the Pacific Ocean, and Asia.

Despite the pervasiveness of shipwreck—as theme, symbol, metaphor, allegory, epistemology, and motor of encounter—in early modern writings and lived experience, no single volume has yet addressed this persistent component of maritime life and imagination in the context of Spain and its overseas pursuits. As part of the mentality of seafaring (and inevitably, but not exclusively, imperial) voyagers, or of those who embrace the realities and metaphors of maritime existence in their writings, shipwreck occupies a prominent place in the conceptual toolbox with which these travelers and writers shaped perceptions of a rapidly expanding globe. It was also a means—as is the case with a figure like Luis de Góngora—for a writer or poet to work at the limits of the literary imagination and to connect with or appropriate aspects of inherited literary traditions. *Shipwreck in the Early Modern Hispanic World* is a major contribution to the field of shipwreck studies and for students and scholars interested in the evolving discipline of the maritime humanities, in which seas and oceans as an object of cultural study reveal affinities and porosities between traditionally discrete modes of thought, such as cosmography and poetry, cartography and historiography, or geography and theology. The essays collected here move between close (literary) analysis, historical specificity, and theoretical postulation and implicitly yet forcefully suggest that, to come to hermeneutic terms with a temporally distant seafaring culture, we must always come to terms with shipwreck.

Josiah Blackmore
Harvard University

Shipwreck in the Early Modern Hispanic World

Introduction

Carrie L. Ruiz and Elena Rodríguez-Guridi

Shipwreck in the Early Modern Hispanic World focuses on the portrayal of nautical disasters in sixteenth- and seventeenth-century Spanish literature and culture and addresses the ways in which the shipwreck motif is inscribed in a larger imaginary that stems from a specific social milieu related to maritime expansion, mercantile interests, and warfare. Indeed, the sixteenth and seventeenth centuries represent the epoch that revolved most heavily around the seafaring enterprise in the history of the Hispanic world. At this peak of maritime activity, the shipwreck motif permeated the entire sociocultural environment. Within this context, the chapters in this book explore the reformulation of the literary tradition of the shipwreck topos within the specific milieu of the Spanish Empire to offer a more global picture of the early modern colonial enterprise. These studies reveal how the symbolic implications of the shipwreck thematic motif operate at multiple levels to question imperial expansion and transoceanic trade, comment on the Christian enterprise overseas, and symbolize the collapse of the dominant social order. The implementation of this motif frequently serves to problematize imperial discourse, but it also functions as a didactic tool to transmit moral messages as well as to reflect the sociopolitical debates of the time. In sum, we contend that shipwreck is a central element in the epistemology of the era. As such, it offers a rich and complex perspective on the fertile oceanic culture of the sixteenth and seventeenth centuries that merits an in-depth analytical approach. Moreover, this volume comes in a timely manner as we commemorate the five-hundred-year anniversary of the first circumnavigation of the globe by Juan Sebastián Elcano and Ferdinand Magellan. This is an opportune moment to explore the role of shipwreck and all of its interstices in Spanish early modern cultural productions.

Despite the centrality of maritime trade and expansion in the Hispanic world during this period and the significance of the ocean in Western art and literature, relatively little has been published on this theme in relation to the Spanish Empire and its transoceanic enterprise. To the best of our knowledge, until now no book-length publication has analyzed the significance of shipwreck in the field of Hispanic studies; existing works explore nautical catastrophes in early modern texts from England, France, the Netherlands, and Portugal. Although sections of the Netherlands, and all of Portugal, were indeed part of the Spanish Empire until the middle of the seventeenth century, the available publications focus on Dutch and Portuguese cultural products and do not analyze texts written in Spanish. Consequently, the literature leaves a gap in Iberian early modern studies, since the maritime disaster theme is examined only through the lusophone lens.

The importance of the shipwreck motif in Spanish textual production has been undervalued, but we contend that its impact marks an entire era that can be designated as the *Naufragocene*, the "Age of Shipwrecks."[1] As such, its pervasiveness in multiple spheres of life and culture demands a macroanalytical approach that places the shipwreck theme at the center of discourse rather than as a disconnected literary, cultural, and historical instance. To do full justice to its pivotal role, we deem a comprehensive approach as most suitable to understanding shipwreck's numerous ideological parameters. This book therefore explores the significance of shipwreck in a variety of cultural products such as theatrical plays, poetry, narrative, and chronicles. The many textual documents examined encompass multiple geographical regions of the Spanish Empire comprising the American and Asian maritime routes. In order to provide an in-depth study of early modern Spanish epistemology around the shipwreck phenomenon and its multifaceted nature, this volume's contributors adopt a variety of analytical perspectives from history, literature, and cultural studies.

These essays are informed by a number of seminal works on the theme of nautical disaster. The most influential of these has been Josiah Blackmore's cultural and historiographical examination of the Portuguese shipwreck narratives compiled by Bernardo Gomes de Brito in *História Trágico-Marítima* (1735–1736). Blackmore's monograph *Manifest Perdition* engages issues of colonialism, historiography, and literary theory to depict how Portuguese shipwreck narratives serve to undermine expansionist endeavors.[2] Moreover, his work stimulated a reemergence of interest in the topic of nautical wreckage across early modern European studies, resulting in such books as Carl Thompson's *Shipwreck in Art and Literature* and James Morrison's *Shipwrecked*, which take a panoramic approach to the topic in different cultural expressions ranging from the *Odyssey* to contemporary popular culture.[3] In *Shipwreck Modernity*, Steve Mentz examines the shipwreck metaphor in literature and culture from the perspective of environmental studies and within the backdrop of English maritime expansion. These admirable and comprehensive works include a wide array of periods, geographical areas, and artistic expressions, but they do not consider the rich shipwreck examples manifested in the Spanish realm.

The aforementioned publications echo the influential study of shipwreck by Hans Blumenberg in his canonical work *Shipwreck with Spectator*, which delineates the development of a logos pertaining to the sea, nautical disaster, and the role of the spectator vis-à-vis violent encounters with the ocean from ancient times through the nineteenth century.[4] Blumenberg points out that the inception of theoretical notions around nautical disaster originated in classical writings, particularly in their use of rhetorical devices. Similarly, some of the chapters in this volume analyze the application of rhetorical topoi of nautical wreckage and its reformulation to critique sociohistorical aspects of the sixteenth- and seventeenth-century Spanish milieu. Regarding the treatment of these nautical topoi, Boris Dunsch, in "'*Describe nunc tempestatem*': Sea Storm and Shipwreck Type Scenes in Ancient Literature," traces the development of shipwreck and sea storm imagery through ancient Greek and Latin culture, especially its significance in relation to rhetorical conventions.[5] Among these, the subgenre of speech of the *psogos nautilias* and the device of *poetica tempestas* are elements whose influence continued to be felt in the seventeenth century but was fed from their articulation in ancient and medieval times. Yet in spite of stemming from older formulations, these rhetorical devices engaged different ideological purposes. Whereas in earlier time periods nautical wreckage had a direct correlation with the wrath of God as divine punishment, in the Spanish Golden Age it acquired different connotations—namely, offering sociopolitical commentary.

As the chapters in this volume elucidate, the multiple expressions that arise in conjunction with the shipwreck motif are informed by a variety of ideological criteria that differ from those of previous eras. Chapter 1, by Carrie L. Ruiz, situates the maritime enterprise within a sociohistorical and literary framework. Beyond this context, Ruiz explores shipwreck as a metaphor for the voyage of life and the turbulent waters of fortune in relation to the actions and emotions of the literary characters in María de Zayas's "Tarde llega el desengaño." Moreover, nautical catastrophe in this work is connected to such notions as reason, madness, gender, and identity, ultimately signaling the decline of the nobility and the empire.

Chapters 2 and 3, by Julio Baena and Elena Rodríguez-Guridi, respectively, further analyze the role of the nautical disaster as examined in the literary production of Iberia. In particular, Baena and Rodríguez-Guridi highlight how the generic peculiarities and literary features of seventeenth-century texts, such as Miguel de Cervantes's *El ingenioso hidalgo don Quijote de la Mancha* and Luis de Góngora's *Soledades*, serve to mine imperial notions of conquest. As both authors indicate, the shipwreck event sets into motion an irreversible process of territorialization by seeking to encompass spatial totality, but this process negates any narrative or historical progression.

Chapters 4 and 5, by Natalio Ohanna and Fernando Rodríguez Mansilla, delve into the polemics and diverse discourses in relation to the colonial enterprise in the New World, considering important moral debates of the early modern period through a transatlantic lens as a means to comment on and reconcile the multiple conflicting stances around such topics as moral truth, colonial domination, pauperism, and labor. Through the study of Alvar Núñez Cabeza de Vaca's *Naufragios*, Ohanna and Rodríguez Mansilla demonstrate how the inscription of the shipwreck narrative within the realm of the Americas triggers an inversion of power dynamics between conquerors and the conquered that impacts sociopolitical debates in Castile.

In chapter 6 Carmen Hsu examines Antonio Enríquez Gómez's play *Fernán Méndez Pinto*, in which China functions as a mirror of contemporaneous political dynamics of the Iberian Peninsula rather than as commentary on the Asian enterprise. The book closes with two chapters that do focus on the colonial enterprise in Asia, in particular on the failure of such endeavor as seen through historiographical chronicles and missionary accounts. Both Ana M. Rodríguez-Rodríguez (in chapter 7) and Noemí Martín Santo (in chapter 8) reveal the precariousness of the Spanish Empire in the geographical realm of the Philippines and Japan. As seen through the religious and political texts they study, it becomes apparent that the shipwreck event forecasts the end of the empire. The following paragraphs summarize each chapter in turn.

In chapter 1, "Turbulent Waters: Shipwreck in María de Zayas's 'Tarde llega el desengaño,'" Ruiz analyzes the symbolic value of the shipwreck motif in Zayas's seventeenth-century novella. Establishing a rich sociohistorical and literary context of the notion of nautical disaster, she examines the significance of the implementation of this trope throughout all fictional frames of the short story. The chapter demonstrates how the nautical theme becomes a rhetorical means to express the correlation between literal and metaphoric collapses of power that occur among all of the story's masculine characters. Consequently, the shipwreck motif serves Zayas's ideological purpose, which is twofold: first, to point to the flaws of the nobility, and second, to question patriarchal order. By tying shipwreck to the masculine realm of human folly and uncontrolled emotions—such as lust, rage, and madness—Ruiz proposes that the narrative points to the inversion of the natural order, which is linked to the decline of the nobility. Furthermore, the chapter exposes how the shipwreck element inverts the economy of power, since the patriarchal order collapses and causes harm. Ultimately, the shipwreck metaphor functions within overarching notions of gender and empire.

Baena, in chapter 2, "Two Small and Two Large Imperial Shipwrecks by Miguel de Cervantes and Luis de Góngora," uses Gilles Deleuze and Félix Guattari's fundamental opposition between "history" and "nomadology" as a starting point to analyze the shipwreck scenes in Cervantes's *Los trabajos de Persiles y Sigismunda*, the second part of *El Quijote*, and Góngora's *Soledades* and *Fábula de Polifemo y Galatea*. Baena argues that shipwreck symbolizes the totalitarian domination, or the dream of totality, to which the Spanish Empire aspires, but that it contains the seeds of its own destruction. He postulates that the colonial enterprise culminates the process of striation of the sea ("smooth space par excellence") in a totality that terminates the empire by turning it into a "smoothed" space. Thus, shipwreck is the event that submerges the striated space of domination by conquest, cartography, commerce, or (hi)story into the smooth and nomadic space of the sea—that is, into an ahistorical, atemporal, mapless movement.

In chapter 3, "The Reader as Castaway: Problematics of Reading *Soledades* by Luis de Góngora," Rodríguez-Guridi studies the function of the reader of Góngora's *Soledades* as a shipwreck victim and the act of reading as analogous to the survivor's struggle to conquer a new land. Beginning with Blackmore's critical remarks about the shipwreck text as a counterhistoriographic narrative of imperialism, Rodríguez-Guridi proposes that the hardship and disorientation the castaway experiences across the geographical hostility and unfamiliarity of the territory are reenacted in the reader's trajectory through the complicated language of the *silva*. The redundant and pointless itinerary of the reader in the conquest of the textual landscape delays the progression of the narrative and the development of a coherent discourse of territorial domination. Readers, constantly cast upon the discursive shores, must reconfigure their intellectual associations indefinitely, allowing other voices into the narrative. Fundamentally, Rodríguez-Guridi advocates that the reading process of *Soledades* exposes alternative historical interpretations to the empire's propaganda of colonial expansion.

Ohanna, in chapter 4, "On Moral Truth and the Controversy over the Amerindians: The *Relación* (1542) by Alvar Núñez Cabeza de Vaca," examines the shipwreck narrative of Cabeza de Vaca in regard to historical discourses of moral truth and the colonization of America. Parting from the shipwreck narrative as an account that inverts the relationship between dominators and the dominated, the conquest is stripped from its epic quality and destabilizes common notions in which coercion was rationalized. Ohanna argues that Cabeza de Vaca solves the paradoxical dilemma of how to fuse spiritual conquest with material gain and expansion without falling prey to doctrinal contradictions. The experience as castaway allows Cabeza de Vaca to position his narrative as an experiential account in which the humanity of Native Americans comes to the forefront and preconceptions are revealed as inaccurate constructions. Ohanna postulates that the account cannot be extricated from its social milieu in which colonial power clashes with the moral reservations of the church. In this light the shipwreck narrative, rather than setting the stage to question the colonial enterprise, allows Cabeza de Vaca to position himself as an example of the peaceful evangelizer.

Therefore, the conflict between the colonizing endeavor of the crown and the moral concerns of the church is reconciled through this figure.

In chapter 5, "The Discourse of Poverty in Alvar Nuñez Cabeza de Vaca's *Naufragios*," Rodríguez Mansilla also analyzes the complex nature of Cabeza de Vaca's text by placing it at the crux of contemporaneous social and religious debates on pauperism. For Rodríguez Mansilla, the entire text should be interpreted as an allegorical voyage in which shipwreck acquires a positive connotation. As such, the shipwreck experience paves the way to find redemption of the body and soul and to acquire the king's favor to embark on another conquest. In this sense, Rodríguez Mansilla contends that *Naufragios* is indeed a shipwreck narrative that arises from a larger debate on poverty, holiness, and manual labor. The nautical catastrophe permits a destabilization of social parameters and an inversion of social status as the conqueror turns into a *pobre vergonzante*. Rodríguez Mansilla points to the pervasiveness of this paradigm in other chronicles of the New World. Shipwreck becomes a springboard to allow the noble to demonstrate ingenious survival methods (i.e., manual labor) to avoid hunger. By establishing this model, Cabeza de Vaca merges two opposite sides of the peninsular debate on poverty in order to secure the favor of the crown: the legitimacy of the beggar as holy, and the value of work to climb out of poverty. Hence, the nautical metaphor is in fact a metaphor for notions of social identity.

Hsu, in chapter 6, "Shipwreck, Exile, and Political Critique in *Fernán Méndez Pinto* (1631) by Antonio Enríquez Gómez," further explores the image of the castaway as a means to reflect on political dynamics of the seventeenth-century Spanish court and society—in particular, on the figure of the *valido* and the position of the conversos. Hsu reveals how the theme of shipwreck and the subsequent vicissitudes of Gómez's main character construe a political allegory to implicitly critique Philip IV's reign and the practice of favoritism. Hsu asserts that although the play is set in the Chinese court in Beijing, it does not present itself as a commentary on the Iberian presence in Asia but instead as a reflection of seventeenth-century Spanish society. Laden with nautical metaphors of catastrophe that link existence to the changes of fortune, Gómez's play projects the theme of disillusionment and cautions against attempting success abroad because, in spite of achievement and loyalty, misfortune is ever present. Simultaneously, Hsu postulates how the figure of the castaway and the plot of the play reflect the difficulties that the author himself confronted as a converso.

In chapter 7, "The Manila Galleon Shipwrecks: Writing Crisis and Decline in the Spanish Global Empire," Rodríguez-Rodríguez examines the role of maritime catastrophe in two central texts in seventeenth-century Filipino historiography—namely, Antonio de Morga's *Sucesos de las islas Filipinas* and Franciso Colín's *Labor evangélica*—that present the archipelago as a failed colonial project foretelling the deterioration of the Spanish Empire. Rodríguez-Rodríguez stresses that shipwrecks were a much more common occurrence on the Manila Galleon Trade Route than in other parts of the liquid space of the empire due to great geographical and climatic obstacles. The ever-present threat of shipwreck fomented the sense of isolation and the adverse image of this colony. Rodríguez-Rodríguez further explains that the nautical wreckages had a larger impact on this colony than in other realms of the empire, since the entire economy of the islands depended on the successful journey of galleons between Acapulco and Manila. Therefore, the shipwreck accounts that prevailed in the political and religious writings of the Spaniards in the Philippines represent a fracture in the colonial discourse and underscore the fragility of the entire colonial enterprise in Asia.

Martín Santo, in chapter 8, "The Shipwreck of the Manila Galleon *San Felipe* in Seventeenth-Century Histories and Accounts on Japan," further asserts the relevance of the relations between the Asia Pacific and Iberia as represented in the underexamined Hispanic texts on Asia. The chapter examines Spanish writings by laypersons and missionaries about the events leading up to the shipwreck of the Spanish galleon *San Felipe* off the shore of the Japanese island of Shikoku. The wreck of the *San Felipe* constitutes a turning point in the relationship between Japan and the Spanish Empire. Using different rhetorical devices borrowed from the legal language of *relaciones* and from shipwreck narratives, the authors of these texts reflect the crown's interest in the commercial and territorial expansion of the empire in East Asia. In this sense, the texts justify their intervention for the evangelization of Japan under divine providence. Martín Santo argues, however, that in spite of projecting this discourse of expansion, the common adherence of these texts to the model of the shipwreck narratives ends up exposing the decline and precariousness of the Spanish Empire's control over the region.

From the microlevel of economic loss on the route from Manila to Acapulco, to the looting of the *San Felipe* galleon off the coast of Shikoku, to the macrolevel of disintegration of colonial domination, shipwreck symbolizes loss and change. Hence, nautical disaster defined by confusion, disorder, and inversion epitomizes the historical shift brought about by transoceanic commerce and conquest during the sixteenth and seventeenth centuries in the Hispanic world. The attraction to the shipwreck motif and its articulation through all cultural manifestations acted as a conduit to express the anxiety caused by the disorientation, fragmentation, and uncertainty of a world whose physical and conceptual boundaries were in constant flux.

It is not surprising that shipwreck narratives and their representations generated an enduring fascination throughout the early modern period given all the intricacies that accompanied the maritime enterprise. In fact, this fascination continues to shape the collective imaginary as it is seen in cultural commemorative events five hundred years beyond the first transoceanic explorations. For example, starting in 2020 Spain has honored Juan Sebastián Elcano and Ferdinand

Magellan's circumnavigation of the globe; many cities around Spain have organized cultural activities to celebrate the impact of maritime exploration and its effect throughout history.[6] The events are projected under an aura of epic accomplishment: the first circumnavigation of the globe had immense repercussions on a global scale, since it opened uncharted dimensions of the world and implied the loss of Portuguese exclusivity on the spice trade; the expedition was rightly named the Armada de la Especiería. Without a doubt, this noteworthy nautical achievement was accomplished largely through the technological and scientific developments of the period, but the cost of the voyage overshadows the maritime feat, since it involved extreme hardship, loss, and death. If one considers the actual details of the endeavor, the epic accomplishment soon becomes tainted: 239 mariners embarked on five ships from Sanlúcar de Barrameda on September 20, 1519; on September 8, 1522, only eighteen of those mariners returned on a single devastated ship. Such numbers confirm the difficulty and harshness behind the mercantile enterprise, which was true of all nautical enterprises of the era (whether mercantile, expansionist, or religious). These enterprises were constantly undermined by obstacles such as nautical catastrophe, changes in route, sea storms, pirate attacks, illness, and lack of technical knowledge. In spite of these challenges, the frequency and significance of the seafaring activity during the sixteenth and seventeenth centuries were remarkable and made the oceanic element integral to the worldview of those within the Spanish Empire.

NOTES

1. We are implementing Steve Mentz's terminology as set forth in *Shipwreck Modernity: Ecologies of Globalization, 1550–1719* (Minneapolis: University of Minnesota Press, 2015), xi.

2. Josiah Blackmore, *Manifest Perdition: Shipwreck Narrative and the Disruption of Empire* (Minneapolis: University of Minnesota Press, 2002).

3. Carl Thompson, ed., *Shipwreck in Art and Literature: Images and Interpretations from Antiquity to the Present Day* (New York: Routledge, 2013); James V. Morrison, *Shipwrecked: Disaster and Transformation in Homer, Shakespeare, Defoe, and the Modern World* (Ann Arbor: University of Michigan Press, 2014).

4. Hans Blumenberg, *Shipwreck with Spectator: Paradigm of a Metaphor for Existence*, trans. Steven Rendall (Cambridge, MA: MIT Press, 1997).

5. Boris Dunsch, "'*Describe nunc tempestatem*': Sea Storm and Shipwreck Type Scenes in Ancient Literature," in Thompson, ed., *Shipwreck in Art and Literature*, 42–59.

6. Some of these activities were interrupted by challenges posed by the COVID-19 pandemic of 2020–2021.

CHAPTER 1

Turbulent Waters

SHIPWRECK IN MARÍA DE ZAYAS'S "TARDE LLEGA EL DESENGAÑO"

Carrie L. Ruiz

In seventeenth-century Spanish literature, shipwreck is a common trope in many works ranging from those of Miguel de Cervantes to those of Luis de Góngora due to obvious historical circumstances. In María de Zayas's work, the trope appears in both her *Novelas amorosas* (1637) and *Desengaños amorosos* (1647), but is most predominant and significant in the story "Tarde llega el desengaño" (from the *Desengaños*), in which it acquires great symbolic implications that have not been studied previously.[1] This chapter will examine how Zayas recurrently employs the motif of shipwreck through multiple fictional frames as a means to invert seventeenth-century gender notions and support her didactic purpose to call into question the patriarchal order of her time. In particular, Zayas implements the literal process of ship deconstruction as a thematic motif to represent a figurative breakdown of the social order. By ascribing a concrete symbol to a conceptual theme, she is able to establish a correlation between literal and metaphoric collapses of power that occur in all her masculine characters. Although in the initial narrative frame shipwreck is associated with the female sphere, at all subsequent narrative levels this relationship is inverted and is linked only to the masculine realm. Thus, the shipwreck element in Zayas's tale shifts symbolically and becomes a key component in relation to the work's exemplary purpose.

THE HISTORICAL, CULTURAL, AND LITERARY CONTEXT OF SHIPWRECK IMAGERY

The recurrence of shipwreck representations in the cultural productions of early modern Europe, and in particular Spain, must be understood as part of a larger

nautical collective imaginary that stems from specific social and historical conditions. Although the importance of the nautical world and its significance for
the Iberian peoples can be traced back to pre-Roman times both in the Atlantic
and the Mediterranean, the imperial expansion of the late fifteenth and sixteenth
centuries triggers an entire maritime enterprise that continues well into the
seventeenth century. As Christopher Connery notes in his essay "Sea Power,"
"Spain and Portugal were the first to conceive of world power as bound by maritime space."[2] For these world powers, oceans, seas, and waterways were the main
conduit through which a worldwide network of imperial and mercantile interests was forged. Hence, the concept of expansion and trade for the Spanish
Empire was directly linked to seafaring and to the notion of Empire in and of
itself. In her study "The Organization of Oceanic Empires," historian Carla Rahn
Phillips exposes how trade was directly linked to political and imperial organization, since both commercial and military fleets were supervised by royal coun-
cils and government administrators so as to delineate "ship sizes, configuration,
and operating norms for voyages between Spain and America . . . and to encourage the construction of ships that could be adapted to military use in wartime."
In order to fully grasp the presence of a nautical collective imaginary, it is useful to note that Phillips estimates that "several hundred vessels and more than
forty thousand men sailed on Spain's commercial and military fleets to Spanish
America each year" during the sixteenth century and that there was "a continued flow of Iberians across the seas—some four or five thousand Spaniards a
year" during the Hapsburg period.[3] These numbers alone should suffice to underscore the tremendous mental, social, and cultural spaces created by the nautical
realm in all levels of Spanish society during the sixteenth and seventeenth
centuries.

Yet along with maritime expansion, control, and commerce came risk, and
the darker side of the nautical exploration and transoceanic trade involved
numerous naval disasters due to natural, technological, and military causes. In
regard to warfare, certain battles would be recalled in Zayas's time as particularly emblematic of shipwreck disaster, such as the loss of the Spanish Armada
in 1588, as well as the more contemporaneous and reoccurring shipwrecks that
took place throughout the Dutch-Spanish struggle between 1621 and 1648. But
perhaps a stronger imaginary than that of shipwreck brought about by naval confrontation among competing powers would have been the continuous loss of
ships due to natural forces and to pirate attacks during routine commerce and
travel. In data collections carried out by the Armada Española it has been registered that during the sixteenth and seventeenth centuries there were 385 Spanish shipwrecks—a number that constitutes almost one-third of all the registered
shipwrecks from the fifteenth to the twentieth centuries.[4] Thus, it can be concluded that the maritime culture of the Spanish Empire exerted constant influ-

ence in both the construction and reception of shipwreck imagery from the Renaissance onward.

Consequently, it is of no surprise that during the sixteenth and seventeenth centuries the shipwreck theme appeared in numerous Spanish cultural products, such as cartography, paintings, emblem books, and literature as a whole. For example, in maps the sea is depicted as a locus for struggle, a wild and treacherous space in which sea monsters lurk. In his study on social construction of the ocean, Philip E. Steinberg notes that the ocean space is represented as unruly and dangerous in European maps well into the middle of the seventeenth century. He offers several examples of early modern European maps, such as that of America by Diego Gutiérrez in 1562, in order to illustrate that seamen are often shown battling with fierce monsters; further, the sea is portrayed as topographically more textured than the land—that is, it is represented as "hardly an inviting environment for navigation."[5] Although some of the representations of the ocean as a perilous space would have been the result of an ideological motive to discourage others to follow the same mercantile routes, such depictions were also very much the reflection of experience and the mental perception of the ocean on the part of early modern seafarers. After all, the sea in early modern Europe was often regarded as "the most profoundly alien and hostile element, with the result that shipwreck is the worst imaginable scenario, evocative of the most extreme fear, horror, and abjection." The unpredictable nature of the sea that could lead to shipwreck incarnated everything beyond humankind's physical control and imaginative comprehension. In fact, this perception was probably fed, to some extent, by the ancient and medieval periods given that, in the Greek and Hebraic traditions, the sea was viewed as the unformed matter and primordial chaos that gave way to the habitable land world.[6]

The hazardous aspect of seafaring also surfaces in the depiction of the sea in the pictorial realm, and becomes a reoccurring theme in the seventeenth century, mostly in Dutch, Flemish, and Venetian art. In his exhaustive study of pictorial representation of tempest and shipwreck in Netherlandish painting, Lawrence Otto Goedde delineates how the storm's prevalence reflects not only the preoccupation of man's interactions with uncontrolled nature but also cosmic disorder.[7] In this sense, the dramatized representation of the tempest reflects early modern notions of opposing elements in nature where seafaring humans are placed at the crossroads of natural discord, directly opposite to the locus amoenus. Although in Spain the pictorial rendering of shipwreck functioned primarily as a background scene to mythological and historical visual narratives, sixteenth- and seventeenth-century painters such as Juan de la Corte, Enrique de las Marinas, and Juan de Toledo focused on naval battles and shipwreck. There were also a number of baroque painters who, even though not of Spanish origin, were present on the Spanish art circuit. For example, in the work of Cornelis de Wael, a seventeenth-century Flemish painter whose patron was Philip III, shipwreck becomes a theme in and of itself as ships are represented fighting the destructive forces of nature while horrified mariners face an imminent death.

The perilous nature of the ocean and sea and the ever-present possibility of shipwreck are also predominant themes in the emblem books of the time. In this literary genre, very popular at the time of Zayas, *pictura* and *poesis* merge, and shipwreck is portrayed as equivalent to human folly. As we see in Andrea Alciato's *Emblemata*, Sebastián de Covarrubias Orozco's *Emblemas morales*, and Juan de Solórzano Pereira's *Emblemas regio-políticos*, the shipwreck motif appears multiple times and is linked to the topics of *vanitas*, the lack of virtue and/or fortune, and the absence of the prince's duties to his people, which serve as a warning to be suspicious of change and as a symbol of uncontrolled amorous passion and impulsive emotions.[8] Some of these associations are reminiscent of classical antiquity topoi in which the ship is a metaphor of the voyage of life and the turbulent waters of fortune. As Goedde remarks, "The tempestuous sea as image of the individual soul in the throes of profound emotion . . . originated in Homer."[9] It thus comes as no surprise that emblem book authors would connect a lack of self-control to nautical disaster, since the image of the conflicted soul as a ship struggling in high seas was already part of a long-standing literary tradition.[10] Furthermore, one of Covarrubias's shipwreck motif emblems (Centuria III, emblema 89) directly echoes the *psogos nautilias* of classical rhetoricians in which navigation is admonished, though here it is reformulated as a criticism to transoceanic trade and the conquest enterprise.[11]

Of course, the topos of shipwreck, predominant in early modern Spanish literature, does not stem only from the sociohistorical circumstance of mercantilism, exploration, and expansion, as it is a theme of importance since classical antiquity; thus, we must also take into account its presence in the classical literary tradition. The most famous shipwrecks in classical literature that inform Renaissance and baroque literatures—in Europe at large, and in Spain in particular—are without a doubt those that appear in Homer's *Odyssey* (the shipwrecks endured by Odysseus), Virgil's *Aeneid* (the nautical disaster of the Trojan fleet in the aftermath of the fall of Troy), and Ovid's *Metamorphoses* (the shipwreck of Ceyx). All these works would have been readily available to any well-educated person, such as Zayas, since they survived in Latin, in translation, and in literary imitations in seventeenth-century Spain. These were important referential oeuvres in early modern literary circles; for example, the *Aeneid* was the foremost epic poem in Spain from the sixteenth century onward.[12]

Although little is known about Zayas's life, it is commonly accepted among scholars, including Marina S. Brownlee, Elizabeth Rhodes, Manuel Serrano y Sanz, and Alicia Yllera, that she came from the nobility—probably from the middle nobility. As Rhodes notes, Zayas participated in the literary salons in Barcelona and Madrid and was well known in the literary circles of her time.[13] We can conclude that she was an extremely educated and well-read person who would have been acquainted with some of the references to shipwreck in classical literature, as well as with those in emblem books and from contemporary authors. Among the more contemporary nautical wreckage references, she would have probably been familiar with Luís de Camões's *Os Lusíadas* (1572), Luis de Góngora's *Soledades* (1613), and Miguel de Cervantes's *Viaje al Parnaso* (1614).[14] The last two works are important because the shipwreck and the castaway characters in them are reformulations of Homeric nautical disaster and Odysseus's voyage;[15] it can thus be concluded that Zayas would have been aware of the value of shipwreck as a literary metaphor to express other themes and messages. The fact that she resorts to the trope of shipwreck in her work—most notably in "Tarde llega el desengaño"—can be understood both as a reflection of her sociocultural milieu and of the literary intertextuality of emblematic genre and contemporary and classical literatures.

Capsizing Power in "Tarde llega el desengaño"

"Tarde llega el desengaño" comprises three narrative frames, and the first reference to seafaring catastrophe appears in the novella's initial narrative frame, that of Lisis's soiree in which multiple female characters partake in storytelling.[16] Within this first fictional frame, the narrator, Filis, offers a long preamble to her narrative contribution in which she defends the intellect of women and invalidates the notion of male "natural" superiority by indicating that women have been restrained socially from acquiring power through their inability to have access to education. In her introduction she asserts that if women were able to access the same education as men, they would be equal or even superior to them. To further support her argument, she lists a number of sixteenth- and seventeenth-century female figures who demonstrate women's capacity to govern and to acquire high intellectual levels. What Filis attempts to transmit to her intradiegetic audience is that noble women and men are equal, and that women only appear inferior because patriarchal society dispossesses them of the power that is naturally inherent in them. As Filis declares, "Los hombres de temor y envidia las privan de las letras y las armas, como hacen los moros a los cristianos que han de servir donde hay mujeres, que los hacen eunucos por estar seguros de ellos" (231). Thus, women are symbolically castrated in order to disempower them, since they threaten male domination. Additionally, Filis relativizes the moral flaws of both genders by stating that not all women or men act in the same manner as their gendered peers but that, rather, they are prey to fortune or misfortune. It is within this dichotomy of fortune and misfortune that shipwreck is associated with the female body and functions as a metaphor for female/male relationships. Filis refers to the following statement by an educated female friend (*bachillera*) in regard to female adversity: "Bueno fuera que por una nave que se anega, no navegasen las demás" (228). In this sense, the ship directly correlates to the female body, and the female experience is that of a ship at sea. This metaphor echoes similar messages in the emblem books of the time: the journey of life as a ship in the sea where the waves of fortune cannot be controlled by humans.[17] At the core of this first shipwreck metaphor lies the motivation for women to continue "sailing the seas" because not all ships' journeys end in wreckage; there are also those that successfully navigate their voyage. In this sense, the shipwreck allusion in the primary narrative frame acquires a somewhat positive connotation as the narrator implements it to encourage women to "sail"—that is, to acquire agency. This concept is reinforced once again right before the tale begins when the narrator encourages her upper-class female audience to leave behind the frivolous pastimes related to beauty and take up their education: "¡Ea, dejemos las galas, rosas, y rizos, y volvamos por nosotras: unas, con el entendimiento, y otras, con las armas!" (231). After all, what Filis proposes here is that female fortune can be shaped to some degree by cultivating one's intellect.

The second reference to shipwreck takes on a primary role in the advancement of the first embedded story (the one told by Filis), and also reconnects to the notion of (mis)fortune. In this second narrative frame the protagonist, don Martín, experiences a drastic change in luck, and the element of nautical danger becomes an imminent possibility that drives the narrative thread for two pages. Here the shipwreck topos functions as a narrative mechanism to advance the story and to connect the narrative levels, since it throws the reader back to the initial narrative frame of Filis in which she comments on the "nave que se anega." In terms of literary structure and content, the detailed and long description of the tempest connects to the classical rhetorical tradition of *poetica tempestas*, which, as Boris Dunsch remarks, belongs to classical Roman poetry in general (and to the epic apparatus more specifically), in which the sea storm scene is a common feature.[18] In the epic tradition, the tempest and shipwreck are narrative devices that launch the protagonist on extraordinary (often fantastical) adventures from which the character returns metaphorically enriched. For a reader of the time, don Martín's tale would be inscribed into this literary tradition, and by the end of the story one would expect him to have learned a moral lesson from his experience.

At a more general level, by integrating the tempest and shipwreck early on in his account, Filis would be creating dramatic suspense for both the intradiegetic audience and also for the extradiegetic readers. As Goedde points out, the dramatized verbal evocations of the storm in literature emphasized the conflict between opposing forces of nature, and "such renderings necessarily involve narrative and a psychological dynamic appeal . . . that seeks to evoke the scene as though before the reader's eyes, thus drawing him psychologically into the account."[19] This dramatization can be clearly appreciated in Zayas's composition:

Pareciéndole el próspero viento con que la nave volaba, perezosa calma. Cuando la fortuna (cruel enemiga del descanso, que jamás hace cosa a gusto del deseo), habiendo cerrado la noche oscura, tenebrosa y revuelta de espantosos truenos y temerosos relámpagos, con furiosa lluvia, trocándose el viento apacible en rigurosa tormenta. Los marineros, temerosos de perderse, queriendo amainar las velas, porque la nave no diese contra alguna peña y se hiciese pedazos; mas no les fue posible, antes empezó a correr, sin orden ni camino, por donde el furioso viento la quiso llevar, con tanta pena de todos ... perdidas las esperanzas de quedar con las vidas, con grandes llantos se encomendaba cada uno al santo con quien más devoción tenía. (232–233)

In this description, which follows early modern conventions for describing a tempest, the protagonist is placed at the crux of weather, where humankind's condition appears in extremis; here, at the focal point where opposing forces meet, one is at the mercy of wind and water—and God. In this sense, men and their ships are represented as vulnerable and fragile bodies as they are caught in a dark and wild space that cannot be controlled. The adjectives implemented to describe the tempest emphasize darkness ("oscura," "tenebrosa"), discord of the elements, ("revuelta"), and uncontrollability of nature ("furioso viento"). All adjectives stress the disharmony and chaotic domain in which man has ended up and which is linked to death ("perdidas las esperanzas de quedar con las vidas"). The predominant elements in the description reflect Renaissance thought in which, according to Goedde, weather was regarded "as a strife between counterforces in the universe" and storms were perceived as the result of "the wind literally entering the sea, resulting in a confusion of the elements approaching primordial chaos."[20] Men thus appear in direct opposition to their stereotypical associations of strength and control, which are also questioned in Filis's defense of women in the preamble. Hence, there is a conceptual inversion of the economy of power: don Martín, who is initially presented as having honorably and valiantly served his king in Flanders with "valeroso ánimo y heroico valor," is thrown into a twist of fate in which his power and agency are completely erased by the forces of nature.

The tempest description continues in a crescendo to heighten the suspense and highlight the precarious condition of the male protagonist:

Tres días fueron de esta suerte, sin darles lugar la oscuridad y el ir engolfados en alta mar a conocer por dónde iban; y ya que esto les aseguraba el temor de hacerse pedazos la nave, no lo hacía de dar en tierra de moros, cuando al cuarto día descubrieron tierra poco antes de anochecer, mas fue para acrecentarles el temor, porque eran unas montañas tan altas que antes de sucederles el mal, ya le tenían previsto ... que la triste nave venía tan furiosa ... dio contra las peñas y se hizo pedazos. ... Don Martín ... animosamente asió una tabla ... con cuyo amparo, y el del Cielo, pudieron, a pesar de las furiosas olas, tomar

tierra ... que como en ella se vieron, aunque conociendo su manifiesto peligro, por llegar las olas a batir en las mismas peñas, por estar furiosas y fuera
de madre, ... don Martín y otro caballero ... se acogieron a un hueco o
quiebra que en la peña había. (233)

Shipwreck, the greatest fear, is materialized, and Filis's audience experiences
heightened danger, becoming spectator of the drama. By incorporating the shipwreck into the account, the audience and the reader become part of the theoretical shipwreck-spectator configuration proposed by Hans Blumenberg in his
pivotal essay, "Shipwreck with Spectator." We, along with the members of Lisis's
soiree, become witnesses to others' nautical crashes; from a safe distance we
observe and fixate on the disaster in an ambiguous role as spectators. As Blumenberg states, "It is only because the spectator stands on firm ground that he
is fascinated by the fateful drama on the high seas."[21] Hence, the spectator's position vis-à-vis the nautical destruction provides a cathartic experience.

In this specific case, Zayas allows her protagonist to survive, and we thus witness a metaphoric rebirth as don Martín and his mate leave the *hueco* in which
they took coverage in a description rich with symbolism:

Estuvieron hasta la mañana, que habiéndose sosegado el aire y quitádose el
cielo el ceño, salió el sol y dio lugar a que, las olas retiradas a su cerúleo
albergue, descubrió una arenosa playa ... de modo que podía muy bien andar
alrededor de las peñas. Que viendo esto don Martín y su compañero, temerosos de que no los hallase allí la venidera noche, y deseosos de saber dónde
estaban, y menesterosos de sustento ... salieron de aquel peligroso albergue,
y caminando por aquella vereda, iban buscando si hallaban alguna parte por
donde subir a lo alto, con harto cuidado de que no fuese tierra de moros donde
perdiesen la libertad que el Cielo les había concedido. (233–234)

As if leaving the confined and dark space of the womb, don Martín and his part-
ner, dispossessed of some of their clothing, exit from their "cóncavo y cavado
hueco" into the bright sunlight offered after the tempest and into a new environment of which they are both curious and fearful. Their initial feelings reveal
disorientation in their new space, and their anxiety to "map out" their geographic
location—that is, to know if they are on Christian or Moorish land—is as strong
as their need for nourishment. They must gain cartographic perspective of the
space of survival by walking and searching for the best pathway to find civilization and nourishment. As Josiah Blackmore states in regard to accounts of shipwreck survivors, their "pedestrian travel bears a cartographic intentionality"
and marks their attempt to regain some control and domain of their new encountered survival space.[22] Although the protagonist is able to deduce that they are
on Christian land by the dress of the first man they see, the disorientation continues because they are still unable to identify their spatial location. The first

question that don Martín asks in their initial encounter is to know in which land they are located; the answer of don Jaime is Gran Canaria. The Canary Islands, within the Spanish Empire but near the African coast, would suggest a liminal space to contemporary readers because, at the time, they were a crossroads between the Christian and Muslim worlds and an important commercial stop for navigation between the Americas and the Iberian Peninsula.

Consequently, the characters experience a spatial crisis after the shipwreck, which had already begun four days prior during the tempest out at sea when their navigation control and orientation was completely lost. As a result, and as Blackmore postulates, "the 'unfortunate hour of shipwreck' moves beyond a single identifiable moment: instead, it refers to a generalized dynamic of loss, estrangement, and disorientation that begins with the wreck of a ship but continues to ripple disastrously outward to encompass the aftermath of disaster."[23] Survivors such as don Martín must find their bearings in a completely unrecognizable space after the sea has devoured all matter and connection to a known space; it is as if their umbilical cord has been severed by the tempest. Zayas draws from the epic literary tradition as don Martín is thrown into a new space and partakes in adventures from which he may never return; at the same time she evokes classical nautical metaphors in which the entire cycle of life and death, including birth itself, is seen through shipwreck. This correlation between birth and shipwreck was not unusual because there was already an established classical tradition. As Blumenberg recalls, the Roman Lucretius, in his cosmic poem *De Rerum Natura* (book 5), presents the birthing act as nature taking the child from the mother's womb and throwing it onto the shores of light, much in the same way a sailor cast onto land after a shipwreck.[24] Yet aside from this classical reference, Filis's description is also reminiscent of the shipwrecked and wandering pilgrim in the first part of Góngora's *Soledades* who must also climb to the rocks above the sea to seek refuge and find his way.[25]

Nonetheless, it must be noted that beyond the literary metaphoric intertexts, Zayas also inscribes the shipwreck trajectory in a sociohistorical context: with the figure of don Martín, the narrative traces the footsteps of thousands of soldiers who serve the king in Flanders in the war against the Dutch and yet, in spite of honorable service, their return to the peninsula is tainted by nautical disaster and loss. Contemporary readers would therefore recognize the journey of don Martín as a common one in their era. A similar trajectory occurs also to the father of don Jaime, the nobleman who takes in don Martín and his mate in Gran Canaria; as don Jaime recounts, his father (of the same name) went to serve the king in Naples and gained great success, becoming a captain; nevertheless, on his return to Spain, he experienced shipwreck due to a sea storm, but managed to live because he, too, seized a board and took shelter in a nook in the rocks. Although the description of don Jaime's father's shipwreck is succinct, because it is part of this character's biographical narrative it serves to establish a

connecting thread among the male characters: both don Martín and don Jaime
(the father) acquired honorable status in service to the king abroad in imperial domains and experienced shipwreck off the coast of Gran Canaria. Consequently, the tale establishes a pattern among its male characters that reflects
the sociohistorical reality of Zayas's time while also establishing a metaphorical
pattern that symbolically undermines strong men. The topos of fortune versus
misfortune is thus once again brought to the foreground and serves to reflect
contemporaneous notions of *vanitas* that imbue many of the emblems referring to shipwreck.[26]

After the shipwreck element has been fully anchored in its literal and metaphoric dimension in the first and second narrative frames, the motif is further
developed in the third frame—that of don Jaime's life story—although this time
it is purely from a figurative perspective. With the story of don Jaime we identify three different metaphorical shipwrecks that pertain to the breakdown or
destruction of the character's personal and socially constructed structures. These
"wrecks" would be his relationship with Lucrecia in Flanders, his later marriage,
and his final loss of reason. In the initial approximation to don Jaime, we can
appreciate that he also partakes, to some degree, in the aforementioned pattern
of fortune and misfortune: valor in serving the king, followed by shipwreck as
he goes off to serve as a soldier in Flanders (like don Martín); and then another
shipwreck (in his case, a symbolic one) before being able to make his way back
home. These metaphoric shipwrecks are presented thematically insofar as the
seafaring disaster represents a loss of control over one's space and trajectory, passion, and emotion, as well as an inversion and disharmony in nature's order.
Moreover, don Jaime's critical experiences are also directly tied to the shipwreck
motif in the description offered by the narrator, Filis, who states that after
recounting his entire life story he invoked "a la memoria los naufragios de su
vida" (250). It should be noted that the narrative voice stresses don Jaime's multiple crises—here shipwreck is spoken of in the plural; he has been through not
one, but several shipwrecks. This serves to underscore the fragility and failure
of this male protagonist.

Don Jaime's first metaphorical shipwreck occurs in his relationship in Flanders with Lucrecia. His narration and the conditions of his encounter with this
female figure inscribe the entire situation within a realm that evokes the features
embedded in seafaring journeys, storms, and shipwreck that we have previously
seen: disorientation, confusion, fear of death, and an attempt to map one's space.
In his initial acceptance to partake in the secretive nocturnal encounter, we
perceive courage as he states "no miraba en riesgos, ni temía peligros, pareciéndome que aunque fuese a los abismos no aventuraba nada, porque no conocía la
cara del temor, acepté la ida" (240–241). But this brave disposition quickly changes
to bewilderment upon meeting the servant who has arranged the rendezvous:
"Lo primero que hizo fue vendarme los ojos con un tafetán. . . . Empezamos a

caminar, pareciéndome, en el tiempo que caminamos, que habían sido dos millas, porque cruzando calles y callejuelas, como por ir tapados los ojos no podía ver por dónde iba, muchas veces creí que volvíamos a caminar lo que ya habíamos caminado" (240). Here the protagonist enters the initial stage of the shipwreck structure: threat. The description is reminiscent of don Martín's account of the initial sea storm in which the ship is engulfed in darkness and they lose control over spatial knowledge and direction. In this case, don Jaime symbolically becomes both the ship and the mariners that enter the uncontrolled and dark space of the sea tempest. His disorientation and confusion quickly give way to dread upon arriving at their final location: "Yo os confieso que en esta ocasión tuve algún temor, y me pesó haberme puesto en ocasión . . . estaba amenazando algún grave peligro . . . ya no podía volver atrás" (240). Like those who have been shipwrecked, don Jaime fears a grave danger, yet he is not able to extricate himself from it since he has already relinquished all power; he no longer has the ability to see, control, or defend himself. He has arrived at the house without his dagger, sword, or gun, and is thus symbolically deprived of both physical and sexual power. In this regard, his arrival at the house is equated to the aftermath of the shipwrecked mariners who reach an unknown space ripped from all their connections and belongings. Just like don Martín and his mate in their first hours on land after the nautical destruction, don Jaime, upon entering the house, attempts to rechart his bearings by touch: "Empecé a procurar por el tiento a conocer lo que la vista no podía" (241). Still, his initial effort to map his new space fails, and he is only able to determine that his encounters occur with a very wealthy noblewoman, since she pays him very generously for his sexual services. In sum, this symbolic shipwreck experience serves to stress the inversion of established social hierarchies because here the brave male soldier is emasculated and disposed of all elements of power: he goes through a spatial crisis and is deprived of all agency, just like a ship tossed by the storm and mariners by shipwreck.[27]

As Goedde states, "The sea possesses . . . profound primordial resonance as symbol of all disorder and conflict, of all that is beyond man's physical control and imaginative comprehension and articulation."[28] All of don Jaime's nocturnal encounters reflect these connotations. Of course, the outcome of the nocturnal meetings ends in a final moment of crisis in which the protagonist comes close to dying due to Lucrecia's order to have him murdered as punishment for his lack of respect of their pact and for his identifying the location of the house. The moment in which he regains spatial control is therefore equated to death, as it is the only way for Lucrecia to remain in power. In this symbolic paradigm, don Jaime as the ship represents the physical structure of patriarchy that is deconstructed by the force of nature (the storm), here incarnated in Lucrecia's destructive power and overt control. This association of the marine natural realm and women was already well established in early modern culture, as the sea itself was linked in antiquity with the goddess Aphrodite as Venus Marina.[29] In this line of thought, Lucrecia is the destructive force that orders his death, but the protagonist's unbridled sexual and economical desire, as well as his desire to know her identity, are destructive forces in the relationship. Moreover, don Jaime does not abide by the honor code, as he does not respect his promise to Lucrecia to keep her identity and their relationship secret. In this regard, don Jaime's bad fortune and figurative wreckage are linked to moral fallacy.[30]

Although he comes close to death, don Jaime is able to escape this figurative shipwreck in Flanders, only to encounter another crisis in his matrimony with Elena. At the beginning of his relationship, the sailing is smooth: Elena is, physically speaking, a carbon copy of Lucrecia, yet she represents a calm sea that don Jaime can easily navigate; he thus remains in control at all times. Nevertheless, his matrimony turns topsy-turvy in what can be considered to be the next shipwreck of his life; indeed, when his female servant accuses his wife of being unfaithful, his known world is questioned and brought into uncharted territory. The crisis and disharmony in this situation are multiple: first, in the sense that the servant takes the place of Elena in the house and marriage, and second, in the lack of control of don Jaime's emotions. The protagonist's unharnessed reaction of anger is taken to the extreme as he creates a situation in which Elena "vive muriendo" and is reduced to a level similar to that of the dogs of the household as she eats from the floor under the table. Even after two years have passed from the initial accusation day, don Jaime's anger still brews uncontrollably, as is evident when he recounts the story: "De haber traído a la memoria estas cosas, estoy con tan mortal rabia, que quisiera que fuera hoy el día en que supe mi agravio, para poder de nuevo ejecutar el castigo" (250). His unrestrained nature is therefore rendered as one of his shipwrecks, and it resonates with how the shipwreck and tempest images are portrayed in the emblem genre of Zayas's time. In the previously discussed emblem books, the ship in the storm serves as a warning against letting one's impulses run wild, and the storm that brings the nautical disaster is linked to man's uncontrollable wrath. In such emblems, the danger of wrath is connected to the position of noblemen, including the prince or king.[31] As we will see later in this chapter, the message of such emblems is that rage can obfuscate princely reason and thus place the state in danger. In the connection between storm, shipwreck, and wrath, the emblems transmit a negative example of the ideal of ataraxia, the domestication of the passions, an ideal that would be expected of the elite class.

Consequently, we can link don Jaime's extreme wrath to the metaphor of an individual in a tempestuous sea and maritime catastrophe. As Goedde points out, "Confusion, sorrows, insanity, and rage are all related to the violence of the moving sea, while the ship struggling in the high seas is seen to resemble a soul in a state of high excitement or torn by conflicting emotions," where such emotions are frequently equated with "an individual's loss of self-control."[32] Indeed, the protagonist is very far from the ideal of ataraxia—so much so that even his shipwrecked guests consider his reaction and punishment too harsh and imprudent: "Espantados iban don Martín y el compañero del suceso de don Jaime, admirándose cómo un caballero de tan noble sangre, cristiano y bien entendido, tenía ánimo para dilatar tanto tiempo tan cruel venganza en una miserable y triste mujer que tanto había querido, juzgando, como discretos, que también podía ser testimonio que aquella maldita esclava hubiese levantado a su señora, supuesto que don Jaime no había aguardado a verlo" (250). Here his figurative shipwreck serves as a narrative platform to transmit one of the central messages of the novella: the importance of the nobility to act discreetly and not trust the servants or allow them to acquire a higher social status. In fact, disharmony in nature's order is here brought about by the destructive force of the servant's lies, as don Jaime foolishly believed a servant (rather than using good judgment) and acted impulsively. For Zayas, the nobility's loss of control is the utmost example of a society gone awry and of disharmony of the "natural" order. Multiple scholars, among them William Clamurro and Elizabeth Rhodes, have argued that Zayas's alliance to the hegemonic ideology of her time drives her narrative in the *Desengaños amorosos*. For Clamurro, the Zayesque oeuvre, and particularly the *Desengaños amorosos*, reflects and criticizes the ideological crisis during an era of political, economic, and social decline.[33] In Zayas's work, the nobility's lack of morals is the cause for imperial decline and for many of the problems facing seventeenth-century Spain. As Rhodes states, "Using the conservative values of the royalist, Catholic nobility as baseline, she points instead to how the elite has strayed from its class ideals."[34] Within this ideological framework, shipwreck serves as a central element in the story to symbolically transmit the moral decline of the aristocracy.

In this embedded tale, the moral decline of the nobility is underscored further when don Martín becomes the spectator of don Jaime's final shipwreck: his madness, which occurs after the servant's confession, his killing of the servant, and the death of Elena. As we have seen, the correlation of insanity with shipwreck was well established in classical literary tradition; further still, the association between the mind and a boat at sea was present in the early Italian Renaissance. In the opening to Dante Alighieri's *Purgatorio*, the epic poet's mind voyages over the open sea: "Per corer miglior acqua alza le vele / Omai la navicella del mio ingegno."[35] From the early Renaissance well into the late seventeenth century, a sound mind was figuratively equivalent to the tranquil voyage in which the ship is in control of the maritime space, whereas the reckless and uncontrollable mind was equated to the ship tossed and destroyed by the tempest, incapable of return from the abyss of the ocean. Furthermore, if we take into account notions of madness in early modern Spain where insanity is interrelated with moral decay—and, conversely, sanity with Christian virtues—the loss of the uncontrollable ship of the mind in the nautical depths would serve Zayas's message regarding the decline of nobility.[36]

In sum, don Jaime's multiple shipwrecks act as a paradigm to be avoided not only by the spectators (and in particular don Martín) but also by the intradiegetic audience and the extradiegetic readers. Such "spectators," as understood under Blumenberg's postulations, are expected not only to have a cathartic experience but also to learn a lesson from observing these wreckages. In the closing remarks provided by Filis, it seems that don Martín has managed to learn from don Jaime's mistakes in his relationships with women, as he has applied the lesson in his own life to avoid further wreckages. Don Martín has returned to Toledo, married his cousin, and lives "contento y escarmentado en el suceso que vio por sus ojos, para no engañarse de enredos de malas criadas y criados" (254). The tale thus ends by emphasizing once more the need to maintain social order and hierarchy, as well as the responsibility of the upper-class male to uphold moral values and guide society in order to avoid future "shipwrecks."

Conclusion

While the recurrence of shipwreck representations in cultural productions of early modern Europe, and in particular Spain, must be examined as part of a larger nautical collective imaginary that stems from a specific sociohistorical milieu, in "Tarde llega el desengaño" this topos serves as an ideal rhetorical device to transmit moral lessons and, indirectly, to offer sociopolitical commentary. Zayas is able to ascribe a vast array of symbolic connections to this motif by drawing from multiple associations of nautical disaster that derive from topoi in classical and early modern literary traditions. As I hope to have shown in this chapter, the shipwreck motif pertains to the topic of human folly and uncontrolled emotions but also ties closely to notions of imperial decline. Such decline is in the text presented in terms of the alteration of the "natural" order in which the nobility does not comply with its moral expectations. The implementation of the nautical wreckage motif thus serves two interrelated functions: on the one hand, it points to the flaws in the nobility, but on the other, it serves to question patriarchal order. For the readers and Filis's audience, shipwreck is circumscribed to the masculine realm of the nobility. As we have seen in the multiple fictional levels, the male figures are not as strong as they seem. In fact, through the shipwreck motif, their power is undermined because they are depicted as frail and vulnerable to the forces of nature and the twists of fortune. Moreover, they have moral flaws that should not exist among the nobility. In the case of don Jaime, his figurative shipwrecks connect to moral decline and the inability to control his impulses; thus, he is not able to attain the ideal of ataraxia that is expected from the elite class.

The connection between the upper nobility and ataraxia appears in the emblem books of the time, and in particular in those that also refer to shipwreck. In Solórzano Pereira's emblems, a lack of control is expressed in the danger of wrath and is mainly connected to the position of the prince or king. For example, in emblem 38, under the motto "Ira animi lutum vomit" (wrath vomits mud from the soul), the image depicts an enraged sea that "vomits" elements onto land while in the background there is a ship that tries to stay afloat. The connection between the maritime storm and royal wrath is clear in the verse section of the emblem: "Cuando el mar tempestuoso combatido de los vientos baraja los elementos y se enoja riguroso, cieno y lodo vergonzoso, arroja mal satisfecho, enfrena, oh rey, del despecho las olas que la ira incita porque si no se limita cieno vomita tu pecho."[37] This emblem, as well as several others in Solórzano Pereira's work and those in the works of Alciato and Covarrubias, connects storms, shipwreck, and wrath to the imperial realm. In this sense, regal control over the passions is crucial for the functioning of the state. The allegory of the state as ship was well established in the works of Plato and Aristotle, and the political writers of the seventeenth century often resorted to such paradigms to demonstrate that the prince or king is pilot of the state and, as such, must lead the ship in the right direction. Under this configuration, the prince or king's rage can obfuscate reason and thus place the state in danger.

In "Tarde llega el desengaño" Zayas seems to indicate that a social breakdown is inevitable; in her narratives, just as in her contemporary society, the patriarchal order of the upper nobility is at an inflection point that warns of the need for greater examination—and correction—of moral behavior within the male nobility. But such an examination is presented as a challenging one because the men in the story have been portrayed as cyclical versions of each other: they are figures that succeed in service to the king but who demonstrate fragility and moral flaws that are exposed during encounters with the forces of nature. Ultimately, in this inversion of the economy of power in which patriarchal order collapses and causes harm, shipwreck functions as a metaphor for the turbulent waters of fortune, which are inscribed within overarching notions of gender and empire.

NOTES

1. María de Zayas y Sotomayor, "Tarde llega el desengaño," in *Desengaños amorosos*, ed. Alicia Yllera (Madrid: Cátedra, 1983); hereafter, page numbers are cited parenthetically in the text.

2. Christopher Connery, "Sea Power," *PMLA* 125, no. 3 (2010): 686.

3. Carla Rahn Phillips, "The Organization of Oceanic Empires," in *Seascapes: Maritime Histories, Littoral Cultures, and Transoceanic Exchanges*, ed. Jerry H. Bentley, Renate Bridenthal, and Kären Wigen (Honolulu: University of Hawai'i Press, 2007), 72–73, 82.

4. These numbers come from a study conducted by the Armada Española as indicated in "La armada documenta 1580 naufragios de buques en aguas españolas o de nacionalidad española desde el siglo XIII," *Europa Press*, January 31, 2013, https://www.europapress

.es/murcia/noticia-armada-documenta-1580-naufragios-buques-aguas espanolas-nacion alidad-espanola-siglo-xiii-20130131112741.html, which houses original documentation from 1767 onward; thus, there are fewer entries prior to that date, and they come from secondary documented sources as well as bibliographies. Therefore, it can be inferred that the shipwreck number would actually be much higher than 385.

5. Philip E. Steinberg, *The Social Construction of the Ocean* (New York: Cambridge University Press, 2001), 99.

6. Carl Thompson, "Introduction," in *Shipwreck in Art and Literature: Images and Interpretations from Antiquity to the Present Day*, ed. Carl Thompson (New York: Routledge, 2014), 6, 8.

7. Lawrence Otto Goedde, *Tempest and Shipwreck in Dutch and Flemish Art: Convention, Rhetoric, and Interpretation* (University Park: Penn State University Press, 1989), 4, 18.

8. In Alciato, these emblems correspond to those on pages 62, 74, 88, 97, and 104 from Manuel Montero and Mario Soria's edition. In Covarrubias they are Centuria II, emblema 32, and Centuria III, emblemas 32, 87, and 89. In Solórzano Pereira, they are emblemas 38, 46, and 90. See Andrea Alciato, *Emblemas*, ed. Manuel Montero and Mario Soria (Madrid: Nacional, 1975); Sebastián de Covarrubias Orozco, *Emblemas morales*, Madrid: Luis Sánchez, 1610, https://archive.org/details/emblemasmoralesdoocovar; and Juan de Solórzano Pereira, *Emblemas regio-políticos*, ed. Jesús María González de Zarate (Madrid: Tuero, 1987).

9. Goedde, *Tempest and Shipwreck*, 36.

10. Both in antiquity and the early modern period, lack of self-control was deemed to entail giving into emotions such as rage, sorrow, confusion, inconsistency, lust, uncontrolled passion, and, of course, madness.

11. For more information regarding the subgenre of speech of the *psogos nautilias*, see Boris Dunsch, "'*Describe nunc tempestatem*': Sea Storm and Shipwreck Type Scenes in Ancient Literature," in Thompson, ed., *Shipwreck in Art and Literature*, 42–59.

12. In regard to the *Odyssey* translations available in sixteenth- and seventeenth-century Spain, see Christopher D. Johnson, "'El Homero español': Translation and Shipwreck," *Translation and Literature* 20, no. 2 (2011): 157–174. In regard to the reception and reference of Virgil, see María Rosa Lida de Malkiel, "Dido y su defensa en la literatura española," *Revista de filología hispánica* 4 (1942): 367–373. For an in-depth account of Ovid's influence and works in early modern Spain, see Vicente Cristóbal, "Ovid in Medieval Spain," in *Ovid in the Middle Ages*, ed. James G. Clark, Frank T. Coulson, and Kathryn L. McKinley (New York: Cambridge University Press, 2011), 231–256.

13. Elizabeth Rhodes, *Dressed to Kill: Death and Meaning in Zayas's "Desengaños"* (Toronto: University of Toronto Press, 2011), 28.

14. In her study on postmodernism, the baroque, and Zayas, Marina S. Brownlee rightly points to the influence of the European novella tradition in her fiction and, in particular, to the work of Matteo Bandello, Giovanni Boccacio, Miguel de Cervantes, Marguerite de Navarre, Masuccio Salernitano, and Giovanni Sercambi. See Marina S. Brownlee, "Postmodernism and the Baroque in María de Zayas," in *Cultural Authority in Golden Age Spain*, ed. Marina S. Brownlee and Hans Ulrich Gumbrecth (Baltimore: Johns Hopkins University Press, 1995), 111.

15. Johnson, "'El Homero español,'" 157, 172.

16. The story comprises three narrative frames.

17. In chapter 6 of the present volume, Carmen Hsu examines the connection between (mis)fortune and nautical metaphors in Antonio Enríquez Gómez's seventeenth-century play *Fernán Méndez Pinto*.

18. Dunsch, "'*Describe nunc tempestatem*,'" 49.

19. Goedde, *Tempest and Shipwreck*, 17.

20. Goedde, *Tempest and Shipwreck*, 33; We can see the same imagery in the emblem books of the time; see, e.g., Alciato, *Emblemas*, 74 and 87, where furious winds move the

ocean waters into battle; Covarrubias, *Emblemas morales*, Centuria II, emblema 32, and Centuria III, emblema 87, where the drastically changing winds endanger ships; and Solórzano Pereira, *Emblemas regio-políticos*, emblema 90, where the violent Noto and Boreas winds alter the state of the waters.

21. Hans Blumenberg, *Shipwreck with Spectator: Paradigm of a Metaphor for Existence*, trans. Steven Rendall (Cambridge, MA: MIT Press, 1997), 39.

22. Josiah Blackmore, "The Sunken Voice: Depth and Submersion in Two Early Modern Portuguese Accounts of Maritime Peril," in Thompson, ed., *Shipwreck in Art and Literature*, 66.

23. Blackmore, "The Sunken Voice," 68.

24. Blumenberg, *Shipwreck with Spectator*, 28.

25. For an exhaustive analysis of Luis de Góngora's *Soledades* "pilgrim" as castaway, see Elena Rodríguez-Guridi's study in chapter 3 of the present volume.

26. We can see an example of this notion in Covarrubias, *Emblemas morales*, Centuria II, emblema 32, in which he warns the readers of the changing winds and the unpredictable sea that surrounds the ship of fortune, cautioning that "muchos hombres se han perdido por no acordarse que lo son y que en esta vida no hay cosa firme ni estable."

27. The implementation of shipwreck as a symbol of power inversion is also evident in other texts of the time period such as Alvar Núñez Cabeza de Vaca's *Naufragios*. For further exploration of this dynamic, see the studies by Natalio Ohanna (chapter 4) and Fernando Rodríguez Mansilla (chapter 5) in the present volume.

28. Goedde, *Tempest and Shipwreck*, 29.

29. In addition to the commonplace of *Venus Marina* as invoked by the Romans, there was also an association of the ever-changing sea with female unpredictability, of erotic passion with storm, and of the lover with the ship. For more on this tradition, see Goedde, *Tempest and Shipwreck*.

30. Along with Lucrecia's name, don Jaime's moral fallacy connects the tale with the Roman legend of Lucretia in classical literature. In Zayas's time, this legend would have been a well-known reference thanks to the writings of Ovid and of Saint Augustine. In antiquity, particularly in Ovid's rendition of the tale, the literature portrayed Lucretia as a representation of pureness and honesty; as such, her suicide is conceived under the parameters of heroism—as well as of *animi matrona virilis*, since this type of death was representative of male honor and not associated with women in antiquity. See A. G. Lee, "Ovid's 'Lucretia,'" *Greece & Rome* 22, no. 66 (1953): 117. According to the legend, Sextus Tarquinius raped Lucretia, and his father lost access to the throne of Rome due to a rebellion to avenge her honor following her suicide. In this sense, the Tarquins' loss of the control over Rome is tied directly to the moral flaw of a male character. Consequently, don Jaime's flaw connects to the Roman legend and, in this sense, the decline of Spanish imperial control—in this case, over Flanders—would connect to the male protagonist's violation of the moral code.

31. Examples of these emblems are Covarrubias, *Emblemas morales*, Centuria III, emblema 87; and Solórzano Pereira, *Emblemas regio-políticos*, emblem 38.

32. Goedde, *Tempest and Shipwreck*, 36.

33. See William Clamurro, "Ideological Contradiction and Imperial Decline: Toward a Reading of Zayas's *Desengaños amorosos*," *South Central Review* 5, no. 2 (1988): 44; and William Clamurro, "Madness and Narrative Form in 'Estragos que causa el vicio,'" in *María de Zayas: The Dynamics of Discourse*, ed. Amy R. Williamsen and Judith A. Whitenack (Madison, NJ: Fairleigh Dickinson University Press, 1995), 229.

34. Rhodes, *Dressed to Kill*, 27.

35. Dante Alighieri, *Purgatorio*, canto 1, lines 1–2, Project Gutenberg, 1997, http://www .gutenberg.org/files/1010/1010-h/1010-h.htm. These opening verses are best understood through the following paraphrasis: "La navicella del mio ingegno, ormai alza le vele per

percorrere acque migliori." In this restructuring, the English equivalent would be "the boat of my intelligence [mind's ability] henceforth raises the sails to cruise better waters"; my translation.

36. For more on the perception of madness in early modern Spain, see María Tausiet, "Taming Madness: Moral Discourse and Allegory in Counter-Reformation Spain," *History* 94, no. 315 (2009): 279–293.

37. Solórzano Pereira, *Emblemas regio-políticos*, emblema 38.

Two Small and Two Large Imperial Shipwrecks by Miguel de Cervantes and Luis de Góngora

Julio Baena

For Gilles Deleuze and Félix Guattari, "the sea is a smooth space par excellence, and yet was the first to encounter the demands of increasingly strict striation."[1] "Striated space" being the proper space of the sedentary (of the polis and of history), and "smooth space" being that of the nomad (of the primordial war machine and of a nomadology), the shipwreck is the event that literally submerges the first into the second, and history (or story) into a mapless movement. Two literary Spanish masterpieces were written at about the same time (1613–1616), both revolving around the theme of shipwrecks and both deviating from all charts about genre: Miguel de Cervantes's *Persiles* and Luis de Góngora's *Soledades*.[2] To what extent they stop being a (hi)story and open the flood gates to a nomadology is the ultimate goal of my long-term investigation. In this chapter, I will indirectly go over some of the main points of the discussion (prose fiction versus poetry; sense/meaning versus polysemy/nonsense; tree versus rhizome, etc.), but I will focus on the triangulations that the small and big shipwrecks offer.

One thing is sure: the same processes of deterritorialization and reterritorialization that produce and develop capitalism in relation to smooth/striated space, according to Deleuze and Guattari, operate in the background of *Persiles* or *Soledades*: the force striating the smooth sea space in them is the Spanish Empire, on the one hand, and the Catholic Church on the other. Both texts are opposites of one another in many respects. In *Persiles* the multiple shipwrecks punctuate the "pilgrimage" from Ultima Thule to Rome of the two love-motivated protagonists, while in *Soledades* what we find is a lonely shipwrecked "pilgrim/lover" coming from nowhere and going nowhere.

Yet, for this chapter, I will combine the big picture of the two big shipwrecks (*Persiles* and *Soledades*) with the closer reading of two smaller shipwrecks, one from Cervantes and one from Góngora: Cervantes in *El Quijote* tells of a brief adventure for the knight-errant and his esquire in "the enchanted boat." It is only a brief incursion on the Ebro River, aboard a small dinghy, but in it Don Quixote's mind manages to circumnavigate the entire cosmos before—of course—hitting the mechanism (the "war machine") of a water mill and capsizing. Góngora, on the other hand, in his other major poem, *Fábula de Polifemo y Galatea*, has the Cyclops singing about how he (of all people) has sheltered a shipwrecked Genoese merchant (of all people). These are minor episodes, indeed, and yet—I will argue—they explain the opposition of nomad/sedentary, or smooth/striated, or capitalism/whatever, in almost the precise way, and often with the same words/tropes, as Deleuze and Guattari do. For instance, they tell us how "smooth space is occupied by intensities [and] tactile qualities" while "striated space . . . is canopied by the sky as measure and by the measurable and virtual qualities deriving from it."[3] Well, Cervantes gives us, precisely, Don Quixote measuring that virtual sky: he will speak of parallels, meridians, the ecliptic, declination . . . and mention—by the way—that lice on sailors die upon crossing the equator, asking Sancho, therefore, to make the tactile experiment himself and see if he finds "something" on himself, to which Sancho replies with inimitable Cervantine wit, "I do feel something, and even somethings!" A lousy empire, indeed.

Because, of course, it is empire (and therefore global striation, capital as reterritorialization at a global scale) that culminates the process of striation of the primordial smooth space (the sea). "The commercial cities," note Deleuze and Guattari, "participated in this striation . . . , but only the States were capable of carrying it to completion, of raising it to the global level of a 'politics of science.'"[4] Perhaps the first symptoms of the imbrication of the striation mechanisms into the properties of the smooth space can be perceived in the old Greek texts: in the way the Greeks—the ultimate "nomadic war machine"—lay siege to Troy while, at the same time, protecting themselves from Trojan counterattacks with a moat, or with the ships themselves, turned into walls. Or, clearer still, and more modern (historical as opposed to prehistorical): the famous oracle, or dream, that told Themistocles how Athens would be defended from the Persians by a "wall made of wood" (its fleet, as it turned out). That Athenian wall, which moves, which dissipates into the wide sea is, obviously, the ancestor of all paradoxical "moving walls" to defend the polis: from the amazing tale—parallel to that of Salamina—of the Spanish Armada fighting the British "wall of wood" to the nuclear submarine fleet (Deleuze and Guattari's favorite example).[5]

The counterpart of this *politization* of the sea is the *nomadification* of the polis—or let us call it (as Deleuze and Guattari do) "appropriation of the war machine," or, more precisely, capitalism. Let us call Potosí—not Madrid, not Seville—the center of the striated space of the empire: ground zero of appropriation of what was not appropriated by the indigenous peoples (nomads in their own land, according to the perverse logic of exploitation). Let us call the countless dead working at "someone else's" mines "the price to pay" for progress. Or let us call them "wear and tear" of the war machine (but the war machine is supposed to be the nomads') of the ultimate, insuperable polis lauded by Hernando de Acuña as early as the 1500s with the famous sonnet "Un monarca, un imperio y una espada," which sounds like an earlier rendition of Francis Fukuyama's *The End of History and the Last Man* (the first lines of the sonnet being "Ya se acerca, señor, o ya es llegada / la edad gloriosa en que promete el cielo / una grey y un pastor solo en el suelo, / por suerte a vuestros tiempos reservada"), as much as of the creepier—but not more ominous—"Ein Volk, Ein Reich, Ein Führer."

The most important shipwreck fictional tales of the Spanish baroque are, almost indubitably, the long *silva* (unorganized poetic forest) by Luis de Góngora, *Soledades*, and Miguel de Cervantes's posthumous novelistic tour de force *Los trabajos de Persiles y Sigismunda: Historia septentrional*. Of how the two of them are close to each other, we have evidence since they were written. In a famous commentary on *Soledades* by Pedro Díaz de Rivas, written in the midst of the intense controversy that Góngora's poem stirred when it began to be disseminated in Madrid after 1613, Rivas, a defender of Góngora, addresses one of the main issues of the controversy—what was the genre of the strange poem— by saying that *Soledades* would be "aquel género de poema de que constaría la *Historia ethiópica* de Heliodoro si se redujera a versos."[6] At the same time, Cervantes was writing his *Persiles*, of which he had advanced, in the prologues of previous publications such as the *Novelas ejemplares*, that it dared compare to Heliodorus ("se atreve a competir con Heliodoro"), adding that this comparison was conditional on its not emerging with its hands on its head ("si ya por atrevido no sale con las manos en la cabeza").[7] Two stories, indeed, of "Byzantine" flavor, in the mode of the then "missing link" in Aristotelian schemes— the long-sought-after model of an epic in prose, which to the inventors of the modern novel was a vital missing link, if the Greco-Latin universe of genres was not to be discarded altogether as useless. But the problem is that one of them, *Soledades*, becomes, if we are to explore Rivas's comment, "Heliodorus in verse"—that is, an epic-in-prose in verse. The other shipwreck tale, *Persiles*, is seen by its own author as a Heliodoran competitor that could very well be born as an octopus: the animal that, by definition, has its hands (or "feet," or "tails"— Cervantes debates this later in the *Coloquio de los perros*) on its head (it is a cephalopod: literally, "feet in head"). *Persiles* curiously dares to penetrate rashly into the realm of the sea monsters (though not quite the same sea monsters that *Soledades* speaks about as adversaries to the beautiful daughters of one of the characters).

In any case, the shipwreck motif, and the monsters, overgrow their classical models and, without abandoning their deep meaning as "pictures of the soul," adopt new, modern, disquieting new meanings. Could it be that the sea is now the here and now of history, instead of that of mythology or psychology? But, if it is the here and now of history, how can it escape being the smooth-space-turned-striated of the Spanish Empire, an empire that has "smoothed," among other things, agriculture—a primordial "striated space"—and the sedentarism of the polis for commerce, for money? The sea, the oldest and newest of "nomadic spaces," brings back the old "war machine" of the nomad, the activity and failure of which the shipwreck most obviously represents.

In another poem by Góngora, *Fábula de Polifemo y Galatea*, lurks an unexpected monster—Galatea, not Polyphemus (I have dealt with this elsewhere)[8]— that, among other calamities, causes Sicilian agriculture to decay. The way Góngora alludes to this is strikingly reminiscent of exactly the same metaphor that Deleuze and Guattari use: striation. This is how Góngora puts it: "Arde la juventud, y los arados / peinan las tierras que surcaron antes."[9]

But the strange monster Galatea also causes the Cyclops, whom we know from the *Odyssey* to be the archenemy of ships and sailors, to shelter in his abode a castaway—a Genoese castaway, of all things. The Genoese were the stereotypical characters to represent greedy moneylending and to cause the breakdown of the Spanish economy. It was in Genoa where the gold, "born" in the Indies, was "buried," as Francisco de Quevedo famously puts it:

Nace en las Indias honrado,
donde el mundo le acompaña;
viene a morir en España
y es en Génova enterrado.[10]

This "small shipwreck" in *Polifemo* accompanies the also relatively small, embedded shipwrecks of *Soledades*. Góngora's major poem presents several embedded shipwrecks: the "main" shipwrecked person (the main character) encounters two old men: a *serrano* (mountain man) and an *isleño* (island dweller). Both tell the main character (described as "náufrago y desdeñado sobre ausente") about how navigation is to be cursed, and of how the navigated sea is the tomb of the imperial commerce. The *serrano* is weeping for his son, lost at/ to sea. He begins his story by cursing whomever invented navigation:

¿Cuál tigre . . .
dió el primer alimento
al que, . . . primero
surcó labrador fiero
el campo undoso en mal nacido pino . . . ?[11]

And navigation is portrayed as a perverse striation (plowing) of the "liquid land." The *serrano* goes on to tell precisely how the entire world is made into "striated space," using almost the same image that Deleuze and Guattari use (and to which I will return when speaking of Cervantes's small shipwreck of the enchanted boat): the globe as a web of meridians and parallels ("Striated space . . . is canopied by the sky as measure").[12] He describes in obsessive detail how the world was turned into a map (every map is a military map, I often insist on remarking, accompanying, and correcting Deleuze and Guattari's insight). Ferdinand Magellan's circumnavigation tops the depiction of the now global calamity.

A second old man (in the second *Soledad*) tells the main character (the original shipwrecked person of the strange poem) of how the sea is, indeed, the maker and destroyer of the empire. While the first old man is a *serrano* (a dweller of the most inland space possible), this second old man is a fisherman: the original nomad of the sea. Just as in a standard eclogue everyone is a shepherd, because sheepherding—not agriculture—brings us back to a mythical golden age before the plow "raped" Mother Earth (the image was a commonplace around 1600), in an *egloga piscatoria* we find the smooth space of the sea before it was "plowed." The fisherman is the hunter-gatherer; no polis for him. And yet, it is a man of the sea who tells the young shipwrecked protagonist about how different the sea is as a space to fish from the sea as a space to conquer. To the old fisherman, the sea is

> ese profundo
> campo ya de sepulcros, que sediento,
> cuanto en vasos de abeto Nuevo Mundo,
> tributos digo Américos, se bebe
> en túmulos de espuma paga breve.[13]

To that sea went his two sons (never heard from again), but to a very different sea go his daughters: fisherwomen. What they do is no less dangerous than circumnavigating the globe. Danger is not the point; if anything, the polis is constructed to avoid danger: "Peace is our business" say the most select forces of states, or of empires; a place has been "pacified" when nobody resists order any longer. These beautiful daughters of the old fisherman are shown as their own father sees them. One hunts/fishes a seal; the other daughter, a more ambiguous kind of sea monster.[14] The prey, although wounded, escapes, so the second daughter has to settle for "un sollo" (a sturgeon): use value of the sea, not exchange value.

Yes, there is the classical component of "shipwreck" as an allegory of a state of the soul, but there is another kind of shipwreck as an allegory of a different state of the soul/body, intimately related to . . . well, capital/state.

In Góngora, then, the Heliodoran motif and allegory of the shipwreck speaks of the sea as that "smooth space that was first striated," proper to the flow of money and commodities. If we compare to Góngora's shipwreck-in-shipwreck poem Cervantes's Heliodoran near-monstrosity, the shipwreck allegory seems to refocus into a non-nomadic travel from the periphery to a "center" (Rome, "el cielo de la tierra," is so called several times in the *Persiles*, just as the expression "nuestras almas están en continuo movimiento y no pueden parar sino en Dios como en su centro" is also repeated often). *Persiles* and *Soledades* are excellent texts to test the fundamental opposition that Deleuze and Guattari pose as the opposition between "history" and "nomadology." A crack in the entire edifice of the baroque, and therefore of modernity—or of, say, G. W. F. Hegel—is at stake. As Deleuze and Guattari note, "History is always written from the sedentary point of view and in the name of a unitary State apparatus, at least a possible one, even when the topic is nomads. What is lacking is a nomadology, the opposite of a history."[15]

The main characters of both *Soledades* and *Persiles* are "peregrinos"—a curious deviation from "the nomadic." A pilgrim goes somewhere, even to a center (roots, arboreal matrix); a nomad is supposed to go nowhere specific (actually, the nomad does not "go" anywhere; the nomad, properly speaking, does not move),[16] and the nomad's "matrix" is rhizomatic, with no center or preordained direction. Apart from the *failed* voyage to the center (the ultimate failure of the *Persiles*, which I have noted with David Castillo,[17] and which would make its "minor strategy" supersede the obvious classical allegory of "the trip, with several shipwrecks, as a self-discovery of the soul") with the radical discovery that there is no center, the *Persiles* is "history" because its pilgrims seem to be real pilgrims on their voyage to the center, but *Soledades* shows no such pilgrim, even if the protagonist is called occasionally "el peregrino," and—more important—the lines themselves of *Soledades* are compared to the steps of a pilgrimage:

> Pasos de un peregrino son errante
> cuantos me dictó versos dulce Musa
> en soledad confusa,
> perdidos unos, otros inspirados.[18]

But this peculiar pilgrimage leading nowhere is one of the main critiques of Góngora's poem: that the protagonist is "un mancebito, . . . y no le da nombre. Este fue al mar y vino del mar, sin que sepáis cómo ni para qué."[19] No pilgrimage. The "mancebito" goes nowhere, and the poem seems to do the same. *Soledades* is a good candidate to be a nomadology.

Another feature that makes *Soledades* a good candidate to be an anti(hi)story (i.e., a nomadology) is the fact that, in spite of being the most literary of artifacts, *Soledades* is a poem—in other words, not literature. I first approached this idea when I was attempting to show how the task to draw a map to a "place to be lost in" is incongruous to the desire to be lost and can only be explained if one wants the opposite (to get out of a labyrinth).[20] I was unknowingly following Deleuze and Guattari's advice to "make a map instead of a tracing," which could be used "for forgetting instead of remembering."[21] Poetry is not literature. One must insist on that obvious but complex fact. Poetry was only reterritorialized in books after literature was invented (millennia after poetry—like dance, music, or myth—existed). Poetry is closer in affinity to smooth space than to striated space. As Deleuze and Guattari put it, in an observation already used through this study, "Smooth space is occupied by intensities, wind and noise, forces, and sonorous and tactile qualities, as in desert, steppe, or ice. The creaking of ice and the song of the sands. Striated space, on the contrary, is canopied by the sky as measure and by the measurable visual qualities deriving from it."[22] Poetry, as Julia Kristeva has shown, is sound before phoneme; semiosis before logos; mother's body before—or against—father's law. But logos is the law of the polis. That is why whereas "history has never comprehended nomadism, the book has never comprehended the outside."[23] When Hegel uses his famous metaphor to refer to history as that which admits no "empty pages" ("The History of the World is not the theater of happiness. Periods of happiness are blank pages in it"),[24] perhaps he does not realize that he uses it because he has no other trope to use. Only a book is as inescapable, as merciless, as cruel, as history. The book has never *compris* (that is the original French word: to understand, but also "to have room for," to hold) the outside. The grand dressing that we call the book constitutes the greatest *detention*—police arrest of what in itself is nomadic. The work of Góngora, however—and in spite of what philologists or neophilologists may say—is *incomprehensible*, and by this I do not only mean that it cannot be understood, but also that it cannot be contained, held, mapped. I once called it *poesía prófuga* (escaped poetry). In Góngora's case, it is obvious that poetry overflows all and any wall that books may impose on it, but it is also true that all poetry is nomadic, *qua* poetry: that only as literature does it belong to the state apparatus. The very word *poiesis* that poetry has retained points toward the activity of craft rather than absconding that very activity in the name we give to, say, art—or "a novel" or any other product. Poetry, through its ancient root *poiesis*, unhides the making, the connection between maker and product. Precisely what the polis, and especially the culmination of the polis in states and empires, hides (let us always remember Max Horkheimer and Theodor Adorno's rendering of the story of Ulysses being able to listen to the sirens only as far as his companions row the boat with their ears plugged).[25] The very story of poetry in, for example, the European Middle Ages shows how it was the itinerant who disseminated poetry. From fair to fair, between kingdoms, and even between religions and local languages, poetry was disseminated. When, for instance, the different kingdoms in the Iberian Peninsula were beginning to adopt their own specific vulgar languages as official, instead of Latin (i.e., when a strong reterritorialization was taking place), poets continued to deliver their singing in, Castilian, Catalan, French, Galician, or Portuguese, even if they were not in "the right kingdom." And audiences "got it." Maybe they did not "understand"—and there is evidence that they understood considerably, especially among Romance languages—but they "got it." By all the gods, they got it, just like we got it entirely in Spain as teenagers, during the years of Francisco Franco, when we listened to the Beatles or Jimi Hendrix. We understood perfectly without "comprehending" the English language.

But, above all, there is a compelling reason for thinking of *Soledades* as nomadology and not history. Like the shipwreck it is—like all shipwrecks—it does not *end* the way a (hi)story is supposed to end. I am not talking about the ongoing controversy over whether Góngora intended to compose four *Soledades* but only finished two. To me, this is secondary to the fact that, as Juan de Jáuregui—Góngora's archenemy and best reader—noticed, its protagonist, together with the text itself, go nowhere. History has an "end" by necessity (Fukuyama in this is merely tautological). In Agustín García Calvo's words regarding Fukuyama's famous dictum, "El Fin de la Historia no es otra cosa que la finalidad de Capital y Estado, juntos los dos en uno: esa finalidad o ideal consiste en la reducción definitiva de la vida a Historia, es decir, la sustitución de la vida por la idea de la vida y su conversión en tiempo, un tiempo vacío y siempre futuro, donde nada pasa, puesto que todo lo que pase ya ha pasado: es Historia en el momento en que sucede."[26] Things end according to what Rafael Sánchez Ferlosio called *tiempo consuntivo* (consumptive time): "El tiempo . . . no dirigido hacia ningún futuro, . . . el tiempo sin sentido de los bienes y la felicidad. [El tiempo] cuyo ahora se desliza por un *todavía* y cesa en un *ya no*."[27] But history is not a thing. If anything, it is the thing of things, like time or like money. As García Calvo notes, "solo se consolida esa existencia o realidad [del tiempo] cuando la idea de 'tiempo' se acerca a adquirir una cierta netitud o certidumbre . . . por medio del establecimiento de su Nombre, *tiempo*, en las lenguas de la Cultura dominante, lo cual implica la facilidad de que se le maneje o nos maneje en los negocios y que venga a asimilarse a la cosa de las cosas, a saber, dinero."[28] History runs by *tiempo adquisitivo* (acquisitive time), the opposite of consumptive time. It is "empty time," which, as Sánchez Ferlosio puts it, "corre, sin ahora, por un *todavía no* y se cumple y corona en un *ya*."[29]

And this is where the other great story about shipwrecks, Cervantes's *Persiles*, diverges from Góngora's *Soledades*. *Persiles* follows a plan—a specific, obsessive plan from Ultima Thule, "debajo del mismo Norte" to Rome, "centro" or "cielo" of the earth. Shipwrecks, like life, end as an ironic "no more" to what was in its origin an "are we there yet?" The survivor, typically hanging to his or her plank for dear life, transforms the "not yets" of the voyager into "I am still here" until . . .

The end of life is as abrupt, as incorrect, as unbookish as the end of my last paragraph. That is why only *irony*, Cervantes's supreme tool, can turn around the obvious historicity of his *Persiles* and leave happiness and life *out of history*, as Hegel would have liked. The novel almost did not *end* in the sense that Cervantes was mortally ill when he rushed to complete the last chapters (one can see that some of them are barely sketches). He knew that he could not give his work a *finish* (in the sense in which artists use the word), but that he had to finish the story. And Cervantes does precisely that: the protagonists arrive at what was supposed to be their destination from page 1, all loopholes are tied, and they marry . . . and live happily ever after, except that such a life of happiness is not part of the story; it belongs to a nonnarrated continuation in which Sigismunda "vivió en compañía de su esposo Persiles hasta que biznietos le alargaron los días, pues los vio en su larga y feliz prosperidad."[30] Elsewhere I have amplified the intense irony of not even putting Persiles and Sigismunda together, as equal subjects of the same sentence.[31] Their time, in the one-thousand-pages-long story has been acquisitive time (with Rome as the object of acquisition). Countless shipwrecks have interrupted it, but "finally" they arrive. "What now?" seems to be the ultimate irony.

Still, the feature that is seldom—if ever—mentioned about *Persiles* (like the proverbial elephant in the room) is the fact that the New World, the basis of the complex Spanish web on navigation, is not an explicit part of the plot in a novel that has at its center the motif of the shipwreck. Scholars have, of course, seen how there are indirect, oblique, or symbolic references to it, whether in the entourage of "barbarians" or in utopias such as King Policarpo's island, but the fact remains that the *Historia septentrional* remains an *allegorical* story of *souls* from north to center, and not a representation of east-west routes of commerce. What is transported, or lost, in those ships is not the all-too-real gold of the Americas. Cervantes seems not to be interested in the subject. Even in *El celoso extremeño*, the one novella in which he has a protagonist who is an *indiano* (a man returned from the New World after having made a fortune), Cervantes only speaks of the empire as a preface to the story, which takes place entirely inside the protagonist's house.

Unless . . . well, unless Carrizales's house, with its extra walls and keys and *celosías* that allow only light from heaven, *is* the epitome of empire: the grotesque picture of the gold-fed polis in its most Deleuzian-Guattarian sense, protected against the war machine of the good-for-nothing Loaysa, the would-be seducer of the well-guarded wife.

So, Cervantes, it seems, does talk about the empire. But he does not do it overtly, like Góngora—in all his obscurity—does. One must look at places— spaces—such as Carrizales's house in *El celoso extremeño*, or the Duke's palace in *El Quijote*—I will shortly go there—to find the ultimate striation of space.

El Quijote, even if it does not speak—almost—of shipwrecks, is perhaps a more promising place to find a nomadology, or at least a critique of striation such as Deleuze and Guattari's (theirs is not a nomadology either; they confess as much). The hero here is the ultimate consumer of time, the ultimate wanderer: *adventure*, not *work*, is the nature of his movement. Part 2 of *El Quijote* explicitly centers on *razón de estado* from the first pages. In the entire book, the classical-allegorical function of the shipwreck as seen in *Persiles* is counterbalanced in

Cervantes by a much more political use of the shipwreck trope and the metony-
mies for empire.

I will focus, then, on a little shipwreck, as a miniature, as a snapshot of
the imbrication of empire and sea, with shipwreck as the submersion—pun
intended—of striated space into smooth space. It is a shipwreck small enough
to be preposterous, even if, in a master stroke, Cervantes has its protagonists
almost seriously drown in the midst of a comic set.

This mini-shipwreck is not in *Persiles*, but in *El Quijote* (just like the lesser-
known shipwreck by Góngora is not in *Soledades* but in *Polifemo*). That "little
shipwreck" is no other than "la Aventura del barco encantado," which is told in
part 2, chapter 29. I will closely read the episode, and simultaneously I will indicate how it interconnects with the entire structure of part 2 of *El Quijote*. Just
like John Beverley showed that *Soledades* is a monumental critique of the Spanish Empire, I will read part 2 as a devastating critique of the Spanish Empire.
A (hi)story, perhaps—not like the nomadology of *Soledades*—but bitter critique
nonetheless, which (unlike *Persiles*) does not avoid the elephant in the room.

To begin: this "political reading" is not mine. Cervantes makes it clear from
chapter 1 of part 2 that a sane Don Quixote engages with his friends in a conversation about "razón de estado" (politics). That, and how there are knights and
there are knights. Then, part 2 will have Don Quixote spend almost half the text
in the real palace of a real duke and duchess, with Sancho Panza being the real (?)
governor of a real (?) Insula Barataria, from where Sancho leaves, in absolute
baroque *desengaño*, to immediately find ethnic cleansing (the expelled *moris-
cos*) before accompanying his master to the "end of the line": the beach of Barcelona and defeat (after crossing a Catalan border marked by a different language
and—mostly—by dead, hanged, bodies), and death.

The adventure of the enchanted boat is placed by Cervantes just before the
encounter with the representatives of Spanish power. But critics have not addressed
this. For example, Francisco Rico's monumental edition of 1998 for the Instituto
Cervantes does not consider the possibility that the enchanted boat and the
empire might be related.[32]

The space of Don Quixote is tensely distributed by Cervantes as one in which
the nomadic madman turned knight-errant lets his horse choose which way to
go (the plain of La Mancha is ideal for that), but constantly comes into conflict
with the striated space of "reality": inns belonging to a specific innkeeper, bar-
ber bowls who are owned by specific barbers. This "smooth" space, in conflict
with striation, is complicated as the novel goes on: Cervantes takes his characters to Sierra Morena, the rugged labyrinth of mountains so different from the
endless plain of La Mancha.

In part 2, Cervantes keeps moving the space from underneath the main characters. First, he will have them go to El Toboso: a real place in which to find an
imagined Dulcinea. Then, to Zaragoza, to joust (i.e., to engage in fake fighting),

and to what could have been the end of the road: the Ebro River. It is now chapter 29 of part 2. A body of water as *limes*. Only a small one, but it suffices, because Don Quixote only needs a dinghy, and knowledge of geography, to completely circumnavigate the world. He is drawing a map of the cosmos—a map with a very poor scale, but a map, nonetheless. It is exactly the kind of striated space "canopied by the sky," "measurable," and "visual" that Deleuze and Guattari speak of. The river itself appears as calm as can be, but, on the other hand, the boat is drifting first, and then channeled toward powerful mills and wheels in a majestic image of striation. It is the millers who, trying to save the boat with Don Quixote and Sancho, turn it over inadvertently, ending the voyage in shipwreck.

It is uncanny how Cervantes, in order to contrast Don Quixote's space "canopied by the sky," has Sancho experiencing *precisely* the "tactile qualities" that Deleuze and Guattari attribute to the smooth space. Don Quixote, in his cosmos, uses the theoretical knowledge of how lice are supposed to die once you have crossed the equinoctial line and asks Sancho to experience for himself: "Y tórnote a decir que te tientes y pesques. Que yo para mí tengo que estás más limpio que un pliego de papel liso y blanco."[33] "To fish oneself." Was "fishing" not the very opposite of "navigating" in Góngora's *Soledades*? "A smooth sheet of white paper." Has Don Quixote not compared Sancho to the "blank page" that opposes history, according to Hegel, and that is as good an image of "smooth space" as that of the sea itself?

Sancho's answer, of course, is the best and most succinct counteraction to the Quixotic striation/mapping of space: "'O la experiencia es falsa, o no hemos llegado adonde vuesa merced dice, ni con muchas leguas.' 'Pues ¿qué?' preguntó don Quijote, '¿has topado algo?' '¡Y aun algos!' respondió Sancho."[34]

To the parallels, meridians, ecliptics, equinoctial lines . . . Sancho opposes the tactile truth of his lice. To the empire, described in cosmological terms even when it was praised (the empire in which the sun never sets), Sancho opposes the reality of poverty and misery. Other striated spaces will be offered to him: the governorship of Barataria, for instance. And, again, he will destroy all pretenses of virtuality/power/domination when he leaves it asking only for a half loaf of bread and a half wheel of cheese.

Cervantes has reduced the entire enterprise of the Spanish Empire to this micronavigation on the Ebro River, which ends in shipwreck. Its striated space dialectically fights with the smooth space it has invaded: "En esta aventura se deben de haber encontrado dos valientes encantadores, y el uno estorba lo que el otro intenta. El uno me deparó el barco y el otro dio conmigo al través. Dios lo remedie, que todo este mundo es máquinas y trazas, contrarias unas de otras. Y no puedo más."[35]

But just in case the reader thinks that this story is about some figment of imagination, Cervantes puts a definite touch that anchors the enchanted boat adventure as an imperial adventure. When the fishermen ask to be reimbursed for their lost boat, Cervantes could simply have had Sancho pay them, but the author wants to make sure that, as he says in relation to the encounter with the *morisco* Ricote, later on, what we are reading "trata de cosas tocantes a esta historia y no a otra alguna." Sancho does not just pay for the destroyed boat. He adds, "A dos barcadas como estas, daremos con todo el caudal al fondo." Cervantes does not forget about whoever is a prisoner in that unknown land ("Amigos, cualesquiera que seáis, que en esa prisión quedáis encerrados"). He simply cannot do anymore. "Perdonadme, que por mi desgracia y por la vuestra, yo no os puedo sacar de vuestra cuita."[36]

The entire part 2 of *El Quijote* is converging into *razón de estado*. Right after the enchanted boat shipwreck, Don Quixote and Sancho meet the Duke and Duchess: the real power, the real "knights" of the state. How the stay at their palace is a sadistic succession of cruelty, ineptitude, and stupidity is too obvious and too long to analyze in this chapter. And Sancho, right after his equally painful governorship of Barataria, encounters ethnic cleansing face-to-face: his neighbor Ricote, expelled from Spain while Cervantes was writing his book. That chapter (chapter 54 of part 2), is the one in which Cervantes remarks that it pertains to "esta historia y no otra alguna." Because, as Sánchez Ferlosio puts it, "No hay más Historia que la Historia de la dominación."[37]

So it would seem that in the same way that the end of history is nothing but the finality of capital and state, as they (capital and state) appear using the idea of time, striated space would have as its dream a totality; let us be careful with Deleuze and Guattari's advice to "make maps, not photos or drawings."[38] While it is clear that *mimesis* is the trap of reproduction, while *poiesis* still has the potential of *making*, it is also clear that the hidden wish of every map is to be total, to be the impossible (or is it still impossible when we already have it and its name is "internet"?) map with a scale of 1:1, made famous by Jorge Luis Borges and discussed by Umberto Eco. Such a map imposes striated space completely. It, on the other hand, finalizes the empire. As Eco puts it (and I do not know if this is a ray of hope in the totalitarian darkness, or the ultimate apocalypse at the hands of Silicon Valley), "Every 1:1 map of the empire decrees the end of the empire as such and therefore is the map of a territory that is not an empire."[39]

NOTES

1. Gilles Deleuze and Félix Guattari, *A Thousand Plateaus: Capitalism and Schizophrenia*, trans. Brian Massumi (Minneapolis: University of Minnesota Press, 1987), 479.

2. For another study that examines the shipwreck motif in relation to the reader as castaway in *Soledades*, see Elena Rodríguez-Guridi, "The Reader as Castaway: Problematics of Reading *Soledades* by Luis de Góngora," chapter 3 in the present volume.

3. Deleuze and Guattari, *A Thousand Plateaus*, 479.

4. Deleuze and Guattari, *A Thousand Plateaus*, 480.

5. Deleuze and Guattari, *A Thousand Plateaus*, 480.

6. Pedro Díaz de Rivas, *Discursos apologéticos por el estilo del "Polifemo" y "Soledades,"* in *La batalla en torno a Góngora (selección de textos)*, ed. Ana Martínez Arancón (Barcelona: Antoni Bosch, 1978), 141.

7. Miguel de Cervantes, *Novelas ejemplares*, ed. Harry Sieber, 2 vols. (Madrid: Cátedra, 1981), 53.

8. Julio Baena, *Quehaceres con Góngora* (Newark, DE: Juan de la Cuesta, 2011).

9. Luis de Góngora, *Fábula de Polifemo y Galatea*, in *Góngora y el "Polifemo,"* vol. 3, ed. Dámaso Alonso (Madrid: Gredos, 1985), lines 161–162.

10. Francisco de Quevedo, *Poesía lírica del Siglo de Oro*, ed. Elías L. Rivers (Madrid: Cátedra, 1997), lines 11–14.

11. Góngora, *Soledades*, pt. 1, lines 366–371.

12. Deleuze and Guattari, *A Thousand Plateaus*, 479.

13. Góngora, *Soledades*, pt. 2, lines 402–406.

14. Góngora uses the verb "pescar" (to fish) when referring to hunting seals, which was common usage during the period.

15. Deleuze and Guattari, *A Thousand Plateaus*, 23.

16. Deleuze and Guattari, *A Thousand Plateaus*, 482.

17. This discussion between Castillo and I is synthesized by William Egginton. See William Egginton, *The Theater of Truth: The Ideology of (Neo)Baroque Aesthetics* (Stanford, CA: Stanford University Press, 2010), 28.

18. Góngora, *Soledades*, pt. 2, lines 1–4.

19. Juan de Jáuregui, *Antídoto contra la pestilente poesía de las "Soledades,"* in *La batalla en torno a Góngora (selección de textos)*, ed. Ana Martínez Arancón (Barcelona: Antoni Bosch, 1978), 156.

20. Baena, *Quehaceres con Góngora*, 128–131.

21. Deleuze and Guattari, *A Thousand Plateaus*, 24.

22. Deleuze and Guattari, *A Thousand Plateaus*, 479.

23. Deleuze and Guattari, *A Thousand Plateaus*, 24.

24. Georg Wilhelm Friedrich Hegel, *The Philosophy of History*, trans. J. Sibree (New York: Willey, 1944), 26.

25. Max Horkheimer and Theodor W. Adorno, *Dialectic of Enlightenment*, trans. John Cumming (New York: Seabury, 1972), 32–37.

26. Agustín García Calvo, *Contra el tiempo*, 2nd ed. (Zamora, Spain: Lucina, 2001), 297.

27. Rafael Sánchez Ferlosio, *God and Gun: Apuntes de polemología* (Barcelona: Destino, 2008), 102.

28. García Calvo, *Contra el tiempo*, 16.

29. Sánchez Ferlosio, *God and Gun*, 102; emphasis in the original.

30. Miguel de Cervantes, *Los trabajos de Persiles y Sigismunda: Historia septentrional*, ed. Juan Bautista Avalle-Arce (Madrid: Castalia, 1969), 475.

31. Julio Baena, *Discordancias cervantinas* (Newark, DE: Juan de la Cuesta, 2003), 171–172.

32. Miguel de Cervantes, *El ingenioso hidalgo don Quijote de la Mancha*, ed. Francisco Rico (Madrid: Crítica, 1998).

33. Miguel de Cervantes, *El ingenioso hidalgo don Quijote de la Mancha*, ed. Thomas Lathrop Newark, DE: Juan de la Cuesta), 2000, pt. 2, 676.

34. Cervantes, *El ingenioso hidalgo don Quijote de la Mancha* (**2000**), pt. 2, 672–678.

35. Cervantes, *El ingenioso hidalgo don Quijote de la Mancha* (**2000**), pt. 2, 678.

36. Cervantes, *El ingenioso hidalgo don Quijote de la Mancha* (**2000**), pt. 2, 827, 678.

37. Rafael Sánchez Ferlosio, *Mientras no cambien los dioses, nada ha cambiado* (Madrid: Alianza Editorial, 1986), 69.

38. Deleuze and Guattari, *A Thousand Plateaus*, 25.

39. Umberto Eco, "On the Impossibility of Drawing a Map of the Empire on a Scale of 1 to 1," in *How to Travel with a Salmon and Other Essays*, trans. William Weaver (New York: Harcourt Brace, 1995), 106.

CHAPTER 3

The Reader as Castaway

PROBLEMATICS OF READING *SOLEDADES* BY LUIS DE GÓNGORA

Elena Rodríguez-Guridi

In *Soledades* (1613), an initial shipwreck on shore gives origin both to the pilgrim's itinerary on a new land and to the reader's intellectual voyage through the text, and the maritime disaster and exploration voyages are constant textual motifs. The shipwreck marks the end of the ship's course on the seas and the beginning of the pilgrim-castaway's route through the different stages of civilization he encounters on the island and, by analogy, the origin of both the narrative and historical discourse.[1] In his influential study about *relatos* of the Portuguese shipwrecks compiled in *Historia trágico-marítima*, Josiah Blackmore asserts that these maritime disaster texts constitute an antihistoriographical narrative that questions a hegemonic reading of empire, "upsetting the imperative of order and the unifying paradigms of 'discovery' or 'conquest' textuality."[2] That destabilization derives from the link Blackmore establishes between misfortune and writing, since shipwreck stories appear defined not just by the thematic presence of this motif but also "by a relationship between calamity and writing, where a certain kind of experience generates a certain kind of text."[3] Hence, shipwreck narratives, by projecting the castaway's physical and psychic state in the rough geography on a new land, reconstruct the experience of loss and disaster through a narrative "of rupture, breakage, and disjunction in which the context of maritime expansion plays a critical role."[4] Starting from these premises, this chapter intends to show how the disorientation characteristic of a shipwreck and the vicissitudes that the survivor experiences in a hostile landscape are reconstructed in the praxis of reading *Soledades* through the instability of meaning encountered amid the textual landscape of the *silva* (forest of verses).[5] In *Soledades*, the relevance of the shipwreck goes beyond its thematic presence and its condition as a violent initiation. The chaos inherent to a shipwreck disaster reveals the dynamics that underlie the whole poem and keep the reader in a constant linguistic and imaginary wreck. Furthermore, while, according to Blackmore and other critics, *relatos* of maritime disaster articulate that which is disjointed and, thus, provide some control and survival through the agency of the narrative, in *Soledades* we have a kind of shipwreck "squared": the poem instigates the experience of loss and disorientation through constant conceptual and syntactic contortions, depriving the reader of referents amid the textual chaos.[6] Ultimately, the destabilization that such tensions create on the reader's interpretative models delays the conformation of a uniform discourse and, as a consequence, a coherent narrative of historical progression and colonial expansion.

At the beginning of *Soledades*, the abduction and rape by Jupiter, described as "el mentido robador de Europa," hint at the subsequent birth of the "mancebito" and his expulsion on the beach. The rape, saturated with mythological and biblical allusions, announces the first incursion into a virgin natural world where the protagonist is shipwrecked—and into the *silva* in which the reader arrives. The birth of the mancebito from the primordial *Chaoskampf* and his first footprint on the sand begin the journey through the island, as well as the textual and historical journey—allegorized in the passage of the pilgrim through the different forms of civilization he observes during his travels.[7] As John Beverley has pointed out, faced with a textual and geographic landscape characterized by difficulty, both the pilgrim's and the verses' trajectory runs parallel to a progressive domestication of the landscape and culturalization of the societies that the protagonist experiences. During the pilgrim's journey this culturalization can be appreciated in the social relations that human beings have established with nature throughout history. In the course of his trek there is a progression from communities, from that of the goatherds, who live in brotherhood with nature, to societies where the natural world has been subjected to the Spanish mercantile obsession of the period. The pilgrim's journey and the progressive culturalization he observes on the island coincide with the gradual manipulation of signs that the reader must employ on the *silva*, the textual landscape, to sort out the textual difficulties and render the poem coherent.[8]

In the pilgrim's travels through different communities, greed appears as the main incentive for humankind's progressive control over nature and for colonial expansion. Ambition forms the backbone of the poem, its main denouncer being the old mountain man protagonist of the "discurso de las navegaciones" of the *Soledad primera*. The old man, like Adamastor in Luís de Camões's *Os Lusíadas*, tells the pilgrim about the history of navigation, lamenting the greed that has prompted the Spaniards to conquer the New World and die in the ocean:

Tú, Codicia, tú pues de las profundas
estigias aguas torpe marinero,
cuantos abre sepulcros el mar fiero
a tus huesos desdeñas.
    —(*Soledad primera*, lines 443–446)

The hubris that lead to the first sailing across the ocean—by the "labrador fiero" who first plows "el campo undoso en mal nacido pino" (*Soledad primera*, lines 370–371)—becomes actualized in the first trace of the shipwrecked pilgrim on the shore and in the first signs on the textual landscape:

Besa la arena, y de la rota nave
aquella parte poca
que le expuso en la playa dió a la roca;
que aun se dejan las peñas
lisonjëar de agradecidas señas.
    —(*Soledad primera*, lines 29–33)

This first incursion into the natural and textual landscapes originates both the *story* and the *history* that will develop throughout the castaway's journey, his itinerary constituting a miniature version of the history of colonial expansion.

Contemporary criticism has adopted a variety of stances regarding the invective of the old mountain man's "discurso de las navegaciones" and its political implications. On the one hand, his negativity is considered a rhetorical exercise that continues a tradition of denouncing navigation based on several classical authors. The tradition of the *psogos nautilias* (denunciation of seafaring) is a subgenre developed by ancient rhetoricians who criticized the invention of navigation as well as the practice of sea commerce.[9] According to Madoka Tanabe, the first passage of the discourse in *Soledades* corresponds to the first eight verses of Seneca's *Medea* and "repite el tópico de la 'maldición al primer navegante,' que nació en la literatura griega como crítica contra la osadía que aspira a cruzar el límite humano."[10] Seafaring denunciation appears related to the belief in a progressive degradation of humanity, which reaches its maximum expression in the Metal Age. Conceiving each of the states of civilization observed by the pilgrim as mimesis of the different cycles of historical change, Beverley asserts that Góngora adopts the version of the myth of the Metal Age from the first book of Ovid's *Metamorphoses*, in which "the fall of the mountain pine into water—navigation and therefore international commerce—marks the descent into the ages of the lesser metals. The tragic epic of the *serrano* (mountain man) in the *Soledad Primera* anticipates the outcome of these new technologies."[11] On the other hand, some critics relate the negativity of the "montañes prolijo" to Góngora's anticonformism toward the emerging capitalist order and thus to an attempt to discredit official history and raise awareness of nonofficial voices.

From this perspective, the poem becomes a commentary on the economic and historical crises of the Spanish Empire at the time and connects Góngora to the sociopolitical thought of pacifists like González de Cellorigo, Fernández de Navarrete, and Pedro de Valencia.

Although the "discurso de las navegaciones" and the shipwreck motif constitute for many the key that explains Góngora's political stance toward the imperialist enterprise, their importance resides in the fact that they expose the mechanics underlying the whole poem. The struggle of the castaway who strives to control unknown lands and societies by imposing the culture and knowledge from the Old World is analogous to the reading process. The reader, trying to render the poem coherent, confronts the difficulty of the textual landscape by applying a series of semantic, linguistic, and imaginary associations from his or her own cultural baggage. Hence, the colonizer's confrontation with the sea and nature through his explorations are mirrored by the reader's struggle with the text which, as we shall see, acquires the same properties as the water and topography of the landscape. Reading the poem through this lens, we find that the thirst for conquest—criticized by the old *serrano* as part of the navigation enterprise—mirrors the ambition of the reader, who strives to cognitively colonize the poem's confusion of signs by transferring his or her own cultural knowledge onto the text. In this sense, the untiring warlike confrontation between the sea and the navigator, who persists in controlling the sea despite the high cost in human lives, is projected onto a similar confrontation between what Betty Sasaki calls a "sea of signs" and the reader,[12] who restarts the textual "conquest" despite the "lastimosas señas" from previous battles:

> No le bastó después a este elemento
> conducir Orcas, alistar Ballenas,
> murarse de montañas espumosas,
> infamar blanquaendo sus arenas
> con tantas del primer atrevimiento
> señas, aun a los buitres lastimosas,
> para con estas lastimosas señas
> temeridades enfrentar segundas.
> —(*Soledad primera*, lines 435–442)

In this bellicose confrontation with a "sea of signs," the reader's travels, like those of the castaway, are characterized by an alternation between conquests and failures—that is, moments of understanding and moments of disorientation, advances and retreats, that expose the futility of conceived knowledge when applied to other realities. Thus, while working through the convoluted syntax to create a cohesive discourse, the reader becomes aware of the artifice that characterizes such an operation and, by extension, all narratives.

The reader, guided by certain European literary and cultural elements in the poem—mythological and biblical allusions, folk rituals, and ceremonies—uses these as coordinates to start an interpretative wandering through the *silva*. And although Góngora appeals to the reader's cultural knowledge and erudition through allusions to common references, he immediately subverts those references by making them point to an unfamiliar content. Such distortion can be found in multiple classical and mythological resonances that the intertextual fabric elicits in the reader. For example, in the following verses, even though the mythological allusions to Bacchus and the "male goat" activate a series of associations in the reader's mind, these are immediately altered by establishing an ironic relationship among such references and the flesh (the "cecina") or the death of Christ, who "redimió con su muerte tantas vid*a*s" (*Soledad primera*, line 160), mixing pagan cult and Christian rituals:[13]

> El que de cabras fué dos veces ciento
> esposo casi un lustro (cuyo diente
> no perdonó a racimo, aun en la frente
> de Baco, cuanto más en su sarmiento,
> triunfador siempre de celosas lides,
> lo coronó el Amor; mas rival tierno,
> breve de barba y duro no de cuerno,
> redimió con su muerte tantas vides),
> servido ya en cecina,
> purpúreos hilos es de grana fina.
> —(*Soledad primera*, lines 153–162)

Another one of the many examples of mythological distortion in *Soledades* is the reworking of one of Góngora's most common emblems, that of the phoenix. The vision of the bride at the wedding in the *Soledad primera* awakens in the pilgrim the memory of his beloved and the misfortune of love that caused his exile:

> Este pues Sol que a olvido le condena,
> cenizas hizo las que su memoria
> negra plumas vistió, que infelizmente
> sordo engendran gusano, cuyo diente,
> minador antes lento de su gloria,
> inmortal arador fué de su pena . . .
> —(*Soledad primera*, lines 737–742)

Although the myth of the phoenix is related to eternal rebirth, in these verses its meaning is altered by referring to the pilgrim's frustrated hope to win back the love of his beloved; as Colin Thompson notes, "The bird normally associated with hope has 'negras plumas' and the 'gusano' it engenders 'infelizmente' is one which will only increase his suffering."[14] In *Soledades* the phoenix's vital cycle thus becomes a mortal cycle that eternally recalls the pain of loss.

This distortion of classical and biblical models, which originally promised to orient the reader through a "sea of signs," is analogous to the ineffectiveness of nautical science that assured a navigator of a clear passage across the seas.[15] *Soledades* introduces several references to rigging and maritime instruments upon which the mariner relies during his seafaring voyages. Among these the compass is of particular interest due to its orienting function in a ship's course and in the pilgrim's expedition. The *serrano* denounces vehemently the audacity of the navigator who, in his colonizing ambition, blindly trusts the compass, which

> lisonjera
> solicita el que más brilla diamante
> en la nocturna capa de la esfera,
> estrella a nuestro Polo mas vecina.
> —(*Soledad primera*, lines 382–385)

The ship,

> En esta pues fiándose atractiva,
> del Norte amante dura, alado roble,
> no hay tormentoso cabo que no doble,
> ni isla hoy a su vuelo fugitiva.
>   —(*Soledad primera*, lines 393–396)

Throughout *Soledades* there are several references that transfer from the naval and maritime semantic fields to the geography crossed by the castaway, thus superimposing the nautical route and its reference points onto his land travels. For instance, when he climbs a mountain, the pilgrim finds his bearings through the "breve esplendor del mal distinta lumbre, / farol de una cabaña" that is at once the lantern lit on the topsail of the ship, which "sobre el ferro está en aquel incierto / golfo de sombras anunciando el puerto" (*Soledad primera*, lines 58–61). Later, once the summit has been reached, the carbuncle on which the pilgrim fixes his gaze to guide him is compared to the North or Polar Star that orients his compass needle:

> Tal diligente el paso
> el joven apresura,
> midiendo la espesura
> con igual pie que el raso,
> fijo, a despecho de la niebla fría,
> en el carbunclo, Norte de su aguja . . .
>   —(*Soledad primera*, lines 77–82)

As previously analyzed in relation to the mythological or biblical models, Góngora provides abundant associations from the Western collective imaginary, but he at once strips these referents of their guiding function, making the reader aware of their artifice and precariousness. In the same vein, the poem exalts the persistence of the explorer, who, entrusting his life to maritime technology, conquers the wildest areas of the planet to later undermine such exaltation in a veiled criticism of the infallibility of the naval doctrine that caused so many shipwrecks and deaths:

> Tantos luego Astronómicos presagios
> frustrados, tanta Náutica doctrina,
> debajo de la Zona aun más vecina
> al Sol, calmas vencidas y naufragios . . .
> —(*Soledad primera*, lines 453–456)

In fact, a constant in the poem is the praise of certain key moments of colonial conquest, which parallel moments of "textual control" and intellectual coherence, as well as their subsequent devaluation or dissolution. As Crystal Anne Chemris points out in her analysis of the poem's obsession with the baroque topic of *mudanza*, the series of images and intellectual associations in *Soledades* happen "in a dialectic with an engulfing void; each creative moment is countered by its inevitable dissolution."[16] This tendency is apparent in the exaltation of the victories achieved thanks to the maritime industry and their subsequent demystification as a result of loss and death. Just as in the rest of the poem there is a scheme against narrative progression—and, by analogy, against a discourse of conquest—here everything seems to conspire against the illusory control that maritime industry provides, since, as the *serrano* laments, greed is "de las profundas / estigias aguas torpe marinero" (*Soledad primera*, lines 443–444).[17] In sum, neither the art of navigation nor the mythological references nor astronomical omens ensures the navigator's control over the sea or the reader's cognitive control of the textual landscape.

The reader's constant effort to interpret the poem through inherited cultural parameters results in a reading that alternates between conquests and failures and between moments of understanding and of loss. This alternation between moments of disorientation and familiarization can be set side by side with notions of the humid and the dry that define Steve Mentz's analytic method.[18] For Mentz, shipwreck narratives alternate between the impact of immersion in the fluidity and chaos of water and the drying-out moments characterized by certain intellectual understanding: "Wet narratives emphasize disorder, disorientation, and rupture; they narrate experiences in which the usual ways of doing things get broken or fragmented. In these moments all forms and fancies of human order dissolve. But narrative cannot bear absolute immersion for long, and nearly all shipwreck stories also contain a dry countermovement that attempts to make sense and meaning out of disorder."[19] Along the same lines, Blackmore adopts Camões's representation of shipwreck texts as sharing characteristics essential to water. According to Camões, while the writing of texts served to perpetuate the hegemony of the Iberian Empire, shipwreck textual production is problematic in that it dissolves the boundaries between success and failure—or, as defined by Blackmore, shipwreck creates a "liquidating of the text"—since shipwreck texts are products of the empire's textual enterprise, a sign of its power, and symbols of its failure and disaster.[20] In *Soledades* the fluidity mentioned by Mentz and Blackmore is apparent in the conceptual dissolution that characterizes the text and transforms the process of reading into a constant nomadism. The "liquidating of the text" is achieved through a hermeneutics and an archeology that, returning language and objects to their origins, deconstruct the reader's cultural references and familiar concepts. This original state is achieved, for example, with the insistence on the etymology of words through an abundance of neologisms and Latinisms. William Ferguson, stressing this point, notices the line "al huésped al camino reduciendo" (*Soledad primera*, line 229) where the verb *reducir* is used in its Latin meaning of "conducir de vuelta."[21] In addition to this emphasis on the ancestral form of words, the return to a "prehistory" or origin can be appreciated in the archeology of some objects, which traces the history and development of a product since its inception. This history of objects "shifts the emphasis away from the end product to the processes by which they come to be" and exposes the relationship among members of a specific community and the natural world.[22]

In the pilgrim's meandering among different societies, this archeology traces an object's manufacturing process by identifying the raw material and craft invested in its production. One of the most frequent references to the utilitarian exploitation of nature is the different variations on the word *leño* that surface throughout the poem. The gradual appropriation of nature by explorers' mercantile and colonizing ambition can be measured in the dimension that the initial synecdoche of "leño" for "navío" acquires with the early modern development of seafaring history. Thus, the "errantes árboles" of classical antiquity have now become "robustas hayas" and "selvas inconstantes": "Piloto hoy la Codicia, no de errantes / árboles, mas de selvas inconstantes" (*Soledad primera*, lines 403–404). Likewise, some commonly used artifacts among the people in the poem are deconstructed through an archeology that identifies each of the elements that influenced their production. As I mention elsewhere, the wooden bowl in which the "peregrino" is offered milk in the "candor primero" of the *Soledad primera* appears embellished through a description that exposes the material and process that created it, as well as the type of relationship between the artisan and nature:[23]

Y en boj, aunque rebelde, a quien el torno
forma elegante dió sin culto adorno,
leche que exprimir vió la Alba aquel día,
mientras perdían con ella los blancos lilios de su Frente bella,
gruesa le dan y fría,
impenetrable casi a la cuchara,
del sabio Alcimedón invención rara.
—(*Soledad primera*, lines 145–152)

In these verses the conceptual unity of the bowl dissolves in a continuum between the final product and all of the elements that have been invested in its production and purpose (from the "boj" and "Alba" to the spoon "del sabio Alcimedón"). This archeology dissects every familiar object and concept into the multiplicity of its components. Such verbal and conceptual fluidity effects a "liquidating of the text" that transforms the poem into a water counterpart, thus exposing a movable reality in a permanent process of formation. As the castaway and the reader advance through history and the story, such conceptual fluidity is gradually territorialized, alternating between a more technical language and an exposure of a natural world that is progressively domesticated.[24] The "watery state" of some objects whose conceptual unity was dispersed in all of the elements invested in their production—be they mythological, human, or natural—gradually acquires "dryness" and cohesion through the practical and commercial value human beings impose on them. The dryness or usefulness transferred to nature by this territorialization runs parallel to the reader's progressively practical and cognitive control of the "sea of signs" to transform what was unfamiliar into a *discurso* that "tiraniza los campos útilmente" (*Soledad primera*, line 201).

Keeping in mind the intersection previously noted between the semantic fields of sea and land, this dry versus wet dichotomy developed by Mentz seems to reveal a certain poetics of *Soledades*. In the poem, imagery related to elements of fire and water abound: from the interaction of humidity and heat from which the "mancebito" emerges in the opening scene—"Del Océano pues antes sorbido, / y luego vomitado / no lejos de un escollo coronado / de secos juncos, de calientes plumas, / alga todo y espumas" (*Soledad primera*, lines 22–26)—to the constant topographic references in which sea and land are shown as flip sides of the same coin. The shifting of landscape images through the use of hypallages makes the solid and aquatic elements constantly merge into one another. Just as the text of *Soledades* dissolves and condenses in a linguistic back-and-forth movement, the fluvial and maritime regions consolidate in the rock and the mountain and the sea transposes its properties to the land, liquifying what was once solid: "Ondas endurecer, liquidar rocas" (*Soledad segunda*, line 41). This migration of natural attributes is apparent in the comparison of the sea to "una Libia de ondas" (*Soledad primera*, line 20) or in the castaway's perception during twilight of a horizon "que hacían desigual, confusamente, / montes de agua y piélagos de montes" (*Soledad primera*, lines 43–44).[25] Throughout the text this dry versus liquid dichotomy operates on several levels. In the alternation between intellectual dryness and chaos, the reader, in a permanent struggle to conquest the textual landscape, must continuously re-elaborate his or her cultural and intellectual associations.

This shifting between conquests and failures, moments of dryness and of conceptual dissolution, delays the consolidation of the images into unitary and defined concepts, thus postponing the cohesion and conclusion of any interpretation. In more ideal circumstances, history and the narrative might progress forward, much as the ship moves forward across the sea; yet here, in textual analogy to shipwreck, Góngora alters the progression of the story and of history through constant deferral, thus impeding any steady movement along the horizontal trajectory of advancement and progress. Pointing out the interweaving of wreckage and text that is characteristic of shipwreck stories, Blackmore considers the concept of *discurso* as a key for discursive and nautical practices: "'Discurso' is the path of the ship and the path of the narrative, and is even a synonym for narrative itself."[26] Consequently, the ship's inevitable renunciation of its *discurso* through the sea as a result of a shipwreck "creates a rupture in a symbolic imaginary where the controlled, forward-moving ship manifests a hegemony of empire or official culture."[27] By distorting all cultural and linguistic associations, the narrative course of *Soledades* avoids stability and permanence. This constant nomadism postpones the consolidation of knowledge and transforms the images into pure presence, thus resisting a discourse of imperial success and historical progress.[28] Consequently, the nautical disasters in the poem, as well as their textual representation, are defined by a movement of verticality and depth opposed to the horizontality implicit in the motto *plus ultra*, the essential referent for imperialism: "[Shipwreck] denotes a disastrous deviation from maritime horizontality and the power this horizontality represents."[29]

In *Soledades*, "the rupture in the symbolic imaginary" related to the imperial enterprise is apparent in the dialectic between a discourse of colonial expansion and progress that details the adventures of Christopher Columbus, Hernán Cortés, and Ferdinand Magellan, and its devaluation through the deaths overshadowed by such heroic deeds. The presence throughout the poem of the losses caused by maritime disaster distorts the epic echoes of naval exploits and destabilizes the official narrative of the empire. *Victoria*, the ship in which Magellan (and, after his death, Juan Sebastián Elcano) circumnavigated the globe, becomes an emblem of this Janus face by being the flagship of imperial domination at the cost of the captain's life. Referring to the baroque subject's peculiar position on the divide between the past imperial splendor and the present deep crisis, Beverley notes that "in such a situation the conventional forms of historical discourse—the chronicle, the imperialistic epic, the sycophantic political biography—have lost their mimetic force, have become more mystifications of history than attempts to render its inner logic."[30] In *Soledades* the destabilization of the temporal and spatial parameters necessary for a forward movement results in a hermeneutical shipwreck that situates the poem in a permanent struggle against the course of the story and of history, thus questioning any official discourse of colonial expansion.

A constant rupture of the maritime *discurso* allows for an emergence of those marginal voices silenced by the official version of history promoted by the empire. In this sense, Sasaki considers *Soledades* "a process which . . . entails the recovery of 'missed' readings—the fragmented accounts, buried beneath or cut off from the state's ideologically coherent edition of history."[31] Through those witnesses of the conquest present in the poem, like the *serrano* and the fisherman, a voice is given to the people already absent. Thus, the losses caused by maritime disaster or by the subjugation of the peoples of the New World emerge, threatening to alter history's official version. The series of tragic naval events eclipsed by the victories of the main protagonists of the conquest surface in the poem as "astillas" through a broken and fragmented syntax that resist the uniformity of imperialist discourse. The old man's monologue exposes in graphic form the human and material devastation caused by the incursion of the three ships of Columbus's voyages upon the sea—"Abetos suyos tres"—transformed in the *Soledad segunda* as

> trágicas rüinas de alto robre,
> que el tridente acusando de Neptuno,
> menos quizá dió astillas
> que ejemplos de dolor a estas orillas.
>   —(*Soledad segunda*, lines 384–387)

In his accusation, the old *serrano* becomes the main town crier of maritime disasters provoked by greed, among whose losses is his son's death,

> en tan inciertos mares,
> donde con mi hacienda
> del alma se quedó la mejor prenda,
> cuya memoria es buitre de pesares.
>   —(*Soledad primera*, lines 499–502)

In the *Soledad segunda* the old fisherman, a mirror image of the old *serrano* and affected likewise by maritime danger with the loss of his sons, characterizes the sea as a mouth that devours the ships and the tributes from the New World:

> ese voraz, ese profundo
> campo ya de sepulcros, que sediento,
> cuanto en vasos de abeto Nuevo Mundo,

tributos digo Américos, se bebe
en túmulos de espuma paga breve.
   —(*Soledad segunda*, lines 403–406)

Thus, through the constant presence of loss and death in *Soledades*, the poem, like the sea, becomes a space where the sedimentation of every unknown story accumulates and where "a hegemonic temporality intersects with other times, with the time of others, through bodies."[32]

The ship's drifting off course and its lack of forward movement also define the poem's structure and the series of advances and retreats in the reader's journey. Through a continuous displacement of meaning, reading *Soledades* is characterized by a back-and-forth movement that contributes to the poem's cyclical structure. The reader paces back and forth in a constant effort to decode a weaving of references and images in the text. Such oscillation, which is characteristic of shipwreck narratives, projects for Blackmore the same confusion and wandering of the castaway, who, lost in a new geographical landscape, constantly walks in circles, returning to the same places he believed he had left behind.

In *Soledades* the historical trajectory itself presents different lapses of time as past, present, and future dissolve into a history without chronology. This overlapping can be seen, for example, through references to a future history of navigation that precedes the chronological development of different historical periods in the poem. Thus, once the pilgrim has left the "bienaventurado albergue" of the primitive goatherds' community, the emblem of the Golden Age, he stops to muse in front of the ruins of an ancient fortress, remainder of a future militarized and warlike Iron Age, "cuando el que ves sayal fué limpio acero" (*Soledad primera*, line 217). The resistance to historical and geographic progression become riverbanks to which the pilgrim returns throughout the poem, revealing a journey that, despite the different stages of civilization described along the way, has no real development from beginning to end.[33] As Beverley observes, the coastline appears first as the context of the pilgrim's initial shipwreck, second as a preamble to the piscatory motifs at the beginning of the *Soledad segunda* ("Naufragio ya Segundo; *Soledad segunda*, 158), and finally as the landscape where the pilgrim ends in the final sequence of the poem:

Vencida se apeó la vista apenas,
que del batel, cosido con la playa,
cuantos da la cansada turba pasos,
tantos en las arenas
el remo perezosamente raya . . .
   —(*Soledad segunda*, lines 938–942)[34]

The coastline is thus both the point of departure and the point to which the pilgrim returns, emphasizing the cyclical structure of *Soledades*.

The circular journey of the pilgrim parallels the series of allusions and clues that move the reader to decode something previously mentioned or to predict a future event. For example, Colin Thompson, noting the interconnection of elements in the dense weave of allusions in *Soledades*, observes that the enigmatic characterization of the castaway at the beginning of the poem—as "náufrago, y desdeñado sobre ausente" (*Soledad primera*, line 9)—is resolved when, at the sight of the bride in the village, the pilgrim appears as "al instante arrebatado / a la que, naufragante y desterrado, / le condenó a su olvido" (*Soledad primera*, lines 734–736). Thus, the reader must go back to understand that the castaway's shipwreck has been motivated by an unrequited love.[35] Similarly, the reader is incapable of perceiving in all its magnitude the semantic resonance of greed until reaching the "discurso de las navegaciones."

The intricate structure of *Soledades* appears in symbiosis with the digressions of the *silva* and with the winding topography, meanderings that in turn mark the reader's mental process by the "torcido discurso" (*Soledad primera*, line 200). For example, analogous to the reader's effort to mentally synthesize the periphrasis and detours of the textual landscape, the *serranas* (mountain women) take a shortcut through the winding path:

> El arco del camino pues torcido,
> que habían con trabajo
> por la fragosa cuerda del atajo
> las gallardas serranas desmentido . . .
>   —(*Soledad primera*, lines 335–338)

In relation to this symbiosis between the textual and geographical digressions of *Soledades*, Marsha S. Collins highlights the characteristics of the *silva* as a visual and textual analogue: "As the silva traces its way across the pages of the Soledades, the poems acquire a sinuous, asymmetrical, meandering silhouette . . . that paints the thematic and structural outline of the works' artistic and natural landscape of labyrinthine sentences, wandering streams, abundant forests, rugged outcroppings, . . . I would suggest that the silva also provides a visual analogue to the movement of the human mind absorbed in the act of reading, grappling with seemingly incongruous images and ideas that flow together in nonlinear, associative patterns produced by sensory impressions conjured by the poetic language of gongorismo."[36] The course of reading through the *silva* is analogous both to the explorer's disorientation in the midst of the wild and abundant nature, described by Alvar Núñez Cabeza de Vaca and Christopher Columbus in their expeditions, and to the castaway's experience in the chaos of maritime disaster.[37]

Soledades's circular structure transforms the multiplicity of days, landscapes, and communities that inhabit the text—a simulacrum of temporal chronology and of historical progression—into a repetition of itself. The image of *Orbis Ter-*

rarum in the *Soledad primera* as a serpent biting its own tail is emblematic of such circularity and coincidence between the beginning and the end of the journey. Mercedes Blanco analyzes the different definitions of this image in antiquity and, adopting one of the meanings that Horapollo attributes to it in his *Jeroglíficos* or *Hieroglyphica*, considers its representation in *Soledades* as an image "de un 'océano siempre uno' que intenta anudar sus dos mitades, cabeza y cola, en el istmo situado en el centro del mapa circular; un istmo que es también el nudo, el gozne o el vínculo entre las dos mitades de América."[38] In fact, the poem insistently places us in such geographical interstices as isthmuses, islands, and straits (Gibraltar, Magellan, and Panama)—split points that produce geographical multiplicity. In *Soledades* everything gives the impression of multiplicity, accumulation, and ambition: acquisition of lands and seas and the succession of historical periods that, in the same way as the east-to-west route of the sun, reveal themselves as repetitions of the same. Thus, despite the progression of days and seasons, and the circumnavigation of the globe in four hundred days started by Magellan, the sun betrays the unity of the planet by returning over and over to the same point:

> Zodíaco después fué cristalino
> a glorïoso pino,
> émulo vago del ardiente coche
> del Sol, este elemento,
> que cuatro veces había sido ciento
> dosel al día y tálamo a la noche,
> cuando halló de fugitiva plata
> la bisagra, aunque estrecha, abrazadora
> de un Océano y otro siempre uno,
> o las columnas bese o la escarlata,
> tapete de la Aurora.
> —(*Soledad primera*, lines 466–476)

Just like the ellipse that the sun traces in its course around the earth on the zodiac, Magellan's expedition circumnavigated the globe crossing the "bisagras" between the Atlantic and Pacific Oceans, revealing in this continuity across the seas the unity of *Orbis Terrarum*. By placing readers directly on these geographical hinges, *Soledades* exposes the artifice of the cartographic lines that divide and territorialize land and sea, as well as that of the narrative and historiographic discourse that classifies and interprets reality.

Throughout its historical and narrative journey, *Soledades* reveals a natural and textual landscape gradually hypostatized and commodified as it submits to both the colonizing domination of civilization and to the cognitive and interpretative control of the reader. Hence, the castle's architecture and the falconry scene that the pilgrim observes in the court at the end of his travels reveal its mercantile fetishism by means of a highly domesticated natural world and a language full of technical and military terminology.[39] In this society the summit of the mountain that housed the goatherds' community in the *Soledad primera* has been transformed into a cultivated garden that surrounds a castle:

> En la cumbre modesta
> de una desigualdad del Horizonte,
> que deja de ser monte
> por ser culta floresta,
> antiguo descubrieron blanco muro,
> por sus piedras no menos
> que por su edad majestüosa cano . . .
> —(*Soledad segunda*, lines 691–697)

Similarly, the peasants' and fishermen's humility has been replaced by the violent and warlike action of a court society entertained by hunting and power games. Throughout the journey, the initial wandering and disorientation of the castaway have gained more agency, "con pie ya más seguro" (*Soledad primera*, line 56), and the reader has channeled the "agradecidas señas" (*Soledad primera*, line 33) of the beginning into a discourse. Once the unknown and the undiscovered have been transformed into the familiar, the poem brings us back to the original condition. The progressive subjection of the new land to the traditions, belief systems, and cultural values of the Old World makes it resemble more and more the present state of the world from which the pilgrim escaped. Hence, the conquest of the natural and textual landscape in *Soledades* shows itself as a solipsistic movement that, throughout the development of history and story, leads the reader/castaway to seek, like Narcissus, his or her own image:

> Esfinge bachillera,
> que hace hoy a Narciso
> ecos solicitar, desdeñar fuentes . . .
> —(*Soledad primera*, lines 114–116)

Conceiving *Soledades* as a reaction to the medieval system of analogies, where everything has its meaning within a divine plan designed by God, Chemris asserts that Góngora equates the "real" with the "represented" when describing objects as a product of the subject's perception and, consequently, as a construct. For Chemris, *Soledades* "portrays human thought, our capacity to perceive and to represent, as inherently solipsistic, revealing more about the nature of the self than about the reality it attempts to apprehend."[40] Once the mercantilist vision and Old World codes have been imposed on the New World, what remains is a territorialized, mapped, and textualized landscape that is assigned a commodity value and devoid of essence.[41]

In *Soledades* the appropriation of the landscape by mediation of culture, commerce, and technology results at the end of the poem in a reality in which everything is artifice because its value is linked to its exchange in the market's economy. This reality without essence, fluid and floating, suggests at the end of the historical and narrative sojourn a new shipwreck off the shore of the beginning.[42] As Beverley notes, if we follow Ovid's historical cycles, at the end of the Metal Age the gods send a flood to submerge all of the violence and corruption that humanity has reached at this point, sending us back to the primordial chaos that generates the first scene of the *Soledad primera*. After the flood, as envisioned by Ovid,

> land and ocean
> Are all alike, and everything is ocean,
> And ocean with no shore-line.[43]

The return to the shoreline at the end of the pilgrim's trajectory in *Soledades* transforms this ending into a textual mouth. Like the thirsty sea described by the old fisherman, this overlap between the journey's beginning and end swallows up the deeds of conquest and the greed that gave origin to the historical, geographic, and narrative *discurso*. While the ending of *Soledades* suggests a return to the beginning, however, after this reading experience neither the reader nor his or her perception of the world before the "textual conquest" appear under the same light. If, as Blackmore points out, the perpetuation of the empire depends on the imposition of its national identity on other lands, in the case of shipwreck stories "this identity has suffered shipwreck and has been left in pieces. The return home is more akin to being washed ashore; as culture and identity travel in the shipwreck tale, they are broken into pieces and rendered unfamiliar and unrecognizable."[44] After the experience of defamiliarization of the conceptual world and the necessary manipulation of the textual landscape, the reader has gained a perception of the inherent artifice in every historical representation of reality. The rebirth from the textual ashes implies a new genesis on the shoreline of the beginning of *Soledades*. Yet Góngora's phoenix comes back once more as a promise of sorrow and decease. Inevitably, the experience of the narrative and the historical conquest along the way have transformed this vital cycle of regeneration into an eternal recollection of loss and death.

NOTES

1. I adopt the notion of "discourse" as defined by Josiah Blackmore. Referring to the imbrication of wreck and text that characterizes shipwreck stories, Blackmore locates the concept of *discurso* as a key for both discursive and nautical practices. Josiah Blackmore, *Manifest Perdition: Shipwreck Narrative and the Disruption of Empire* (Minneapolis: University of Minnesota Press, 2002), 29.

2. Josiah Blackmore, "Foreword," in *The Tragic History of the Sea*, ed. and trans. C. R. Boxer (Minneapolis: University of Minnesota Press, 2001), xii. *Historia trágico-marítima*

is an anthology of a dozen stories of shipwrecks compiled and published by the Portuguese editor Bernardo Gomes de Brito in 1735–1736.

3. Blackmore, *Manifest Perdition*, xxi.

4. Blackmore, *Manifest Perdition*, 40.

5. Even though *Soledades* does not inscribe itself as a shipwreck narrative per se, this study considers that it shares many of the metaphoric, thematic, and symbolic dimensions that Blackmore explores in Portuguese shipwreck texts, especially in regard to the relationship he establishes between calamity and writing.

6. Steve Mentz, *Shipwreck Modernity: Ecologies of Globalization, 1550–1719* (Minneapolis: University of Minnesota Press, 2015), xxxi, notes that "anthropotechnic efforts to imagine order within disorder, or to reconceive disorderly experience within orderly frames, illuminate the struggles of premodern writers, thinkers, and mariners to comprehend their encounters with the global ocean." For Blackmore, *Manifest Perdition*, 29, this type of salvation is provided by the narrative and the reality of the printed text: "The shipwreck narrative is a second, or reenacted loss, and there exists an attempt on the part of the shipwreck authors to recuperate or repair loss through the agency of narrative . . . the fact that the shipwreck story can be told at all is a sign of a certain kind of salvation."

7. While examining the place that the sea occupies in poetic and religious traditions in order to understand the cultural importance of shipwreck stories, Mentz, *Shipwreck Modernity*, 28, points out that "many Western religions, including but not limited to Christianity, imagine a primal 'Chaoskampf' between a usually male God of the Sky who conquers a usually female Goddess of the Sea."

8. See John Beverley, "Introducción," in Luis de Góngora, *Soledades*, ed. John Beverley (Madrid: Cátedra, 1998), 20. Hereafter, Góngora's work will be cited parenthetically in the text, as *Soledad primera* or *Soledad segunda*.

9. Boris Dunsch, "'*Describe nunc tempestatem*': Sea Storm and Shipwreck Type Scenes in Ancient Literature," in *Shipwreck in Art and Literature: Images and Interpretations from Antiquity to the Present Day*, ed. Carl Thompson (New York: Routledge, 2013), 42–59, offers a detailed study of the subgenre of the *psogos nautilias*.

10. Madoka Tanabe, "Imágenes del mar en Góngora" (PhD diss., Universidad de Córdoba, 2016), 141.

11. John Beverley, *Aspects of Góngora's "Soledades,"* Purdue University Monographs in Romance Languages (Amsterdam: John Benjamins, 1980), 97.

12. Betty Sasaki, "Góngora's Sea of Signs: The Manipulation of History in the *Soledades*," *Calíope* 1, nos. 1–2 (1995): 150.

13. See Paul Julian Smith, *Writing in the Margin: Spanish Literature of the Golden Age* (Oxford: Oxford University Press, 1978), 89.

14. Colin Thompson, "Myth and the Construction of Meaning in the *Soledades* and the *Polifemo*," *Bulletin of Spanish Studies* 90, no. 1 (2013): 91.

15. The association we establish between the reference points that guide the reading and the instruments that guide the sailor in the ocean and the pilgrim on the ground is related to the comparison established by Roman poets between the composition of a text and the sea voyage.

16. Crystal Anne Chemris, *Góngora's "Soledades" and the Problem of Modernity* (Woodbridge, UK: Támesis, 2008), 93.

17. As Carrie L. Ruiz highlights in chapter 1 of the present volume, this critique of the conquest enterprise and of transoceanic trade is also present in the emblematic genre of the time in such authors as Sebastián de Covarrubias.

18. Bradley J. Nelson, "Góngora's *Soledades*: Portrait of the Subject," *Romance Languages Annual* 8 (1996): 611, situates the dry versus humid duality in terms of struggle: "We can see this struggle between the symbolic order and the real that it attempts to capture in its

net in the constant oppositions between *escollo* and *mar, pluma* and *espuma, leño* and *agua, pino,* or *pluma,* and *viento,* the yugo of marriage and the extra-nuptual [*sic*] bachannal."

19. Mentz, *Shipwreck Modernity*, 11.

20. Blackmore, *Manifest Perdition*, 27.

21. William Ferguson, "Visión y movimiento en las *Soledades* de Góngora," *Hispanófila* 86 (1986): 17.

22. Betty Sasaki, "Góngora's Sea of Signs: The Manipulation of History in the *Soledades*," *Calíope* 1, nos. 1–2 (1995): 154.

23. Elena Rodríguez-Guridi, "La orilla del discurso: Una topografía del desorden poético en las *Soledades* de Luis de Góngora," *Hispanic Review* 80, no. 1 (2012): 46–47.

24. For a detailed study of the global striation and territorialization produced by the Spanish Empire on the smooth space of the sea as processes operating in the background of *Soledades*, see chapter 2, by Julio Baena, in the present volume.

25. As Chemris, *Góngora's "Soledades,"* 79, notes, the alternation between the clear perception of the boundaries between regions and its dissolution projects an instability of the limits of perception and the order of things in the ancien régime: "Boundaries appear and disappear, delimiting and dissolving like the fishermen's net, which is 'siempre murada, pero siempre abierta.'"

26. Blackmore, *Manifest Perdition*, 29.

27. Blackmore, *Manifest Perdition*, xxvi.

28. In chapter 2 of the present volume Baena analyzes the shipwreck event in *Soledades* as effecting a *nomadification* of both story and history as a result of the imbrication of empire and sea.

29. Josiah Blackmore, "The Sunken Voice: Depth and Submersion in Two Early Modern Portuguese Accounts of Maritime Peril," in Thompson, ed., *Shipwreck in Art and Literature*, 64.

30. Beverley, *Aspects of Góngora's "Soledades,"* 87.

31. Sasaki, "Góngora's Sea of Signs," 162.

32. Ian Chambers, "Maritime Criticism and Theoretical Shipwrecks," *PMLA* 125, no. 3 (2010): 5.

33. As Juan de Jáuregui, one of the main detractors of *Soledades*, would criticize in his *Antídoto contra la pestilente poesía de las "Soledades,"* the protagonist himself is an atypical pilgrim who wanders without a particular destination.

34. John Beverley, "Soledad Primera, Lines 1–61," *MLN* 88 (1973): 235.

35. Thompson, "Myth and the Construction of Meaning," 90–91.

36. Marsha S. Collins, *The "Soledades," Góngora's Masque of the Imagination* (Columbia: University of Missouri Press, 2002), 55.

37. For an in-depth study on how Cabeza de Vaca's experience as a castaway shapes his new positionality, see the studies by Natalio Ohanna (chapter 4) and Fernando Rodríguez Mansilla (chapter 5) in the present volume.

38. Mercedes Blanco, *Góngora heroico: "Las Soledades" y la tradición épica* (Madrid: Centro de Estudios Europa Hispánica, 2012), 356.

39. As Beverley, *Soledades*, 154, points out, in the description of this stage of civilization found at the end of the *Soledad segunda*, Góngora begins to introduce military terms such as "duro son, foso, puente levadiza, tropa inquieta contra el aire armada, etc."

40. Chemris, *Góngora's "Soledades,"* 76. This solipsism is the product of a historical moment when empiricism and scientific developments make everything susceptible of being created and produced, and therefore devoid of truth or essence. In short, everything is perceived as artifice; the world can no longer be measured with reference to universal archetypes; there is no essence in things and phenomena, and everything can be manipulated and transformed.

41. The subjection of what is unknown to the reader's thought and to the mentality of a mercantilist society creates a reality in which, according to Andrés Sánchez Robayna, the representation of the world on a map that the pilgrim observes, which "si mucho poco mapa le despliega" (*Soledad primera*, line 194), and the textual map of the representation overlap: "El peregrino ve desde las rocas un mundo gráfico, un mapa, un mundo escrito." Andrés Sánchez Robayna, quoted in Enrica Cancelliere, "Las rutas para las Indias y la imaginación poética de Góngora," in *Actas del XIV Congreso de la Asociación Internacional de Hispanistas*, vol. 2, ed. Isaías Lerner, Roberto Nival, and Alejandro Alonso (Newark, DE: Juan de la Cuesta, 2004), 80.

42. Hans Blumenberg, *Shipwreck with Spectator: Paradigm of a Metaphor for Existence*, trans. Steven Rendall (Cambridge, MA: MIT Press, 1997), 8, points out that in Christian iconography "the sea is the place where evil appears, sometimes with the Gnostic touch that it stands for all-devouring Matter that takes everything back into itself." The sea is thus related to "Matter"—the maternal, the womb, the semiotic, always threatening because of its fluidity, wetness, and nomadism—and to death.

43. Ovid, *Metamorphoses*, quoted in Beverley, *Aspects of Góngora's "Soledades*," 91.

44. Blackmore, *Manifest Perdition*, 39.

CHAPTER 4

On Moral Truth and the Controversy over the Amerindians

THE *RELACIÓN* (1542) BY ALVAR NÚÑEZ CABEZA DE VACA

Natalio Ohanna

In an effort to trace the origins of Latin American literature in the first contacts between Europeans and Amerindians, studies of early chronicles and histories of the conquest often express a need to identify elements of primary sources that belong more to fiction than to the field of historiography. Considering the case of the *Relación* by Alvar Núñez Cabeza de Vaca—in which the author narrates the adventure of his shipwrecks, captivity, and arrival in New Spain after crossing the North American continent on foot between 1528 and 1536—the concern for taxonomy was such that it often led to the neglect of sociopolitical factors involved in its production, and to misrepresentation, if not to a reductionist reading of events.[1] The most commonly accepted opinions about the author align with the way he portrays himself: a faithful Christian, a strong leader, loyal to the interests of the crown, and an altruistic benefactor of the vulnerable inhabitants of America. Diametrically opposed readings have, however, been suggested—readings that, in their focus on a single aspect, tend to overlook the polyvalent nature of Cabeza de Vaca's writings. This chapter investigates two complex dimensions of the *Relación*: the first is the early modern notion of moral truth as historical license, serving a self-praising discourse that ponders the so-called *polémica de los naturales*, the moral and theological controversy that surrounded two conflicting ways of conceiving the colonization of America; the second is the disruptive character of the shipwreck narrative, in which the conquest loses its epic and chivalrous aura, the relationship between dominators and the dominated is reversed, and the conqueror ends up living with those who were to be his victims. In other words, this chapter focuses on the fundamental fact that the *Relación* transcends self-referentiality. In the pursuit of a moral truth of history, exposing an imperial failure that gives rise to a firsthand experience, the text destabilizes common prejudices and generalizing ideas with which coercion was rationalized.[2] In so doing the 1542 account—regardless of intention—offers powerful insight to the polemics on the legitimacy of Spanish actions in the New World.

In his proem, Cabeza de Vaca claims to have written the *Relación* in service to Emperor Charles V, so that his majesty can most benefit from the author's experience in America. Cabeza de Vaca refers to all that he saw and learned in the time he walked—lost and naked—through so many strange lands, the locations of those territories, the foodstuffs and animals produced in them, and the diverse customs of the many and most barbarous peoples with whom he conversed and lived.[3] He then adds that he held everything seen and lived for so many years in his memory, only in order to report back, "Porque aunque la esperança que de salir entre ellos tuve siempre fue muy poca, el cuidado y diligençia siempre fue muy grande de tener particular memoria de todo, para que si en algún tiempo Dios nuestro Señor quisiesse traerme adonde agora estoy, pudiese dar testigo de mi voluntad y servir a Vuestra Magestad" (18). Finally, he specifies the nature and usefulness of such service: "La relación dello es aviso, a mi parescer no liviano, para los que en su nombre fueren a conquistar aquellas tierras; y juntamente traerlos a conosçimiento de la verdadera fe y verdadero Señor y servicio de Vuestra Magestad" (18–20). The didacticism stands out here: the *Relación* can be used as a guide for future military campaigns in the region, while simultaneously providing guidance on how to convert Indigenous peoples into Christians and faithful subjects of the emperor. In this sense, Cabeza de Vaca seems to propose an answer to the great dilemma of his time: how to reconcile the material and spiritual conquests in the New World (i.e., the expansion of the empire and the spreading of faith) without incurring legal or doctrinal contradictions. This exordium is extremely relevant. In the years when the *Relación* was written and first published (1536–1542), the polemics on the legal, moral, and ethical legitimacy of Spanish actions in America reached an inflection point.[4] Cabeza de Vaca's narrative would shed new light on the matter: as a survivor of the disastrous Pánfilo de Narváez expedition to La Florida, his word is rooted in direct knowledge, and, as he makes clear, he experienced numerous cultures from within, and thus the emphasis on the seen and the lived. After announcing this purpose, Cabeza de Vaca adds that his account was written with documentary rigor: "con tanta çertinidad que aunque en ella se lean algunas cosas muy nuevas y para algunos muy difíciles de creer, pueden sin dubda creellas, y creer por muy cierto que antes soy en todo más corto que largo, y bastará para esto averlo yo offrescido a Vuestra Majestad por tal" (20). In this way he warns readers about the unusual nature of some passages, which, in some scholarship have given rise to a long-standing debate about whether the text belongs more to fiction than to the field of history or ethnography.

Under the premise that any work from the past can be read with contemporary criteria, David Lagmanovich finds that, beyond the general model of the chronicle or account, there are elements of modern realism that anticipate some aspects of the picaresque novel, a doctrinal attitude in favor of the Native American, and a presence of the marvelous that is impossible not to connect to some writers of the twentieth century.[5] From another angle, José Rabasa observes a tension between the particular (the true account) and the universal (the meaning of events), and concludes that Cabeza de Vaca seeks to develop a textual alternative that allows him to communicate an inapprehensible experience that does not participate in the temporality of Western narrative. Rabasa also shares a favorable opinion of the author: "No cabe duda de que Alvar Núñez es un colonizador benévolo, con las mejores de las intenciones."[6] Later, though, Rabasa amended this judgement, expressing reservations: "It seems to me that the seductive powers of the *Naufragios*, that is, what makes it a brilliant literary piece, have led historians and critics alike . . . to argue that Cabeza de Vaca underwent a personal transformation that enabled him to formulate and exemplify a 'peaceful conquest.'"[7] For his part, Robert Lewis detects a series of tensions between the historical and the fictional qualities of the work, which seem to originate in three circumstances. First, there is a persuasive function: as Cabeza de Vaca was lacking in military conquests and riches, he had to resort to the construction of a story that, through its compelling and strong narrative qualities, would help him win the favor of the monarch and the desired honors. Second, Lewis considers the dependence on memory at the time of conferring order and meaning to some strange and chaotic experiences. Finally, he addresses the problem of verisimilitude: to become credible, Cabeza de Vaca had to use the discursive resources necessary to incorporate experiences of Indigenous culture into his story, elements that could hardly be explained within the European cognitive and value system.[8]

Clearly inclined toward the defense of truthfulness, other readers underscore the ethnographic value of the text. As Enrique Pupo-Walker explains, the author illuminates many aspects of nomadic life and tribal relations, such as war actions, the exchange of goods, and the eating habits of Amerindian cultures. Even more, following Claude Lévi-Strauss, Pupo-Walker credits the passages referring to the miraculous cures performed by the survivors.[9] In a similar vein, Silvia Spitta interprets such moments in terms of a symbolic overlay: "Aunque él se vuelve curandero indio de mucho éxito, a la hora de relatar sus experiencias sólo logra hacerlo apelando a un discurso religioso occidental, y sólo de paso y de vez en cuando deja traslucir la extensión de sus prácticas chamánicas."[10] This would point, in Spitta's opinion, to two overlapping planes: Cabeza de Vaca's "shamanic

experiences" and their formulation in a Christian religious discourse that invalidates and obfuscates them.[11] The most radical position belongs to Juan Francisco Maura, for whom literary creation prevails and discredits any ethnographic
value the text may have. Maura finds a link between the persuasive function of
the work and its fictitious resources—literary elements that do nothing more
than introduce the narrator and protagonist as the good shepherd of the Native
American in a *Vita Christi* aimed at convincing Charles V of the importance of
his actions. But this assumed devoted and philanthropic vision would not align
with some facts of Cabeza de Vaca's life, a man who "consiguió la Gobernación
y la Capitanía General del Río de la Plata, y no precisamente para seguir haciendo
de 'mártir,' sino para sojuzgar a los indios rebeldes e imponer su autoridad frente
a sus compatriotas."[12]

Considering the positions collated here and elsewhere,[13] it becomes apparent
that there was an excessive concern for categorization as it relates to the problem of truthfulness. Yet history, ethnography, and the novel, as they are understood today, are modern concepts whose literary precepts did not apply to
sixteenth-century authors in the same way, and with the same rigor, as they are
imposed on us. As David A. Boruchoff points out, the persistence of the roman-
tic concern for the taxonomic affects the understanding of a past in which there
was really no distinct boundary between literature and historiographical genres:
"Early modern authors continually stretched the traditional concept of history
as a documentary medium by employing fictional devices to attain to higher
truths that exist not in the facts of history as for Hegel, but beyond these facts in
philosophy and religion."[14] The idea of higher truth was well defined by Jerónimo
de San José in terms of a moral benchmark or point of reference in history
writing, which at times required nothing less than a deviation from actuality:
"Parecerá dificultoso que haya narración verdadera, y que sea de cosas falsas."
Though there is a point, he notes, at which the sides of the oxymoron become
compatible, because "bien considerada la naturaleza de la verdad y de la falsedad, hallaremos que se puede juntar en algún modo y sentido la verdad de la
narración con la falsedad de las cosas que se narran." He then clarifies, "La verdad moral consiste en un ajustamiento y conformidad de las palabras con la
mente o concepto e inteligencia de las cosas, como la natural en el ajustamiento
de las palabras y mente con las cosas mismas en la realidad de su ser."[15] This is
to say that moral truth requires that words adapt to the mentality, concept, and
intelligence of things as they should be, while, in natural history, words must
attend to the concept and intelligence of things as they are, as facts. Challenging in this manner the Aristotelian precepts, San José believed that human history should not adhere to an accurate reference of what was, but instead to the
reconstruction of what should have been, since only the latter could conform
more faithfully to a higher and universal truth, to a moral truth of things.

San José's ideas did not originate in an isolated philosophy. In the same way, in search of the seed of history, the Italian poet Torquato Tasso highlights the value of writing *poetando*, not to narrate the particular as a historian but to formulate universals as a philosopher: "Non volle narrare come istorico i particolari, ma come filosofo formare gli universali: la verità de' quali è molto più stabile e molto più certa."[16] In search of equally didactic purposes, in that same century Gonzalo Fernández de Oviedo also sought to enunciate universals. Examples abound throughout his *Historia general y natural de las Indias*, but it should be emphasized that at the beginning of the narration based on the joint report that Cabeza de Vaca, Alonso del Castillo Maldonado, and Andrés Dorantes de Carranza offered to the viceroy of New Spain in 1536, the chronicler presents the reader with a moral lesson about greed: "Paresce que les da el tiempo su pago a los hombres que no se contentan con lo honesto, en especial aquellos a quien Dios les da de comer e los pone en buen estado y edad para reposar e darle gracias, sin que la cobdicia debiese alterarlos ni mover a buscar nuevos trabajos."[17] Fernández de Oviedo refers to Narváez's tragic end as an example for the reader, and then concludes, "Deben los hombres, para perpetuarse, no en esta mortal morada, sino en la que para siempre ha de permanecer, conformarse, e fundarse en limpios deseos que no discrepen del servicio de Dios."[18] The universal lesson is thus perfectly delineated. Not surprisingly, decades later, a similar concept of history would inspire José de Acosta. In the prologue to the fifth, sixth, and seventh books of *Historia natural y moral de las Indias* (1590), he announces that "el intento de esta historia no es sólo dar noticia de lo que en Indias pasa, sino enderezar esa noticia al fruto que se puede sacar del conocimiento de tales cosas, que es ayudar aquellas gentes para su salvación, y glorificar al Creador y Redentor." In this fashion, Acosta expounds on the historical license that guides the narrative so that a moral benefit can be harvested: "No es mi propósito escribir ahora lo que españoles hicieron en aquellas partes, que de eso hay hartos libros escritos; ni tampoco lo que los siervos del Señor han trabajado y fructificado, porque eso requiere otra nueva diligencia; sólo me contentaré con poner esta historia o relación a las puertas del Evangelio, pues toda ella va encaminada a servir de noticia en lo natural y moral de las Indias, para que lo espiritual y cristiano se plante y acreciente."[19]

Like other authors of the time, Cabeza de Vaca pursued a moral truth of history when writing the account of his adventure in America. Didacticism transcends the particulars of his experience in search of a higher and universal truth and permeates the narrative in a calculated way. And, to that end, the most effective and well-known reference was the Bible. Let us consider an episode that takes place after his arrival to the Avavares tribe. Cabeza de Vaca tells us that one day, having gone out to look for a fruit from some trees, he got lost: "La gente se bolvió y yo quedé solo, y veniendo a buscarlos, aquella noche me perdí. Y plugo

Dios que hallé un árbol ardiendo, y al fuego dél passé aquel frío aquella noche, y a la mañana yo me cargué de leña, y tomé dos tizones y bolví a buscarlos" (156). The passage infers a moment of initiation for Cabeza de Vaca, who subtly outlines the allegory of a providential journey. In all likelihood, sixteenth-century readers would not have hesitated to connect the tale with the moment in the book of Exodus when Moses, alone in the desert (like Cabeza de Vaca), is presented with the angel of Jehovah under the guise of a burning bush (Exod. 3:2). The allusions to the bare feet (Exod. 3:5) and the snake (Exod. 4:3) emphasize this parallel and add symbolic value to the narration. Other passages of moralizing effect also refer to scripture—for example, in the episode of captivity under the Arbadaos: "No tenía, quando en estos trabajos me vía, otro remedio ni consuelo sino pensar en la Passión de nuestro Redemptor Jesuchristo y en la sangre que por mí derramó, y considerar quánto más sería el tormento que de las espinas él padesçió que no aquel que yo entonces suffría" (172). Cabeza de Vaca's comparison to Christ cannot be more explicit; yet the most audacious and controversial cases are those related to the miraculous healings performed by the survivors of the shipwreck, and, among those, the resurrection parable stands out: "Dixeron que aquel que estava muerto y yo avía curado en presencia dellos se avía levantado bueno y se avía passeado y comido y hablado con ellos, y que todos quantos avía curado quedavan sanos y sin calentura y muy alegres. Esto causó muy gran admiración y espanto, y en toda la tierra no se hablava en otra cosa" (163–164).[20] Although Cabeza de Vaca distances himself from the source of this information—it was the natives who said that he had raised a dead man—the matter would not go unnoticed by the author's contemporaries. Fernández de Oviedo treats the subject with ambiguity. When he begins the story of the unfortunate expedition, the chronicler states that "subcedieron cosas de mucho dolor y tristeza, e aun miraglos en esos pocos que escaparon o quedaron con vida, después de haber padescido innumerables naufragios e peligros." He then relativizes the issue by referring to what the natives believed, but without completely discarding its truthfulness: "En estos indios había muchos ciegos, e muchos tuertos de nubes en grand cantidad, . . . mas allí curaron todos los ciegos e tuertos e otras muchas enfermedades, e a lo menos si los cristianos no los sanaban a todos, los indios creían que los podían sanar." Finally, Fernández de Oviedo highlights the moral truth of history:

¿Paréceos, lector cristiano, que es contemplativo este paso y ejercicio diferente de los españoles que estaban en aquella tierra, e de los cuatro peregrinos: que los unos andaban haciendo esclavos e a saltear, como de suso es dicho, e los otros venían sanando enfermos e haciendo miraglos? . . . De que podéis colegir cuánta parte destos trabajos consiste en la buena o mala intención e obras de los mismos cristianos, e por el número de los muertos e de los vivos, podéis conjeturar lo que os pareciere. Pues no los tengáis a todos los que por acá

andan e han andado por españoles, aunque la mayor parte de ellos lo son, sino
de diversas naciones, que llamándose cristianos, acá han pasado en busca deste
oro, e algunos lo hallan por su mal, e otros nunca lo topan, sino la muerte e
angustias tales como las que podéis haber entendido de aquesta lección.[21]

For his part, and without signs of skepticism, the Spanish historian Francisco
López de Gómara attributes the miraculous cures to the survivors themselves:
"Los cuales anduvieron perdidos, desnudos y hambrientos nueve años y más por
las tierras y gentes aquí nombradas, y por otras muchas, donde sanaron calen-
turientos, tullidos, mal heridos, y resucitaron un muerto, según ellos dijeron."
He refers to the matter again in the chapter on South America: "Año de 41 fue al
mismo río de la Plata, por adelantado y gobernador, Alvar Núñez Cabeza de
Vaca, natural de Jerez, el cual como en otra parte tengo dicho, había hecho milagros."[22] It should be noted that if López de Gómara substantiates miracles, confirming and ascribing them to the survivors, he does so to serve the moral truth
of his *Historia general de las Indias* (1552). In the broadest sense, this is a tribute
to the conquerors and, above all, a glorification of the American enterprise as
an act of providence in which the Spaniards are the chosen people who will do
the supreme work of spreading faith. Years later, Inca Garcilaso de la Vega does
not question the veracity of these passages, by then canonized, but he does criticize the attitude of the wayfarers, and comments with irony, "Escapó con otros
tres españoles y un negro y, habiéndoles hecho Dios Nuestro Señor tanta merced que llegaron a hacer milagros en su nombre, con los cuales habían cobrado
tanta reputación y crédito con los indios que les adoraban por dioses, no quisi-
eron quedarse entre ellos, antes, en pudiendo, se salieron a toda prisa de aquella
tierra y se vinieron a España a pretender nuevas gobernaciones."[23]

In his own reading, Jacques Lafaye offers a sound interpretation of these healing practices and the way they were understood by Cabeza de Vaca's contemporaries. From the viewpoint of the communities of northern New Spain, the image
and fame of shamans enjoyed by the survivors would be stimulated by local
forms of spirituality and cosmology: "Puesto que lo sagrado impregnaba los actos
más anodinos de su existencia, vivían en clanes, practicaban ritos colectivos y
su vida individual era muy reducida, los indios tenían que presentar un terreno
selecto para las oleadas de entusiasmo religioso."[24] Such a rationale makes far
more sense if one remembers that Cabeza de Vaca attributes no miracle to himself. In fact, time and again he makes clear that neither he nor his companions
were healers by their own will and initiative, but that they were so at the stub-
born demand of the natives themselves: "Dorantes y el negro hasta allí no habían
curado, mas por la mucha importunidad que teníamos, veniéndonos de muchas
partes a buscar, venimos todos a ser médicos" (164).[25] On the other hand, from
the chroniclers' perspective, an explanation for their own gullibility emerges
from a well-known context: the providentialism that permeates the ideals of the

American enterprise. Once the Moors were thrown out of Spain or converted, and while the front against Lutheranism was maintained, there was no doubt that Catholicism would soon coincide with the limits of the universe itself. The European encounter with America, together with its material and spiritual conquests, embodied a holy endeavor of Christianity that would renew and expand the church and, in so doing, earn it its miracles and martyrs. As Lafaye observes, conquerors and evangelizers were convinced that they were instruments, if not protagonists, of a providential plan. They saw themselves as witnesses of the most formidable moment of humankind since the Incarnation.[26] Such an ideological and spiritual background explains the sensibility of Cabeza de Vaca's contemporaries to interpret and digest the moral truth of history, especially at a time when chronicles and accounts, or *relaciones*, were considered effective vehicles for the dissemination of edifying examples for the glorification of national or religious heroes and, above all, as ways to exalt moral values that were often intermingled with political or even personal agendas.[27]

Just as Toribio de Benavente Motolinía equates the twelve Franciscans who arrived in the New World in 1524 with the twelve apostles of Christ in his *Memoriales*,[28] and as decades later Acosta does in his *Historia natural y moral*, so Cabeza de Vaca guides his *Relación* toward a higher truth. To do so effectively, one of his most frequent strategies is to portray the Amerindians as human groups that are naturally inclined to piety and faith. Given what he has seen and experienced among so many cultures, intimidation and violence would be pointless. In this sense, it is important to keep in mind the disruptive nature of the shipwreck narrative, which reverses the perspective, enabling for the first time a view of the Amerindian from within. In the direct encounter with a different cultural universe and its peculiarities, ways of thinking and feeling, myths and beliefs, there is a compulsory effort of interpretation, of translation. Perhaps the most clear example in this regard is the well-known episode of a bizarre figure that, as reported by the natives, frightened the people of the region: "Un hombre que ellos llaman mala cosa, y que era pequeño de cuerpo, y que tenía barvas aunque nunca claramente le pudieran ver el rostro, y que quando venía a la casa donde estavan, se les levantavan los cabellos y temblavan, y luego paresçía a la puerta de la casa un tizón ardiendo." The portrait concludes with a most suggestive comment: "También nos contaron que muchas vezes le dieron de comer y que nunca jamás comió, y que le preguntavan [de] dónde venía y a qué parte tenía su casa, y que les mostró una hendedura de la tierra y dixo que su casa era allá debaxo" (166). The allusions to the evil character of Mala Cosa—the fear he aroused among the natives, the burning firebrand, and, of course, the fact that he had his dwelling beneath the earth—signal a rather overt image of Christian mythology.[29] As Rolena Adorno points out, Cabeza de Vaca did not have to attribute the visits of Mala Cosa to satanic intervention for his readers to understand that this was his way of interpreting it.[30] Naturally, cultural transfer is unavoidable in this translation of the supernatural to the European code of beliefs, but the mere selection of the incident serves a very deliberate purpose as it attests to the evangelizing efforts of the survivors: "Nosotros les diximos que aquél era un malo. Y de la mejor manera que podimos les dávamos a entender que si ellos creyessen en Dios nuestro Señor y fuessen christianos como nosotros, no ternían miedo de aquél ni él osaría venir a hazelles aquellas cosas" (168). Oddly enough, this is not a random and disconnected episode. It contributes to the moral truth of the *Relación*, as Cabeza de Vaca will emphasize time and again the natives' ability to understand and embrace the principles of faith: "Dixímosles por las señas, porque nos entendían, que en el cielo avía un hombre que llamávamos Dios, el qual avía criado el cielo y la tierra, y que éste adorávamos nosotros y teníamos por Señor, y que hazíamos lo que nos mandava, y que de su mano venían todas las cosas buenas, y que si ansí ellos lo hiziessen les iría muy bien dello. Y tan grande aparejo hallamos en ellos que si lengua huviera con que perfetamente nos entendiéramos, todos los dexáramos cristianos" (232–234).

The way in which the evangelization motive relates to moral truth becomes even more conspicuous along the corn route, when the survivors are harassed by a crowd that is thirsty for spirituality. Such passages highlight a seemingly personal conviction that spreading the gospel without coercion is not only feasible but also needed, as the natives display a tremendous eagerness to be protected by faith.[31] The futility of violence is further exemplified in the march of the survivors, which leaves a pacifying effect in its wake: "Por todas estas tierras los que tenían guerras con los otros se hazían luego amigos para venirnos a resçebir y traernos todo quanto tenían. Y desta manera dexamos toda la tierra" (232).[32] The key moment, however, arises toward the end of the adventure, when Cabeza de Vaca refers to the communities of New Spain's northern border that had already experienced the colonial presence:

> Y preguntados en qué adoravan y sacrificavan y a quién pedían el agua para sus maizales y la salud para ellos, respondieron que a un hombre que estava en el çielo. Preguntámosles cómo se llamava. Y dixeron que Aguar, y que creían que él avía criado todo el mundo y las cosas dél. Tornámosles a preguntar cómo sabían esto. Y respondieron que sus padres y abuelos se lo avían dicho, que de muchos tiempos tenían notiçia desto, y sabían que el agua y todas las buenas cosas las embiava aquél. Nosotros les diximos que aquel que ellos dezían nosotros lo llamávamos Dios y que ansí lo llamassen ellos y lo sirviessen y adorassen como mandávamos y ellos se hallarían muy bien dello. Respondieron que todo lo tenían muy bien entendido y que assí lo harían. (258)

In the spirit of the moral truth of the story, the parallel between the ancestral beliefs of these societies and Christianity is such that their conversion could begin with something as simple as an onomastic adjustment. As Cabeza de Vaca emphasizes the natives' ability to understand and consent to what they are taught, he highlights the value of a constructive approach, providing a solution to the problem of violence and recommending that, when the Spaniards arrive, the natives go out to welcome them with crosses in their hands and invite them into their homes (260). The viability of an interaction that avoids bloodshed is confirmed by positive results.[33] In this light, the survivor of the Narváez expedition addresses the emperor with the assertion that, given what he has seen and lived among so many peoples in so many regions, peaceful evangelization is achievable: "Lo qual tenemos por çierto que assí será, y que Vuestra Magestad a de ser el que a de poner esto en effeto" (262). Such a task, he claims, "no será tan diffíçil de hazer, porque dos mil leguas que anduvimos por tierra y por la mar en las barcas, y otros diez meses que después de salidos de cativos sin parar anduvimos por la tierra, no hallamos sacrificios ni idolatría" (262).

It goes without saying that the *Relación* makes an effort to amend stereotyped views and prejudices about Indigenous peoples. In the face-to-face encounter enabled by shipwreck and subsequent coexistence with the Amerindians, imagination gives in to reality, direct knowledge overpowers assumption, and preconceptions reveal their constructive nature. Generalizing ideas thus lose the appearance of certainty from which they operate, which leads to their adjustment or, in the best-case scenario, an active urge to revoke them. As presented by Cabeza de Vaca the inhabitants of these lands are not all equal; they are neither angels nor demons, they do not lack in judgment or intellectual maturity: they are simply human beings, worthy of human treatment[34]—hence his resolve to criticize the violence that becomes increasingly explicit as the survivors approach New Spain: "Anduvimos mucha tierra y toda la hallamos despoblada, porque los moradores della andaban huyendo por las sierras sin osar tener casas ni labrar por miedo de los christianos" (238). This comment invites commiseration while raising the problem of material resource waste: "Fue cosa de que tuvimos muy gran lástima, viendo la tierra muy fértil y muy hermosa y muy llena de aguas y de ríos, y ver los lugares despoblados y quemados y la gente tan flaca y enferma, huida y escondida toda" (238).[35] From this perspective, the *Relación* highlights the level of cultural development of these societies that, like other civilized nations, built their homes and worked the land, clearly showing that they are people of reason, capable of embracing faith and self-governance. In stark contrast is the level of barbarism of those who hunt them for material gain: "Y aun contáronnos como otras vezes avían entrado los christianos por la tierra, y avían destruído y quemado los pueblos y llevado la mitad de los hombres y todas las mugeres y mochachos, y que los que de sus manos se avían podido escapar andavan huyendo, como los víamos tan atemorizados sin osar parar en ninguna parte, y que ni querían ni podían sembrar ni labrar la tierra, antes estaban determinados de dexarse morir, y que esto tenían por mejor que esperar ser tratados con tanta crueldad como hasta allí" (238–240). The denunciation of violence, so evident in these and other passages, could lead one to infer, as does Beatriz Pastor, that Cabeza de Vaca sympathized with the ideas of Bartolomé de las Casas.[36] Certainly, Bishop Juan de Zumárraga publicly used Cabeza de Vaca's experience to oppose war in America, and, in fact, Bartolomé de las Casas himself paraphrased and directly quoted Cabeza de Vaca's testimony in preparing his *Apologética historia sumaria*.[37] Yet such a radical statement would not be accurate, especially considering the utilitarian aim of Cabeza de Vaca's work, written in Castile between 1536 and 1537. It becomes clear that, bearing in mind the polemics over the treatment of Amerindians and the Spanish actions in the New World, Cabeza de Vaca knew how to craft his *Relación* with content that would brand him a good conqueror, peaceful evangelizer, and faithful follower of the church and the crown's commands. Precisely, the capitulations for the conquest of La Florida granted to Hernando de Soto in April 1537 included instructions for behavior toward Native Americans, given "los males y desórdenes que en descubrimientos y Poblaciones nuevas se han fecho y hacen, é para que nos con buena conciencia podamos dar licencia para los hacer."[38] The leadership of this new conquest, intended to be carried out in good conscience, was none other than that requested by Cabeza de Vaca upon his return to Spain. One month later, on May 29, Pope Paul III wrote to Cardinal Tabera, ordering him to forbid the enslavement of Indigenous peoples and the expropriation of their lands, under penalty of excommunication *ipso facto incurrenda*.[39] On June 2, the famous bull *Sublimis Deus* would be promulgated, thus recognizing the humanity of the Amerindians and outright reproving their slavery. In this regard, the *Relación* cannot be extracted from a context in which colonial power, struggling to preserve its privileges and *encomiendas*, clashes with the moral reservations of the church and an absolutist trend that seeks to centralize the governance of the Indies with regulations such as the New Laws of 1542. In light of this, let us understand the emphasis of the *Relación* on peaceful evangelization as a way of handling both lived experience and textual materials in a manner that suited the political milieu in which it was written. Nonetheless, this utilitarian aspect does not in any way inhibit the conscious effort to communicate, from an internal perspective and with firsthand knowledge, the humanity of the Amerindian, nor does it reduce the effect that Cabeza de Vaca sought to have with his shipwreck narrative, "por donde claramente se vee que estas gentes todas, para ser atraídos a ser christianos y a obediençia de la Imperial Magestad, an de ser llevados con buen tratamiento, y que éste es camino muy çierto y otro no" (240). The utilitarian and self-centered aspect of the *Relación* worked for the acquisition of some privileges and titles that Cabeza de Vaca was able to enjoy, but only for a short time. Just a few years after obtaining the *adelantamiento* of the Río de la Plata, he would return to Spain without honor—disgraced, dismissed, and imprisoned. The moral truth of history, on the other hand, endures to this day.

NOTES

1. The compulsive search for literary models in Cabeza de Vaca's text owes more to the intrinsic nature of the periodization of Spanish-American literature than to the discursive logic itself. Since the generation of Alfonso Reyes and Pedro Henríquez Ureña, Latin American critics have tended to bestow a literary vocation to the historiographical writing of the conquest, embracing it as the foundational corpus of their object of study. Such an attitude responds to the search for an autochthonous cultural space in which colonial writing, originally branded as a deficient imitation of the peninsular culture, should be claimed and incorporated into the canon. For more on this, see Santiago Juan-Navarro, "Constructing Cultural Myths: Cabeza de Vaca in Contemporary Hispanic Criticism, Theater, and Film," in *A Twice-Told Tale: Reinventing the Encounter in Iberian/Iberian American Literature and Film*, ed. Santiago Juan-Navarro and Theodore Robert Young (Newark: University of Delaware Press, 2001), 69–79; Walter Mignolo, "Cartas, crónicas y relaciones del descubrimiento y la conquista," in *Historia de la literatura hispanoamericana: Epoca colonial*, vol. 1, ed. Iñigo Madrigal (Madrid: Cátedra), 57–116; and Rolena Adorno, "New Perspectives in Colonial Spanish American Literary Studies," *Journal of the Southwest* 32, no. 2 (1990): 173–191.

2. For a different approximation on how Cabeza de Vaca's text engages with other contemporaneous sociopolitical debates, such as those on pauperism, see Fernando Rodríguez Mansilla's study in chapter 5 of the present volume.

3. Alvar Núñez Cabeza de Vaca, *Relación* (1542), in *Alvar Núñez Cabeza de Vaca: His Account, His Life, and the Expedition of Pánfilo de Narváez*, vol. 1, ed. Rolena Adorno and Patrick Charles Pautz (Lincoln: University of Nebraska Press, 1999), 18; hereafter, page numbers will be cited parenthetically in the text. The first report on the Narváez expedition is the joint testimony by Cabeza de Vaca, Alonso del Castillo Maldonado, and Andrés Dorantes presented in 1536 to the viceroy of New Spain, Don Antonio de Mendoza. This document has been lost, but is indirectly preserved in the thirty-fifth book of *Historia general y natural de las Indias, islas y tierra firme del mar Océano* by Gonzalo Fernández de Oviedo. The second report was written by Cabeza de Vaca and Dorantes between 1536 and 1537, when Hernando de Soto's expedition was being arranged; this text was used years later by Alonso de Santa Cruz as a source for his *Crónica del emperador Carlos V*. The first full version of the work was published in 1542, in Zamora, with the title *La relación que dio Alvar Núñez Cabeza de Vaca de lo acaecido en las Indias en la armada donde iba por Gobernador Pánfilo de Narváez, desde el año de veinte y siete hasta el año de treinta y seis que volvió a Sevilla con tres de su compañía*. Finally, the Valladolid edition of 1555, titled *La relación y comentarios*, is the text on which most modern editions are based—now known as *Naufragios*. For all quotes in this chapter, I have opted to use Adorno and Pautz's edition, which transcribes the 1542 text.

4. In 1536, Fray Bernardino de Minaya traveled to Rome with a letter from Queen Isabella of Portugal, seeking the intercession of Pope Paul III on the issue of slavery. This coincided with the initiative of the Bishop of Guatemala, Fray Juan Ramírez, who also traveled to the Holy See to expose this problem to the pope, alongside the letter of Fray Julián Garcés, Bishop of Tlaxcala, which was sent to the pontiff from Mexico with the same goal. See Alberto Pérez-Amador Adam, *De legitimatione imperii Indiae Occidentalis: La vindicación de la Empresa Americana en el discurso jurídico y teológico de las letras de los Siglos de Oro en España y los virreinatos americanos* (Madrid: Iberoamericana-Vervuert, 2011), 91. In response to these efforts, the *Pastorale officium* and the bull *Sublimis Deus* were promulgated at the end of May and beginning of June 1537, respectively, asserting that the Indigenous peoples were not animals but human beings capable of understanding and embracing Catholic doctrine. These actions gave sustenance to the ideas of Francisco de Vitoria for his *Relectio de Indis* (1539), a declaration of the illegality of the conquest as demonstrated

by numerous arguments. The most comprehensive official attempt to abolish the *encomiendas* and regularize colonial law took place in the same year in which the *Relación* was first published—that is, when the New Laws of 1542 were issued. See the full document of "Leyes y ordenanzas nuevamente hechas por S.M. para el gobierno de las Indias y el buen trato y la conservación de los indios" in *La conquista espiritual de la América española: 200 documentos del siglo XVI*, ed. Paulo Suess (Quito: Abya-Yala, 2002), 355–360. For a study that traces Las Casas's footprints in the writing of the New Laws, see Isacio Pérez Fernández, "Hallazgo de un nuevo documento básico de Fray Bartolomé de las Casas: Guión de la redacción de las Leyes Nuevas," *Studium* 32, no. 3 (1992): 459–504.

5. David Lagmanovich, "Los naufragios de Alvar Núñez como construcción narrativa," *Kentucky Romance Quarterly* 25, no. 2 (1978): 35–36. For how the picaresque genre connects to Cabeza de Vaca's text in relation to shared themes of hunger and need, see the study by Fernando Rodríguez Mansilla in chapter 5 of the present volume.

6. José Rabasa, "De la allegoresis etnográfica en los *Naufragios* de Alvar Núñez Cabeza de Vaca," *Revista iberoamericana* 61, nos. 170–171 (1995): 181, 180.

7. José Rabasa, *Writing Violence on the Northern Frontier: The Historiography of Sixteenth-Century New Mexico and Florida and the Legacy of Conquest* (Durham, NC: Duke University Press, 2000), 31.

8. Robert E. Lewis, "Los Naufragios de Alvar Núñez: Historia y Ficción," *Revista iberoamericana* 48, nos. 120–121 (1982): 693.

9. Enrique Pupo-Walker, "Los Naufragios de Alvar Núñez Cabeza de Vaca: Notas sobre la relevancia antropológica del texto," *Revista de Indias* 47, no. 181 (1987): 760, 768.

10. Silvia Spitta, "Chamanismo y cristiandad: Una lectura de la lógica intercultural de los *Naufragios* de Cabeza de Vaca," *Revista de crítica literaria latinoamericana* 19, no. 38 (1993): 321.

11. See Silvia Spitta, *Between Two Waters: Narratives of Transculturation in Latin America* (Houston: Rice University Press, 1995), 29–54.

12. Juan Francisco Maura, "Veracidad en los *Naufragios*: La técnica narrativa de Alvar Núñez Cabeza de Vaca," *Revista iberoamericana* 61, no. 170–171 (1995): 188. These ideas are further developed in Juan Francisco Maura, *El gran burlador de América: Alvar Núñez Cabeza de Vaca* (Valencia, Spain: Universidad de Valencia, 2008), 77, which outlines the panorama of two conflicting views about the life and work of Cabeza de Vaca: "Ambas son apasionantes. Una de ellas por ensalzar la figura del conquistador hasta las cotas más altas que las virtudes cristianas puedan llevar a un caballero, llegándolo a hacer poseedor de virtudes sobrenaturales. La otra, la que nos muestra a un individuo que quiere hacerse pasar por santo habiendo cometido los crímenes más abominables hacia sus propios compañeros y hacia los indígenas que ser humano haya podido cometer, tras haber abusado de la confianza y el dinero de su mujer y amigos para conseguir llevar adelante sus delirios de grandeza. No existe lugar posible para una postura intermedia." For an opposing perspective, see Mary Docter, "Enriched by Otherness: The Transformational Journey of Cabeza de Vaca," *Christianity and Literature* 58, no. 1 (2008): 19–20, which asserts that "Cabeza de Vaca's long years in the New World have enabled him to readjust his identity in order to receive and embrace the other. They have opened his eyes and transformed his heart. He concludes his pilgrimage a changed man, one 'enriched by otherness.' Distancing himself from the imperial ideology that shaped the conquest—and his own identity a decade earlier—the 'healer' will dedicate the rest of his life to defending Indian rights and promoting peaceful relationships for all. The long odyssey of Cabeza de Vaca proves to be a transformative spiritual journey both of self-discovery and of deepening love for the other."

13. See Bernardo E. Navia, "Colón y Cabeza de Vaca: Su encuentro con el Nuevo Mundo," *Hispanófila* 172 (2014): 9–24; Claret M. Vargas, "'De muchas y muy bárbaras naciones con quien conversé y viví': Alvar Núñez Cabeza de Vaca's *Naufragios* as a War Tactics Manual,"

Hispanic Review 75, no. 1 (2007): 1–22; Alberto Prieto Calixto, "Aculturación en las fronteras de América: Cabeza de Vaca, el primer mestizo cultural," *Estudios fronterizos* 8, no. 16 (2007): 123–143; Robert T. C. Goodwin, "Alvar Núñez Cabeza de Vaca and the Textual Travels of an American Miracle," *Journal of Iberian and Latin American Studies* 14, no. 1 (2008): 1–12; Carlos A. Jáuregui, "Cabeza de Vaca, Mala Cosa y las vicisitudes de la extrañeza," *Revista de estudios hispánicos* 48, no. 3 (2014): 421–447; and Carlos A. Jáuregui, "Going Native, Going Home: Ethnographic Empathy and the Artifice of Return in Cabeza de Vaca's *Relación*," *Colonial Latin American Review* 25, no. 2 (2016): 175–199.

14. David A. Boruchoff, "The Poetry of History," *Colonial Latin American Review* 13, no. 2 (2004): 276.

15. Jeronimo de San José, *Genio de la historia*, ed. Higinio de Santa Teresa (Vitoria, Spain: Ediciones El Carmen, 1957), 263.

16. Torquato Tasso, *Opere*, vol. 5, *Apologia in difesa della Gerusalemme liberata*, ed. Bruno Maier (Milan: Rizzoli Editore, 1965) : 655.

17. Gonzalo Fernández de Oviedo, *Historia general y natural de las Indias*, vol. 4, ed. Juan Pérez de Tudela Bueso (Madrid: Atlas, 1959), 285.

18. Fernández de Oviedo, *Historia general*, 4:286.

19. José de Acosta, *Historia natural y moral de las Indias*, ed. José Alcina Franch (Madrid: Dastin, 2002), 297–298. Let us understand "a las puertas" as preparatory text that would provide Indigenous peoples with the possibility of being understood by European readers. For more on this, see Gregory J. Shepherd, *An Exposition of José de Acosta's "Historia natural y moral de las Indias," 1590: The Emergence of an Anthropological Vision of Colonial Latin America* (Lewiston, NY: Edwin Mellen, 2002), 60–62.

20. Margo Glantz, "El cuerpo inscrito y el texto escrito o la desnudez como naufragio: Alvar Núñez Cabeza de Vaca," in *Obras reunidas*, vol. 1, *Ensayos sobre literatura colonial* (Mexico City: Fondo de Cultura Económica, 2006), 102, notes the progression of a hagiographic account: "El texto proporciona abundantes datos para verificar las comparaciones esbozadas: las espinas, las cruces, las llagas, los malos tratos, la sangre, el sufrimiento corporal y su paralelismo con los sufrimientos del Redentor: la pasión como camino de la redención—la imitación de Cristo—, las marcas corporales como signos de una hagiografía. Ya está listo para ser chamán, la purificación ha terminado. Alterna la mención de datos concretos—realismo que puede leerse como un discurso etnológico—y la excesiva frecuentación de los milagros, la conciencia de su santidad, el arribo de la sacralización. La predestinación lo hace elegible para la santificación y le otorga poderes sobrenaturales: como Cristo, tiene su Lázaro y resucita a un muerto."

21. Fernández de Oviedo, *Historia general*, 4:287, 4:306, 4:313. Oviedo underlines this moralizing effect with a providentialist interpretation: "encomendándose todos tres a Nuestro Señor, hobieron por mejor hacer aquello que eran obligados como cristianos (e como hidalgos, que cada uno dellos lo era) que no vivir en vida tan salvaje e tan apartada del servicio de Dios e de toda buena razón. E con esta buena voluntad, como hombres de buena casta determinados, salieron; e así Jesucristo los guió e obró de su infinita misericordia con ellos, e abriéndoles los caminos, sin habellos en la tierra, e los corazones de los hombres tan salvajes e indómitos, movió Dios a humillárseles e obedescerlos" (4:304).

22. Francisco López de Gómara, *Historia general de las Indias*, ed. Jorge Gurría Lacroix (Caracas: Biblioteca Ayacucho, 1979), 69, 134.

23. Inca Garcilaso de la Vega, *La Florida del Inca*, ed. Sylvia L. Hilton (Madrid: Historia 16, 1986), 77–78.

24. Jacques Lafaye, "Los 'milagros' de Alvar Núñez Cabeza de Vaca (1527–1536)," in *Notas y comentarios sobre Alvar Núñez Cabeza de Vaca*, ed. Margo Glantz (Mexico City: Grijalbo, 1993), 24–25.

25. Other scholars tend to read these events as adaptations of experienced reality to create an intelligible discourse for the European reader. In Spitta, "Chamanismo," 322, for

example, the parallels between Cabeza de Vaca and Christ would indicate a process of trans-culturation: "El discurso bíblico que él manipula ofusca no sólo la realidad americana que vivió sino también los códigos chamánicos a los que recurrió para sobrevivir. Lo que no queda en claro ya que no podemos determinar si Cabeza de Vaca creía en el chamanismo o no, es si este ofuscamiento se debe a que escribía para la corona y no quería aparecer como predicador de idolatrías o si fue el resultado de la imposibilidad de formular sus experiencias ya que los términos discursivos a su alcance no abarcaban experiencias como la suya." Adorno and Pautz do not cast doubt on the healing issue, but do reverse the point of view: "Cabeza de Vaca and his companions might not have been perceived as great shamans because they performed cures but rather performed cures because they were taken to be great shamans"; Adorno and Pautz, in *Alvar Núñez Cabeza de Vaca: His Account, His Life*, 1:163.

26. Lafaye, "Los 'milagros,'" 25–26.

27. Beyond the healing motive, other passages highlight the humanity of the Amerindian. Among them, consider the well-known incident of the crying of the Malhado people (98–100), or the moments that serve to undermine generalizations about sacrifices and anthropophagy (100–106)—practices that conferred the right to armed intervention, even in the opinion of Francisco de Vitoria, a clear opponent of the conquest (145). As Juan Ginés de Sepúlveda, *Demócrates segundo o de las justas causas de la guerra contra los indios*, ed. and trans. Angel Losada (Madrid: Consejo Superior de Investigaciones Científicas, Instituto Francisco de Vitoria, 1984), 43, notes, extermination would be legitimate in such cases: "Así, pues, si se hubiese de haber obrado en justicia con ellos para que fuesen castigados en razón de sus crímenes públicos, y no se hubiese decidido anteponer la equidad y misericordia a la severidad, no sólo de sus bienes, sino hasta de su vida podían ser privados para que recibiesen el mismo castigo que aquellos cuyos pecados imitaron." In this respect, the shipwreck narrative has a devastating force in the role reversal illustrated by the Malhado calamity (where Christians eat Christians and natives are scandalized), at a time when anthropophagy was perceived as a privative feature of paganism; see Peter Hulme, "The Cannibal Scene," in *Cannibalism and the Colonial World*, ed. Francis Barker, Peter Hulme, and Margaret Iversen (Cambridge: Cambridge University Press, 1998), 1–38. Such passages did not go unnoticed; as Garcilaso de la Vega, *La Florida del Inca*, 81, notes, "Los que dicen que comen carne humana se lo levantan, a lo menos a los que son de las provincias que nuestro gobernador descubrió; antes lo abominan, como lo nota Alvar Núñez Cabeza de Vaca en sus *Naufragios*, capítulo catorce y diez y siete, donde dice que de hambre murieron ciertos castellanos que estaban alojados aparte y que los compañeros que quedaban comían los que se morían hasta el postrero, que no hubo quién lo comiese, de lo cual dice que se escandalizaron los indios tanto que estuvieron por matar todos los que habían quedado en otro alojamiento."

28. Juan Toribio de Motolinía, *Memoriales*, ed. Nancy Joe Dyer (Mexico City: El Colegio de México, 1996), 133–134.

29. Beatriz Pastor, *El segundo descubrimiento: La conquista de América narrada por sus coetáneos (1492–1589)* (Barcelona: Edhasa, 2008), 278–279, sees a process of transculturation in the transfer of the supernatural to the European notion of the devil: "Ante las señales de las cuchilladas dadas por Mala Cosa, los cristianos no pueden seguir echando a burla la leyenda indígena y se ven obligados a aceptar la posibilidad de su veracidad. Pero lo hacen después de haberla reformulado de acuerdo con las categorías de conceptualización de lo sobrenatural propias de una ideología cristiana. . . . El diablo sustituye a 'lo inexplicable,' reinstaurando la verosimilitud que esta última categoría amenazaba." For Rolena Adorno, *The Polemics of Possession in Spanish American Narrative* (New Haven, CT: Yale University Press, 2007), 257, the story of Mala Cosa "can be identified with one of humanity's oldest inventions, the trickster figure. With a nearly universal distribution that included the ancient Greeks, the Chinese, the Japanese, and the Semitic world, the figure had its earliest

and most archaic forms among the Indians of North America, and its patterns have apparently changed little over time." In the opinion of Daniel Reff, "Text and Context: Cures, Miracles, and Fear in the *Relación* of Alvar Núñez Cabeza de Vaca," *Journal of the Southwest* 38, no. 2 (1996): 166, Mala Cosa suggests an allusion to colonial violence in New Spain. Going even further, Jáuregui, "Cabeza de Vaca, Mala Cosa y las vicisitudes de la extrañeza," 429, proposes that Mala Cosa represents Cabeza de Vaca himself, "como puede indagarse mediante la lectura comparativa de las coincidencias entre estas dos figuras, en lo que toca a sus particularidades físicas, travestismo, extranjería, malignidad, rapacidad, práctica de la curandería y ejercicio del terror."

30. Adorno, *The Polemics*, 260.

31. In the aforementioned letter by Bishop Julián Garcés to Pope Paul III, beyond the Amerindians' aptitude to voluntarily receive Christianity a particular predisposition is described, especially among children: "Los niños de los indios no son molestos con obstinación ni porfía á la fe católica . . . antes aprenden de tal manera las verdades de los cristianos, que no solamente salen con ellas, sino que las agotan, y es tanta su facilidad, que parece que se las beben. Aprenden más presto que los niños españoles y con más contento los artículos de la fe, por su orden, y las demás oraciones de la doctrina cristiana, reteniendo en la memoria fielmente lo que se les enseña. . . . No son vocingleros, ni pendencieros; no porfiados, ni inquietos; no díscolos ni soberbios; no injuriosos, ni rencillosos, sino agradables, bien enseñados y obedientísimos á sus maestros. Son afables y comedidos con sus compañeros, sin las quejas, murmuraciones, afrentas y los demás vicios que suelen tener los muchachos españoles. Según lo que aquella edad permite, son inclinadísimos á ser liberales. Tanto monta que lo que se les da, se dé á uno como á muchos; porque lo que uno recibe, se reparte luego entre todos. Son maravillosamente templados, no comedores ni bebedores, sino que parece que les es natural la modestia y compostura. . . . Tienen los ingenios sobre manera fáciles para que se les enseñe cualquier cosa." See "Información de Julián Garcés O.P., primer Obispo de Tlaxcala a Paulo III sobre la buena disposición de los indios para la fe cristiana," in *La conquista espiritual*, 129–130. In this way Garcés refutes both the need for coercion and the Aristotelian notion of natural slavery applied to the Native American, because even Sepúlveda himself contemplated the exception in the case of a people who "hiciese naturalmente sin la ley aquellas cosas que son de la ley." See Juan Ginés de Sepúlveda, *Demócrates Segundo o de las justas causas de la guerra contra los indios*, ed. and trans. Angel Losada (Madrid: Consejo Superior de Investigaciones Científicas, 1984), 44. For a systematic refutation of natural slavery, see Bartolomé de las Casas, *Apologética historia sumaria*, 2 vols., ed. Edmundo O'Gorman (Mexico City: Universidad Nacional Autónoma de México, 1967).

32. Concerning this pacifying effect in the period between the Narváez expedition and the second publication of the *Relación* (1527–1555), Ralph Bauer, *The Cultural Geography of Colonial American Literatures: Empire, Travel, Modernity* (Cambridge: Cambridge University Press, 2003), 48, tracks a transformation of colonial policy in the Americas and a cultural "retroping" of Spanish imperial identity in the course of which the Renaissance dream of conquest is exposed as falsehood: "This discursive shift from 'conquest' to 'pacification' in official political discourse . . . must primarily be seen in the context of a geo-political dialectic between Habsburg absolutism promoting a discourse of 'pacification' and a colonial (*criollo*) neo-feudalism promoting a discourse of 'conquest.'" According to Bauer, Cabeza de Vaca therefore "ascribes the reasons for the Florida expedition's failure to certain participants' 'false' chivalric ideology of *caballería* while firmly aligning himself with the absolutist and mercantilist values of the Habsburg state" (48).

33. This is illustrated toward the end of the *Relación*, where Cabeza de Vaca writes: "Y nosotros les mandamos que hiziessen iglesias y pusiessen cruzes en ellas, porque hasta entonces no las avían hecho. E hezimos traer los hijos de los principales señores y bautizarlos. Y luego el capitán hizo pleito omenaje a Dios de no hazer ni consentir hazer entrada

ninguna ni tomar esclavo por la tierra y gente que nosotros avíamos assegurado, y que esto guardaría y compliría hasta que Su Magestad y el governador Nuño de Guzmán o el visorey en su nombre proveyessen en lo que más fuesse serviçio de Dios nuestro Señor y de Su Magestad. Y después de bautizados los niños, nos partimos para la villa de San Miguel, donde como fuimos llegados vinieron indios que nos dixeron como mucha gente baxava de las sierras y poblavan en lo llano y hazían iglesias y cruzes y todo lo que les avíamos mandado" (260).

34. The *Relación* highlights extraordinary cultural diversity. Cabeza de Vaca stresses that throughout his journey he did not live a uniform experience among the peoples of America, having found among them "más de mil diferencias" (232). In contrast to this humanizing image, consider the perception offered by the sixteenth-century Spanish historian López de Gómara in his chapter dedicated to the issue of freedom; see López de Gómara, *Historia general de las Indias*, 310.

35. Regarding the fertility of these lands, Nan Goodman, "Mercantilism and Cultural Difference in Cabeza de Vaca's *Relación*," *Early American Literature* 40, no. 2 (2005): 236, identifies in the *Relación* a stimulus for the establishment of an agrarian-based colonialism: "Cabeza de Vaca turns his attention to the idea of settlement and cultivation in what one can only assume was an effort to establish a productive infrastructure in which profits for the king might flow not only from metals but also from a self-sustaining agriculture." Nevertheless, in the descriptions of La Florida, the *Relación* refers mainly to the roughness of the land. This is questioned in Garcilaso de la Vega, *La Florida del Inca*, 214–215: "De ver esta diferencia de tierras muy buenas y muy malas me pareció no pasar adelante sin tocar lo que Alvar Núñez Cabeza de Vaca, en sus *Comentarios*, escribe de esta provincia de Apalache, donde la pinta áspera y fragosa, ocupada de muchos montes y ciénagas, con ríos y malos pasos, mal poblada y estéril, toda en contra de lo que de ella vamos escribiendo." Pastor, *El segundo descubrimiento*, 246–247, suggests that the topography provides a demystifying element, disarticulating Columbus's idealization: "La América fabulosa del Almirante, que reunía los atributos de Tarsis y Ofir, Japón y China—por no mencionar los del Paraíso Terrenal—desaparece en el texto de Alvar Núñez para dejar paso a una presentación que busca ser fiel a la experiencia personal de las tierras que recorrió a lo largo de nueve años de peregrinación. La América de Alvar Núñez ya no es un mito. Es una tierra vastísima, salvaje e inhóspita, cuya naturaleza la hace apenas habitable para los naturales e inhabitable por completo para los europeos. . . . Lo característico de esta nueva representación de la naturaleza es aquí—como en otros textos del discurso del fracaso—la desmesura, que asume con frecuencia carácter de caos originario que la dota de un aspecto que alternativamente maravilla y sobrecoge al que la contempla."

36. Pastor, *El segundo descubrimiento*, 273.

37. Las Casas, *Apologética historia sumaria*, 1:651–652, 2:354, 2:360–361, 2:375.

38. "Asiento y capitulación hecho por el Capitán Hernando de Soto con el Emperador Carlos V para la conquista y población de la provincia de la Florida, y encomienda de la gobernación de la isla de Cuba," in *Colección de varios documentos para la historia de la Florida y tierras adyacentes*, ed. Buckingham Smith (London: Trübner, 1857), 145.

39. See "Paulo III escribe al cardenal toledano, Tabera, para que los indios no sean reducidos a esclavitud," in Francisco Javier Hernáez, *Colección de bulas, breves y otros documentos relativos a la iglesia de América y Filipinas*, vol. 1 (Vaduz, Liechtenstein: Kraus, 1964), 101–102.

CHAPTER 5

The Discourse of Poverty in Alvar Núñez Cabeza de Vaca's *Naufragios*

Fernando Rodríguez Mansilla

The reader of Alvar Núñez Cabeza de Vaca's *Naufragios*, in its second and definitive edition in a single volume, along with the *Comentarios*,[1] would have found—at the end of the text after the "tabla," or index of chapters—an emblem that represented poverty: a man with one arm lowered, drawn to the ground by the stone tied to his wrist, and the other arm raised with a pair of wings. The emblem has two epigrams: one reads *Ingenium volitat* (Wit flutters), referring to the winged hand; the other reads *Paupertas deprimit ipsum* (Poverty oppresses), pointing to the stone that hangs from the other hand.[2] Certainly this colophon to *Naufragios* was not used exclusively, as it seems to have also been the emblem of the Valladolid printer Francisco Fernández de Córdoba. Yet it is quite relevant in terms of revealing an aspect of Cabeza de Vaca's narrative discourse that has not been sufficiently observed by the critics: poverty and its effects on the subject. Through the course of *Naufragios*, Cabeza de Vaca experiences a transformation from conqueror to beggar, then to merchant and healer. At all times his particular epic is one of hunger, and his interactions with the natives are shaped by his new condition as beggar.[3] A quintessential shipwreck narrative, Cabeza de Vaca's text is a hybrid account that makes use of the diverse discourses that converge in this textual modality.[4] In this way, poverty as a narrative topic is a result of the shipwreck itself. In this chapter, I am particularly interested in analyzing the images of poverty—such as nudity and the ritual of giving blankets—presented within the text, since these images belong to the medieval religious iconography that deals with the virtues of poverty and holiness in the Christian subject.[5]

In Golden Age Spain, the debate on poverty as a social and religious issue was called pauperism, and it was the subject of a remarkable textual production, including proposals made by intellectuals (notable, among others, are Juan Luis Vives and Cristóbal Pérez de Herrera), as well as laws and documents that show social commitment, utopian thought, and a critical look at the status quo.[6] One of the questions raised was what to do with the poor. Basically, there were two opposite positions: the first, advocated by progressive thinkers, was to make the poor work and turn beggars into the proletariat (as happened in the countries of northern Europe); the second, embraced by orthodox thinkers, defended the existence of the poor, whom they considered "a necessary evil," while simultaneously censoring false beggars and proposing their eradication. Evidently these two positions shared interest in recognizing the legitimately poor person while seeking to eliminate social parasites, the vagrants.

Naufragios was first published in Zamora in 1542, two years after Cardinal Tavera's *Ley de pobres* was established. Among other provisions, this law required an examination of the poor (in order to distinguish between legitimate and false ones) and expelled foreign vagrants. This legislation generated the 1545 debate between Domingo de Soto, who represented the traditional perspective about the poor, and Juan de Robles, who defended the new legislation.[7] This panorama of the debate on poverty also explains the presence of some issues depicted in *Lazarillo de Tormes*, whose first known edition is from 1554. As Miguel Herrero states, "The *Lazarillo* . . . was composed at a time when the problems of poverty and vagrancy had captured the attention of most of the Spanish urban population."[8] Its protagonist is a child who, given up by his mother to a blind man, must navigate a cruel world, exposed to hunger and deprivation. In *Lazarillo* the reader also finds the *escudero*, an impoverished nobleman from Valladolid (precisely where the second edition of *Naufragios* will later be published). This man is starving in Toledo, unable to work (because of his social status) but at the same time forbidden to beg for food (and thus his servant Lázaro does it for him). In sum, *Lazarillo* is the founder of a genre—the picaresque—that re-creates the use of ingenuity to fight adversity, all the while denouncing the hypocrisy and selfishness of those who are above the poor in the social pyramid.[9]

Until now the approaches that have explored the connections between picaresque discourse and colonial texts have paid attention to subjects such as the appropriation of legal discourse or the development of an autobiographical self before the state.[10] I believe, however, that the most tangible points of contact are the shared themes: the protagonist of *Naufragios* faces extreme experiences that expose him to hunger and great need. To survive he employs ingenuity and develops a religious symbolism that he imbues into the narrative. In his work on *Naufragios*, Enrique Pupo-Walker claims that the experience of isolation resulting from the shipwreck leads to introspective reflection, which in turn transforms the unfortunate adventure into a "spiritual shipwreck" that tests the individual.[11] Following this path of thought, Cabeza de Vaca's text could be interpreted as an allegorical voyage, starting from the ruins of a shipwreck, leading toward a tough survival in misery and, finally, a redemption of both body and soul.

It is possible that contemporary readers of *Naufragios* would have had in mind the problem of the poor when reading about the protagonist and his adventures in the New World. Between 1551 and 1559, Valladolid experienced a period of economic prosperity, coinciding with its time as royal court. This wealth is precisely what attracted the beggars, who, in the words of French historian Bartolomé Bennassar, were a luxury that the city could afford. About 10 percent of the population was poor, meaning that these people depended on charity to meet their needs. The majority of them did not work. They were *pobres solemnes*, which meant that they begged openly. In response, the city created an assistance system that took care of the maintenance of between approximately two thousand and three thousand people in hospitals and parishes.[12] Considering this situation in the streets of Valladolid and other Castilian cities (Salamanca, Toledo, and Zamora), we can imagine how corresponding narrative details would catch the attention of a reader of *Naufragios* around 1550. Accordingly, the publication of both *Naufragios* and *Lazarillo* during this time period (1542–1554) may be better understood by taking into account the role pauperism was simultaneously playing. Indeed, the printer Fernández de Córdoba also published the eye-opening treatise *Provechoso tratado de cambios y contrataciones de mercaderes y reprobación de usuras* (1546) by Cristóbal de Villalón, a text that deals theologically with the legitimacy of interest and the sin of usury,[13] issues related to alms and the definition of poverty.

Although *Naufragios* re-creates the image of the mendicant saint of medieval roots extensively, the self-configuration of Cabeza de Vaca also employs an image associated rather with the coeval debate about pauperism: the ingenuity to survive through work. In the second part of *Naufragios*, the protagonist moves forward among the Indigenous people's towns, becoming a trader and a healer, something that would have appeared novel to sixteenth-century readers, even if it may today seem natural to us. The ingenuity that underlies his actions is the same that is found in *Lazarillo de Tormes*, only here its purpose is not to swindle or steal. The use of the hands in *Naufragios* is dignified and becomes authentic virtue, in contrast with the social prejudice of its age.[14] As is well known, the essential characteristic of the *pícaro* is the use of ingenuity in the face of adversity (i.e., hunger and abuse) that provokes the character to complain about his fortune, which vacillates as much as the rogue's creative instinct to survive.[15] Considering this ingenious dimension of the poor protagonist of *Naufragios*, my analysis aims to supplement the interpretations of colonial scholars who have highlighted this text as an exploration of the project of military conquest, evangelization, or authorship or who have emphasized how this text allows a reflection on the discovered other as an equal, thus decentering the subject.[16] These are all typical approaches of colonial criticism that disregard how Cabeza de Vaca's *Naufragios* was received in the Iberian Peninsula as a shipwreck narrative when it was originally published.

The image of a resolute Cabeza de Vaca, capable of confronting any obstacle that lies in his path, is clearly shown in the very beginning of *Naufragios*. In the "proemio," or prologue, the writer explains that he wishes to receive compensation for his service in Florida, because, though his campaign was not successful, his testimony constitutes a valuable experience for the information it provides. To dignify failure, Cabeza de Vaca remarks that poverty is a fundamental condition of one who has survived shipwreck: "Suplico la resciba [the *relación* he writes] en nombre de servicio, pues este solo es el que un hombre que salió desnudo pudo sacar consigo."[17] He introduces himself as naked, which is an image par excellence of poverty in Romanesque medieval art.[18] This is a constant motive throughout the text, though it apparently contradicts the innumerable mentions of the blankets that were given to him in his narrative. Nevertheless, nudity is a fundamental aspect of the configuration of his character's mythology: naked and therefore poor and homeless, but still having survived to tell the tale. In this way, poverty and ingenuity are marked as inseparable in *Naufragios*.

Pauperism within the discourse of Cabeza de Vaca comes to the surface when we pay attention to how the subject negotiates the two aforementioned visions of the poor: the orthodox perception of the poor as holy, following Job; and the modern perception, which considers the poor as subjects who must work to survive. Cabeza de Vaca merges these contradictory visions in the text, displaying a religious piety that redeems him. Pupo-Walker recognizes in Cabeza de Vaca aspects of the pilgrim saint who performs miracles and is followed by believers, much like Bernardo and other saints in the Middle Ages.[19] While this idea explains the miraculous aspect of the character, it does not explain his suffering and poverty—key elements of Cabeza de Vaca's story—and how they might be influenced by the tradition of Job, particularly when considered within the context of the pauperism prevalent in the middle of the sixteenth century.

Let us take the image of the poor as saintly, which is the result of a pilgrimage that neither Cabeza de Vaca nor his companions expected when they set out for Florida. The adventure started as an epic enterprise: "Yo quería más aventurar la vida que poner mi honra en esta condición [doubting his bravery]" (193). But things soon turn upside down. The conquerors have no interpreters, the terrain is difficult, and nobody knows how to navigate. The disastrous leadership of Pánfilo de Narváez coincides with the onset of hunger, which becomes the main theme of the narrative in chapter 5 and continues until chapter 32, when they reach the "camino del maíz." The lack of food transforms the conquerors, as Cabeza de Vaca details chapter by chapter. In chapter 5 he reports that they devoured a horse, thereby depriving themselves of the symbol of their knighthood. Additionally, their weapons weighed too much, and carrying them injured the men. The conquerors start a pilgrimage to satiate their hunger. As a result, the search for gold or other precious metals is set aside; now wealth is food. After arriving in Apalache and recognizing that "la tierra era mal poblada" (99),[20] the natives recommend that the conquerors go to Aute, since "los indios dél [Aute] tenían mucho maíz y que tenían frisoles y calabazas" (99). The truth is that, in *Naufragios*, Aute is as poor as Apalache and they find the land destroyed. After this discouraging news, many begin to desert. The narrator asserts that "muchos hijosdalgo y hombres de buena suerte" (103) are among those who leave the army. The men who stay intend to make ships to save themselves; this constitutes the first time in the text that the characters employ ingenuity to fight adversity. After building a ship with his hands, Cabeza de Vaca will become a merchant and later a healer. Building a ship implies a challenge to the subject's own social status, and with this the author points to the theme of honor and the paradoxical status of the needy conqueror who becomes a *pobre vergonzante*—that is, one who cannot ask for money or work because his social class prevents it.

The moment when the nobleman works with his hands in order to survive is a commonplace scene in the chronicles of the New World, yet despite this it has been insufficiently observed.[21] While such an action would be unfathomable on the other side of the ocean, in the shipwreck narrative it denotes a turning point. Other examples of this kind of scene are subsequent to *Naufragios*. In an episode of the conquest of Mexico narrated by Bernal Díaz del Castillo in *Historia verdadera de la conquista de la Nueva España*, Cortés urgently looks for people to paddle the brigs they just built to escape: "Y aunque más hidalgos dijesen que eran, [Cortés] los hizo ir a remar; y desta manera juntó ciento cincuenta hombres para remar."[22] Narrating the conquest of Peru, Inca Garcilaso de la Vega explicitly shows the solution to the same problem: "Gonzalo Pizarro [the leader of the army], como tan gran soldado, era el primero en cortar la madera, en forjar el hierro, hacer el carbón y en cualquiera otro oficio, por muy bajo que fuese, por dar ejemplo a todos los demás, para que nadie se escusase de hacer lo mismo."[23] Cabeza de Vaca might be among the first authors to expose this kind of scene, one whose motivation is none other than extreme need. After this first experience with his hands, Cabeza de Vaca will use them again—sometimes with more fortune, sometimes with less—throughout his long trip: he dedicates himself to exchanging objects as a merchant, he acts as a healer, and he even ends up as a manufacturer of objects for the Indians.

Chapter 10 is crucial to understanding the religious pilgrimage of the protagonist. Narváez leaves the army and Cabeza de Vaca takes control of the expedition with his famous statement, "Tomé el leme" (115). Next the narrator observes that the Spaniards have become pitiful beggars; they are no longer soldiers, nor are they valiant. The natives look like giants, or in any case "nuestro miedo les hacía parecer gigantes" (117). In chapter 12 a new shipwreck leaves them "desnudos como nacimos y perdido todo lo que traíamos, y aunque todo valía poco, para entonces valía mucho" (120). They look like the "propria figura de la muerte" (120). Here we find an invocation to God, from whom the survivors beg for mercy and forgiveness of their sins. The answer comes with the arrival of a group of natives who treat them with kindness, promise them food, and even cry: "De ver el desastre que nos había venido y el desastre en que estábamos, con tanta desventura y miseria, se sentaron entre nosotros, y con el gran dolor y lástima que hubieron de vernos en tanta fortuna, comenzaron todos a llorar recio, y tan de verdad, que lejos de allí se podía oír, y esto les duró más de media hora" (121). Here it is worth noting the meaning of the word *fortuna*, which is figuratively equivalent to "misfortune."[24] Along with other terms, such as "desventura" and "miseria," Cabeza de Vaca depicts a scene in which he is far away from God's mercy. God is constantly invoked throughout the story and sends help in the form of generous Indians or favorable natural conditions. Humanists of the sixteenth century, when discussing astrology, claimed that *fortuna* was a residue of pagan thought, and, though they considered the influence of stars, they also recognized that the only real *fortuna* was the providence or will of God.[25] Thus, complaining about *fortuna* was an ancient custom or commonplace in rhetoric to evoke emotion in the reader.[26] The chain of negative meanings (*desventura, miseria,* and *fortuna*) in the text of Cabeza de Vaca is consolidated with the island of Mal Hado (chapters 15 and 16), whose name, so emblematic, is attributed to our author. *Hado*, or fate (the force that arranges facts), is another concept from antiquity that was used extensively in the Renaissance, even with full acceptance that it did not exist.[27] For the circumstances of Cabeza de Vaca, of course, *hado* can only be bad. *Desventura, miseria, fortuna,* and *mal hado* are opposed to divine providence, which is the only legitimate will for the Christian. Moreover, in the sixteenth century, the poor were identified with the melancholic or unfortunate who were the victims of daily setbacks. In his literary dialogues, the humanist and Christian scholar Erasmus of Rotterdam states that "a la pobreza acompaña la soledad, e pobreza e soledad abren puerta a muchos males."[28]

In this way the imprecations toward *fortuna* or *mal hado* in Cabeza de Vaca's text have a rhetorical origin: these concepts shape his self-portrait as a poor man. Since the Middle Ages, "la pobreza y la enfermedad se asocian a la penitencia y la fortaleza de la fe en la figura de Job."[29] These evils are a test for the believers, who will only save themselves through their faith, no matter how hard the difficulties may be. In chapter 26 of *El libro de Job*, according to the translation by Fray Luis de León, the protagonist reminds the audience of the inscrutable plans of God:

De lo que sabe y hace el Soberano,
es esta una pequeña y breve parte.
Es poco lo que alcanza el seso humano;
que a todas sus grandezas, ¿quién es parte?[30]

It is there, on the inauspiciously named island of Mal Hado, where Cabeza de Vaca begins his career as merchant and then as healer. Trade, which in his age was associated with usury and therefore with Jews, contradicts the identity of the Christian conqueror; at the same time, however, it reveals his ingenuity in response to hunger.[31] His occupation as healer is also related to that urgency, as Cabeza de Vaca describes it: the natives urge him to heal by praying, and he does so to earn their favor. Cabeza de Vaca effectively re-creates an adverse environment—hungry, defenseless, poor as he is—in which he cures other homeless people afflicted with similar hardships and evangelizes at the same time. As Lygia Rodrigues Vianna Peres points out, "Cabeza de Vaca como taumaturgo es también evangelizador."[32]

In chapter 17, Cabeza de Vaca encounters Dorantes, Castillo, and Estebanico, an event that he attributes to the grace of God, who begins to show him favor. Cabeza de Vaca recommends that his comrades escape to the lands of the Christians and, entrusting himself to divinity, he manages to move forward. In chapter 21 the protagonist perceives the presence of God in the burning tree (which emulates the bush that Moses sees in the book of Exodus) and is then saved from hunger. God does not abandon the poor nor the survivors of the shipwreck. Chapter 38 of *El libro de Job* evokes the power of God over the sea, which obeys his orders:

¿Quién, di, con puerta y llave, quién cerrado
detuvo el mar, al punto que nacía
de golpe y con tropel soberbio, hinchado . . . ?[33]

The narrative atmosphere of *Naufragios* relies on this biblical certainty so that the religious experience of the protagonist can be meaningful.

At a similar time, but in a different part of the world, the experience of captivity in Algiers was presented with a comparable religious significance; in Fray Diego de Haedo's writing, for example, captivity is described as hell on earth and the sufferings of the captives are compared with the passion of Jesus Christ.[34] For this reason, Cabeza de Vaca employs a similar image: "No tenía, cuando estos trabajos me veía, otro remedio ni consuelo sino pensar en la pasión de nuestro redentor Jesucristo" (162).[35] The protagonist works for the natives: he makes combs and mats "que son cosas de que ellos tienen mucha necesidad" (162). Holiness, poverty, and manual labor are intertwined: "Esta es la vida que allí tuvimos, y aquel poco sustentamiento lo ganábamos con los rescates que por nuestras manos hicimos" (163).

There is a change of tone in chapter 24. Cabeza de Vaca and his comrades are already saints and have purged themselves of their sins. As the story progresses, there is "un progresivo estado de gracia en el que la misericordia divina se hace cada vez más patente."[36] Consequently, putting aside his misfortunes, the protagonist elaborates *avant la lettre* ethnographic notes on the native groups that he meets. Natives welcome the Spaniards and show respect through ceremonies that Cabeza de Vaca diligently describes but barely understands. Mentions of hunger or of suffering are given a less prominent role. Now he and his companions are respected characters who have "tres o cuatro mil personas" (185) as followers.

A first sign of improvement in Cabeza de Vaca's condition of life is expressed through the blankets, which are referenced an almost implausible number of times in chapter 30. Blankets metaphorically mean charity and comfort to poverty, so the references in this regard are not necessarily literal. In medieval Romanesque art, the mantle represents inner prosperity, and Job (the sick and poor saint) is usually represented with wounds and as a dejected beggar wrapped in a blanket.[37] In a text such as Bernal Díaz del Castillo's *Historia verdadera de la conquista de la Nueva España*, mantles have various narrative functions: they are finery, as in the *Poema de Mío Cid*; a spoil of war; and gifts for the natives. Montezuma gives Díaz del Castillo blankets and gold ingots; Cortés does the same to win the favor of Guatemuz.[38]

In this cultural context the numerous references to blankets in *Naufragios* should not necessarily be understood as realistic utterances but as elements of the models of poverty and holiness that Cabeza de Vaca designs in his writing. The natives are so generous that the protagonist finds that, in addition to food and water, they bring him "mantas de vacas" (190). His pilgrimage is now marked by this gift, as the next day he meets another group that is likewise generous: "De aquí en adelante comenzaron a darnos muchas mantas de cueros y no tenían cosa que no nos diesen" (190). Another group of Indigenous people encourages them, saying that "nos darían muchas mantas de algodón y cueros y otras cosas de las que ellos tenían" (191).[39] With these signs of progress, the protagonist reaches the "camino del maíz," where the natives seem more civilized. Corn was a sacred food for Indigenous peoples, a deity connected by the southern routes.[40] For Cabeza de Vaca this also implies prosperity and the end of his adventure as a mendicant pilgrim. In the following chapter, 31, the story's ending approaches. The allusions to blankets are constant in the "camino del maíz": "Por todas ellas [their travel days] el río arriba nos dieron muchas mantas de vacas" (193). At the end of the chapter, Cabeza de Vaca begins to preach about the existence of God to the natives, who supply him with gifts and food. Blankets are a relief to the poor and comfort them in their nakedness.

At this point in his shipwreck narrative, Cabeza de Vaca and his companions have hunger under control. They perform a job that is recognized by the multitude and have already consolidated their professions as healers and saints and established themselves as pilgrims who evangelize and understand languages. In chapter 33, when they meet Christians, there seems to be a prelude to a history that repeats itself: these Spaniards walk, lost, and are going through "necesidad y hambre" like another group of shipwreck survivors (297). In the next chapter it is Cabeza de Vaca who gives blankets to those other Christians as charity gifts. In addition, the natives closely empathize with the captives because of their actions and appearance, in contrast to their response upon seeing the Spaniards: "Que nosotros sanábamos los enfermos y ellos mataban los que estaban sanos; y que nosotros veníamos desnudos y descalzos, y ellos vestidos y en caballos y con lanzas. Que nosotros no teníamos codicia de ninguna cosa, antes todo cuanto nos daban tornábamos luego a dar y con nada nos quedábamos" (205). Cabeza de Vaca is apparently on the other side, since he cares about the natives and steps back from the Spaniards.[41] In chapter 35, he is presented as a cultural mediator between the Indigenous peoples and the Europeans and proposes a plan to civilize the territory, which involves compelling the natives to populate and cultivate the land (208). As a pinnacle to his evangelizing, in chapter 36 he says that they built churches, which combines the ingenuity applied to work and holiness. His text includes all these hagiographic elements to construct a persuasive speech for an informed reader on the issues of pauperism while advocating in favor of evangelizing missions in the new territories.[42]

In conclusion, Cabeza de Vaca's journey is marked by his use of ingenuity to survive shipwreck: he uses his hands, he works, and he heals; at the same time, he represents himself as poor and holy by means of his suffering. Like Job, he is the victim of the vacillations of fortune. He never loses faith, and he identifies his experience with the passion of Christ. His poverty is transformed by the natives' charity, which they offer to him as thanks for his work as a merchant and then as a healer. The use of blankets confirms the sanctity of his life: he is a poor man who receives a reward for his suffering, a test he has passed. Cabeza de Vaca composes a discourse that is replete with powerful images of medieval origin: poor and sick like Job, a beggar, naked and holy.[43] At the same time, he proposes ingenuity as a means of survival as he rids himself of the prejudices of nobility by using his hands for pragmatic purposes; this is in strong contrast to the satire of the picaresque that links manual labor to the service of mockery and theft. Cabeza de Vaca occupies the crossroads of the debate on pauperism through the legitimacy of the beggar, the meaning of poverty, and the value of work. He makes an effective use of the concepts at stake by means of an engaging narrative and plenty of religious symbolism—this as he seeks to win the favor of the crown in order to start a new conquest enterprise.

All in all, it would be difficult to consider Cabeza de Vaca a transcultural subject in real life or to understand his text as an organic proposal of cultural hybridization in the New World. As the protagonist is returning to Spain at the end of *Naufragios*, the scene where he runs into the Portuguese, who are in pursuit of the French, reiterates that a latent return of the epic enterprise—a neverending struggle of ambition and power—persists. This last adventure damages any alleged questioning of the imperial project or of the conqueror's enterprise in the text: "Veníamos de la Nueva España y . . . traíamos plata y oro" (217). Cabeza de Vaca did not obtain any gold or silver on his rugged trip to Florida, but he wanted to try again. Years later, he would be able to set up his own illfated expedition to Paraguay, thanks in part to the impact of his adventures in North America, as narrated in *Naufragios*. Cabeza de Vaca was granted the exploration and pacification of Río de la Plata. In this respect, he would turn the failings enumerated in *Naufragios* into a relative success: "Alvar Núñez da un paso más cuando reivindica explícitamente el valor de la palabra frente al de la acción."[44]

Through the perspective of my analysis, which identifies themes and their narrative expression in *Naufragios*, I would like to highlight the use of "peripecia," a concept that, according to Alonso López Pinciano, consisted of "una mudanza súbita de la cosa en contrario estado que antes era."[45] This merit in the discourse of Cabeza de Vaca was easily identified and appreciated by the readers of his epoch, and it is evident in the dedication of both works to the infant Don Carlos: "[*Comentarios*] van juntos con mis primeros sucesos [*Naufragios*], porque la variedad de las cosas que en la una parte y en la otra se tractan y la de mis acontescimientos detenga a Vuestra Alteza con algún gusto en esta lección. Que cierto que no hay cosa que más deleite a los lectores que las variedades de las cosas y tiempos y las vueltas de la fortuna, las cuales, aunque al tiempo que se experimentan no son gustosas, cuando las traemos a la memoria y leemos son agradables."[46] This digression makes sense considering that *Comentarios* is very different from *Naufragios*: narrated in the third person and penned by his secretary, Pedro Hernández, the adventures of Cabeza de Vaca in Río de la Plata are not those of the survivor of a shipwreck but of a governor who must show leadership when confronted with the natives (who are always suspected of lying, in his view) and with the other Spaniards who are susceptible to mutiny (as does occur at the end of the story). *Comentarios* is therefore nothing more than an official report explaining how and why its protagonist returned to Spain under arrest. In this latter text, there is hardly anything that reminds the reader of the holy and mendicant Cabeza de Vaca depicted in *Naufragios* with the exception of the ethnographic notes. In *Comentarios* there is only one crisis due to hunger; the natives are usually generous (which does not mean that they are any less suspected of lying), there are language interpreters, and the governor—Cabeza de Vaca—is constantly making decisions regarding supplies and logistics to avoid being criticized for any lack of expertise.[47]

According to Josiah Blackmore's *Manifest Perdition*, shipwreck narratives go beyond the mere act of telling how the shipwreck occurs to expand on the calamity, survival, and metaphorical character (sometimes allegorical) of the experience. Considering the Latin etymology of the word *naufragio* (ship that breaks), the shipwreck narrative presents a broken dream or crisis, a transformation from order to chaos that the protagonist faces as a test of life.[48] As one of the greatest examples of the genre, the protagonist of *Naufragios* faces this breakage or rupture. The way in which Cabeza de Vaca articulates his confrontation with this challenge engages with contemporary debates on pauperism of the mid-sixteenth century such as *Lazarillo de Tormes*. Curiously, in the prologue of the latter work, an explanation is provided for the origin of its autobiographical account. This explanation is a nautical metaphor that hides the crisis (another shipwreck) that surrounds the protagonist. Lázaro says that he writes "porque consideren los que heredaron nobles estados cuán poco se les debe, pues Fortuna fue con ellos parcial, y cuánto más hicieron los que, siéndoles contraria, con fuerza y maña remando salieron a buen puerto."[49] As Francisco Rico explains in his edition of this work, the image of *fortuna*—in the sense of "maritime storm"—is implicit in the words *remar* and *buen puerto*; thus, the text alludes to the danger of shipwreck in a rough sea.[50] Only at the conclusion of *Lazarillo* do readers understand the irony of the phrase: the love triangle in which the protagonist is trapped causes a moral disorder that employs the image to comically re-create a real event that the narrator aims to hide at all costs.[51] Yet in *Naufragios*, a text pervaded by religiosity, there is no place for such irony. Perhaps this is because, conversely, the experience that disrupts the protagonist is a real shipwreck—one that transcends into an existential metaphor.

NOTES

1. Alvar Núñez Cabeza de Vaca, *Relación y comentarios del gobernador Alvar Núñez Cabeça de Vaca, de lo acaescido en las dos jornadas que hizo a las Indias* (Valladolid, Spain: Francisco Fernández de Córdova, 1555). Although originally entitled *Relación*, Cabeza de Vaca's text about his experience in Florida is commonly known as *Naufragios*. In the 1555 edition, the *Relación*'s page headers say *Naufragios*. Inca Garcilaso de la Vega already calls Cabeza de Vaca's text *Naufragios* in the early seventeenth century: "Como lo cuenta en sus *Naufragios* Alvar Núñez Cabeza de Vaca . . . ," *La Florida del Inca*, edited by Emma Susana Speratti Piñero (Mexico City: Fondo de Cultura Económica, 1956), 16.

2. The emblem originally appeared in Andrea Alciato's *Emblemata*, a work well known in early modern Spain due to the translation by Bernardino de Daza published in 1549. See Andrea Alciato, *Los emblemas de Alciato traducidos en rimas españolas*, edited by Rafael Zafra (Barcelona: J. J. Olañeta, 2003), 35.

3. Regarding hunger as a topic in the conqueror's captivity experience, see Olaya Sanfuentes, "Morirse de hambre. El hambre del conquistador," in *El cautiverio en la literatura del Nuevo Mundo*, ed. Miguel Donoso, Mariela Insúa, and Carlos Mata (Madrid: Iberoamericana/Vervuert, 2011), 233–251.

4. Josiah Blackmore, *Manifest Perdition: Shipwreck Narrative and the Disruption of Empire* (Minneapolis: University of Minnesota Press, 2002), 45.

5. For another interpretation on how Cabeza de Vaca's text engages with other sociopolitical debates of the sixteenth century, such as those on moral truth, colonial domination, and peaceful evangelization, see the study by Natalio Ohanna in chapter 4 of the present volume.

6. Michel Cavillac, *Gueux et marchands and le "Guzmán de Alfarache" (1599–1604): Roman picaresque et mentalité bourgeoise dans l'Espagne du Siècle d'Or* (Bordeaux, France: Institut d'Etudes Ibériques et Ibéro-Américaines de l'Université de Bordeaux, 1983), 201–210, provides a catalog of texts appearing in Castile in the sixteenth century dedicated to alms as a topic closely linked to mercantilism and the problem of usury. The origin of Cavillac's approach, which explores the relationship between poverty and the picaresque genre, can be found in a seminal article by Miguel Herrero, "Renaissance Poverty and Lazarillo's Family: The Birth of the Picaresque Genre," *PMLA* 94, no. 5 (1979): 876–886. Another relevant book about the connection between pauperism and the picaresque is Anne Cruz, *Discourses of Poverty: Social Reform and the Picaresque Novel in Early Modern Spain* (Toronto: University of Toronto Press, 1999).

7. Cruz, *Discourses of Poverty*, 21–29.

8. Herrero, "Renaissance Poverty and Lazarillo's Family," 878.

9. Claudio Guillén, "Toward a Definition of the Picaresque," in *Literature as System* (Princeton, NJ: Princeton University Press, 1971), 71–106.

10. Roberto González Echevarría, *Myth and Archive: A Theory of Latin American Narrative* (New York: Cambridge University Press, 1990), 46–71; Pierre Darnis, "Génesis de la picaresca, absolutismo e individuo en las *Vidas* de Lázaro de Tormes y Guzmán de Alfarache," *Creneida* 2 (2014): 316–348.

11. Enrique Pupo-Walker, "Pesquisas para una nueva lectura de los *Naufragios*, de Alvar Núñez Cabeza de Vaca," *Revista iberoamericana* 53, no. 140 (1987): 526.

12. Bartolomé Bennassar, *Valladolid en el Siglo de Oro* (Valladolid, Spain: Maxtor, 2015), 141–144, 292–293, 401–415.

13. Marcel Bataillon, *Erasmo y España* (Mexico City: Fondo de Cultura Económica, 1979), 658–659.

14. Américo Castro, *De la edad conflictiva* (Madrid: Taurus, 1963), 144, explores the representation of this social prejudice in Cervantes. Concerning the rejection of manual work in Spanish society (which is diagnosed in the mid-sixteenth century, precisely), see José Antonio Maravall, *La literatura picaresca desde la historia social (siglos XVI y XVII)* (Madrid: Taurus, 1986), 176–181.

15. Jesús Cañedo, "El curriculum vitae del pícaro," *Revista de filología española* 49, nos. 1–4 (1966): 180.

16. Beatriz Pastor, *Discursos narrativos de la conquista: Mitificación y emergencia* (Hanover, NH: Ediciones del Norte, 1988), 243; Pupo-Walker, "Pesquisas para una nueva lectura," 517–539; Lisa Voigt, *Writing Captivity in the Early Modern Atlantic: Circulations of Knowledge and Authority in the Iberian and English Imperial Worlds* (Chapel Hill: University of North Carolina Press, 2009), 57–66; Francisco Javier López Martín, *Representaciones del tiempo y construcción de la identidad entre España y América* (Huelva, Spain: Servicio de Publicaciones de la Universidad de Huelva, 2012), 93–98.

17. Alvar Núñez Cabeza de Vaca, *Naufragios*, ed. Juan Francisco Maura (Madrid: Cátedra, 1989), 180. All the quotations from *Naufragios* come from this edition; hereafter, page numbers will be cited parenthetically in the text. Writing as a service offered to the royal authority was commonplace. For instance, this technique was also used by Hernán Cortés to justify his letters, which were military reports; see Pastor, *Discursos narrativos de la conquista*, 237. The practice was not limited only to the New World, as evidenced by the fact that a contemporary humanist, Alfonso de Valdés, used the same technique to compose his works on European politics while addressing Charles V.

18. Ana Belén Muñoz Martínez, "Pobreza, enfermedad y exclusión en la iconografía bíblica románica," in *Relegados al margen: Marginalidad y espacios marginados en la cultura medieval* (Madrid: Consejo Superior de Investigaciones Científicas, 2010), 178.

19. Pupo-Walker, "Pesquisas para una nueva lectura," 529–531.

20. Garcilaso de la Vega, *La Florida del Inca*, 183, re-creates this same town with a totally opposite view, for he remarks about "la abundancia y fertilidad de la provincia de Apalache." This quote suggests that we are dealing with representations rather than documentary truth. Regarding this difference between Cabeza de Vaca and Garcilaso when writing about Florida, Juan Francisco Maura, "Introducción," in Cabeza de Vaca, *Naufragios*, 61, comments: "Pese al realismo evidente de su obra, Cabeza de Vaca parece recrearse en las descripciones de la pobreza y desolación de las tierras por las que pasa."

21. Pastor, *Discursos narrativos de la conquista*, 217–219, pays attention to this scene, but her assessment is focused on the destruction of the conqueror prototype coined by Hernán Cortés's texts.

22. Bernal Díaz del Castillo, *Historia verdadera de la conquista de la Nueva España* (Madrid: Espasa-Calpe, 1982), 347.

23. Garcilaso de la Vega, *Historia general del Perú*, 3 vols., ed. Angel Rosenblat (Buenos Aires: Emecé, 1944), 2:248.

24. Real Academia Española, "Fortuna," in *Diccionario de autoridades*, 1726–1739, https://apps2.rae.es/DA.html, gives as definitions "tempest" or "storm." Cabeza de Vaca is using the word metaphorically.

25. Antonio Torquemada, *Jardín de flores curiosas*, ed. Giovanni Allegra (Madrid: Castalia, 1982), 355.

26. This is evident in a poem from the fifteenth century that was canonical both in its time and in the time of Cabeza de Vaca, Juan de Mena's *Laberinto de Fortuna*, in which the narrator complains about fortune while also recognizing the absolute power of divinity. See Frank Domínguez, "Laberintos, mappae mundi y geografías en el *Laberinto de Fortuna* de Juan de Mena y en la edición de las *Trezientas* de Hernán Núñez," *La Corónica* 40, no. 1 (2011): 155.

27. Torquemada, *Jardín de flores curiosas*, 359.

28. Erasmus of Rotterdam, *Coloquios*, ed. Ignacio Anzoátegui (Buenos Aires: Espasa Calpe, 1947), 167.

29. Muñoz Martínez, "Pobreza, enfermedad y exclusión," 183.

30. *El libro de Job*, trans. Fray Luis de León (Lima: Pontificia Universidad Católica del Perú, 2007), 116. The English translation, according to the Jerusalem Bible, reads as follows: "All this but skirts the ways he treads, a whispered echo is all that we hear of him. But who could comprehend the thunder of his power?" (Job 26:14).

31. Only later, in the seventeenth century, would Spanish literature explore (and timidly) the character of the *hidalgo-mercader* as a reaction to this social debate. See Michel Cavillac, "L'hidalgo-mercader dans la littérature du siècle d'or," in *Hidalgos & hidalguía dans l'Espagne des XVIe–XVIIIe siècles: Théories, pratiques et représentations* (Paris: Centre National de la Recherche Scientifique, 1989), 105–124.

32. Lygia Rodrigues Vianna Peres, "El cautivo, el taumaturgo: Caminos y caminantes en la escena de la vida y de la muerte," in Donoso, Insúa, and Mata, eds., *El cautiverio en la literatura del Nuevo Mundo*, 202. The role of preacher was so attached to Cabeza de Vaca's character that, decades later, Garcilaso de la Vega, *La Florida del Inca*, would criticize the conqueror and the three other survivors of the expedition for not staying in Florida to teach the natives about religion. Additionally, among the texts about captivity in the Americas, *Naufragios* has an outstanding status because of its originality in the depiction of both thaumaturgy and poverty. The only account that is closer to Cabeza de Vaca concerning these two topics belongs to Hans Staden, a German captive who narrated his experience as healer in Brazil to survive among the natives. A useful anthology about this writing genre is Fer-

nando Operé, comp., *Relatos de cautivos en las Américas desde Canadá a la Patagonia: Siglos XVI al XX* (Buenos Aires: Corregidor, 2016).

33. *El libro de Job*, 163. The Jerusalem Bible translates this passage as "Who pent up the sea behind closed doors when it leapt tumultuous out of the womb?" (Job 38:8).

34. George Camamis, *Estudios sobre el cautiverio en el Siglo de Oro* (Madrid: Gredos, 1977), 109–114.

35. This is one of the first references about Florida as a land of Christian martyrdom, and this characterization of the territory would influence colonial writing in the following decades. By the early seventeenth century, missionaries would be the main protagonists of the expeditions to Florida. See Amy Turner Bushnell, "A Requiem for Lesser Conquerors: Honor and Oblivion on a Maritime Periphery," in *Beyond Books and Borders: Garcilaso de la Vega and La Florida del Inca*, ed. Raquel Chang Rodríguez (Lewisburg, PA: Bucknell University Press, 2006), 66–74. On the other hand, the connection between captivity as a result of shipwreck and the suffering of the Christ's passion might have a medieval origin. As Blackmore, *Manifest Perdition*, 12–13, notes, Alfonso X's *Cantigas* bind together images of shipwreck with some others from the passion, making them similar.

36. Pupo-Walker, "Pesquisas para una nueva lectura," 258.

37. Muñoz Martínez, "Pobreza, enfermedad y exclusión," 171. This meaning of the blanket as a wealthy product appears in key scenes of *Poema de Mío Cid*: there were "mantos e pielles e buenos çendales d'Andria" (line 1971) in King Alfonso's court; later, when the Cid arrives in Valencia, the narrator describes local people, admiring "tanta buena capa e mantos e pelliçones" (line 1989). *Poema de Mío Cid*, ed. Colin Smith (Madrid: Cátedra, 1998).

38. Díaz del Castillo, *Historia verdadera*, 315, 318, 333, 208, 378.

39. A useful contrast to understand the value of these blankets are the "mantas de martas" in comparison to the "lazos de labores de unas pieles leonadas, que parecían muy bien" (112), worn by the natives in the first stage of the journey (chapter 10). The latter are quite sumptuous, while Cabeza de Vaca's blankets are charity gifts.

40. Fernando Operé, *Historias de la frontera: El cautiverio en la América hispánica* (Mexico City: Fondo de Cultura Económica, 2001), 58.

41. Here I say "apparently" because, as I will discuss later, the character of Cabeza de Vaca fully empathizes with the natives in *Naufragios*, but in *Comentarios* he will become a diligent conqueror who is willing to show political and military skills—a model that is very different from that of the poor saint in Florida. Regarding this shifting sense of "nosotros" (the captives) and "los otros" (the Spaniards) in relationship with knowledge, see Voigt, *Writing Captivity*, 58–60.

42. This is part of Cabeza de Vaca's permanent legacy in the representation of Florida. In Garcilaso de la Vega's *La Florida del Inca*, published almost fifty years after Cabeza de Vaca's *Naufragios*, evangelization on this land is still a pending task; see, for example, Garcilaso de la Vega, *La Florida del Inca*, 5–6.

43. Pastor, *Discursos narrativos de la conquista*, 225, also notes Cabeza de Vaca's nudity but interprets it as the origin of a new consciousness that is proper to Spanish American culture, since "indica el punto de origen de una conciencia nueva . . . que se desarrolla sobre la liquidación simbólica de los modelos ideológicos europeos." Blackmore, *Manifest Perdition*, 55–56, also perceives the symbolic value of Cabeza de Vaca's nudity, though he follows the colonial interpretation: "This body [naked or half naked] represents a stripping away of European identity and a return to a utopian innocence."

44. Pupo-Walker, "Pesquisas para una nueva lectura," 237.

45. Alonso López Pinciano, *Filosofía antigua poética*, 3 vols., ed. Alfredo Carballo Picazo (Madrid: Consejo Superior de Investigaciones Científicas, 1973), 2:25–26. Detecting this literary sensitivity in Cabeza de Vaca's writing, Voigt, *Writing Captivity*, 63–64, finds in it a double strategy: "Cabeza de Vaca seeks to author-ize himself in both senses: as an author

able to captivate his readers and as an authoritative source on American geography and ethnography."

46. Alvar Núñez Cabeza de Vaca, *Naufragios y comentarios*, ed. Roberto Ferrando (Madrid: Historia 16, 1984), 147.

47. Voigt, *Writing Captivity*, 62, highlights Cabeza de Vaca's role as successful mediator in *Comentarios* in contrast with his inexpert men. Yet even with such positive depiction before the crown, the protagonist cannot hide his failure, due to poor judgment in the leadership of this new enterprise of conquest.

48. Blackmore, *Manifest Perdition*, 51–53.

49. *Lazarillo de Tormes*, ed. Francisco Rico (Madrid: Cátedra, 2000), 11. For some examples of this type of nautical metaphor, see Ernst R. Curtius, *Literatura europea y edad media latina*, vol. 1 (Mexico: Fondo de Cultura Económica, 1998), 189–193. Blackmore, *Manifest Perdition*, 7, notes its presence in the medieval *Milagros de Nuestra Señora* by Gonzalo de Berceo.

50. For further elaboration and examples of the literary implementation around the nautical metaphor in relation to fortune/misfortune, see the study by Carrie L. Ruiz, in chapter 1 of the present volume.

51. Bruce Wardropper, "El trastorno de la moral en el *Lazarillo*," *Nueva revista de filología hispánica* 15, nos. 3–4 (1961): 441–447. The status of *Lazarillo de Tormes* as a "funny" book was widely accepted among readers during early modern times in Europe. After assessing numerous contemporary testimonies and bibliographic data, Maxime Chevalier, *Lectura y lectores en la España de los siglos XVI y XVII* (Madrid: Turner, 1976), 192, concludes that "la amargura y desesperación que leen los críticos del siglo XX en el libro no parece que la perciban los que leen la novela entre 1554 y 1630."

CHAPTER 6

Shipwreck, Exile, and Political Critique in *Fernán Méndez Pinto* (1631) by Antonio Enríquez Gómez

Carmen Hsu

Fernán Méndez Pinto by Antonio Enríquez Gómez begins with an actual shipwreck and ends with the prospect of a turbulent sea voyage.[1] The main character in one of Spain's most representative converso work describes how his "valiente leño" was overtaken by a vicious hurricane and turned into a metaphorical "ave del cielo" in stormy seas, and how it attempted to steer through large billows of black clouds that covered the "región tronante" as thunderbolts darted to and fro, waterfalls poured down from the sky (1.1.258–263), livid wind scourged the "mísera nave" (1.1.271), and fierce waves burst the ocean apart (1.1.261–262). Finally, the battered vessel "chocó con la roca" and the crashing was such that it split the ship, releasing an "intrépido ruido" (1.1.297), allowing only six affrighted men to escape on salvage that is described as the "iris desta desdicha" (1.1.309). In this nightmarish seascape—composed of an eerie darkness and terrifying sounds—the visual effect of a diminutive vessel juxtaposed with the destructive forces of an adverse world is powerful: it serves to foreshadow the theme of man's essential helplessness in the face of a threatening world whose scale and energy are about to wreck him. On the other hand, the play ends on an apocalyptic note when the hero prepares to set sail for his homeland. The Chinese monarch generously sends off the hero with twenty ships "cargados de todo cuanto / gira el sol y el alba llora" (2.3.2809), an astonishing fortune that promises a future of prosperity. His parting words, however, seem to suggest uncertainty as to whether Fernán could conclude his voyage successfully. The

Chinese king envisions that "olas furiosas" (2.3.2808) await. Thus, the coda of *Fernán Méndez Pinto* poetically foresees another imminent shipwreck in storm-tossed seas.

That the play begins and ends with maritime metaphors is in many ways appropriate. Composed around 1631–1635, *Fernán Méndez Pinto* emerged from a baroque culture that, in Spain, was coterminous with the campaigns of maritime imperial expansion that began in the Americas in the fifteenth century and extended to Asia in the mid-sixteenth century. It is one of the many testimonies to this historical and cultural milieu. As such, the play recasts material from the travelogue *Peregrinaçam* (1614) of Fernão Mendes Pinto, who was one of the earliest European travelers to visit Japan and author of "Información de algunas cosas acerca de las costumbres y leyes del reino de la China," as several scholars have demonstrated.[2] Like Mira de Amescua's *La conquista de las Malucas* (1624–1625[?]) and Lope de Vega's *Los primeros mártires del Japón* (1621), Enríquez Gómez's *Fernán Méndez Pinto* also draws on earlier and contemporary Iberians' historico-imaginative engagement with the ocean and the dangers that it represents. Indeed, the storm and shipwreck images that open and close the play reflect the author's awareness of violent storms at sea and the shipwrecks that Spanish transpacific seafarers were forced to face in that age.[3] Heeding this early modern maritime context, this chapter argues that the maritime scenes not only reveal Enríquez Gómez's indebtedness to the Portuguese author's writings and Iberian maritime enterprise but also, when juxtaposed with the continuous metaphorical storms and wrecks throughout the play, reveal a dramatic structure through which Enríquez Gómez contemplates the life of Fernán Méndez Pinto, an unfortunate shipwrecked character. The chapter also explores the manner in which the dramatist employs the Portuguese character's life as an analogue for the constant and abrupt changes in circumstances endured by many Iberian conversos who, like him, are forced to seek solace, honor, and recognition abroad. In addition, my study aims to show how the seafaring images are also intimately linked to Enríquez Gómez's notions about the *valido*'s extreme vicissitudes of fortune.

The play, divided into two parts,[4] uses storm and shipwreck images to dramatize and give shape to the eventful life of a Portuguese castaway, named Fernán Méndez Pinto, at the court in Beijing. In the opening scene of part 1, Fernán's first words are "¡Cielos, piedad!" (1.1.69). Thus, Enríquez Gómez introduces Fernán's presence on stage as a cry for mercy to the heavens before he is physically pulled out of a hole and seen, thus making his entrance. From the start, Fernán's plea sums up perfectly his life as a victim of misfortune. The pathetic supplication also serves as a brief yet symbolic prelude to a long speech to the king and his daughter, Princess Pantalisa of China, in which Fernán gives a full account of his birth and misfortune and describes how he survived the misery and wretchedness of a shipwreck and was washed ashore in Pattani (Thailand),[5] near the land of the Chinese. Being someone "en quien los cielos supremos / depositaron desdichas, / y llovieron desconsuelos" (1.1.152–154), Fernán emphasizes his determination to steer his own course and, for that reason, he has voluntarily fled an oppressive homeland that is "terrible" to its own people (1.1.518–519). With an "espíritu invencible" (1.1.515) he is determined to battle against the "estrella adversa" (1.2.1923); and during fourteen years of self-exile, he has been drifting restlessly in "ochenta y seis reinos" across Europe and Africa (1.1.386–389). He ends by insisting that in such a world, man is a frail "bajel" that cannot remain afloat for long as the turbulent sea will eventually engulf him. It is therefore imperative to find "un emperador supremo" who would be the

> entre sus tormentas puerto,
> escollo entre sus desdichas,
> sol en sus abismos densos,
> nave entre tantas borrascas,
> bajel entre tantos vientos,
> roca entre tantas fortunas.
> —(1.1.394–399)

In this romance that combines hyperbatons and a vocabulary that superimposes the seafarer's world onto that of a "triste desdichado" (2.2.850), Fernán conflates his personal odyssey with maritime terror: his life is one that is perennially dogged by drifting on tempestuous seas. What begins as a simile comparing the realms of shipwreck survivor and man of constant sorrow culminates here as a metaphor in which the two realms of experience overlap: life becomes seafaring. To be at sea is to be unprotected; only a "monarca excelso"—"puerto," "escollo," "sol," "nave," "bajel," and "roca"—can protect him from such powerful forces as "tormentas," "abismos densos," and all kinds of violent winds including "borrascas," "vientos," and "fortunas," which are, in the playwright's time, synonymous with "borrasca, tempestad en mar o tierra."[6]

Fernán's quest is not, however, motivated entirely by self-preservation. Despite being a victim of constant strokes of adversity, he is ambitious and determined to find a "monarca excelso" to also

> [dar] luz a mis intentos,
> [favorecer] mis ansias,
> y [realzar] mis sucesos.
> —(1.1.403–410)

There is, then, a remarkable mixture of self-preservation and ambition in Fernán's speech. The monologue reveals that his wandering is an action taken not out of despair alone but also because of hope, passion, and the drive to satisfy his ambitions ("intentos," "ansias," "sucesos"). In other words, Fernán is not merely a victim of peripatetic existence; he is also a kinetic participant in it. He escapes from his homeland looking for a supreme prince to serve not because he has to but because he dares to dream.

Moved by this story of toil and determination, the Chinese monarch makes Fernán his royal guard. At the court in Beijing, Fernán is able to demonstrate his aptitudes and seems to succeed in leaving his unfortunate past behind. In part 1, act 2, Fernán's capabilities soon earn him the appreciation and trust of the monarch, who expresses great satisfaction with Fernán's loyalty and talents:

> De tu amor estoy pagado,
> . . . .
> Conozco tu valentía,
> tu valor y atrevimiento,
> y puede tu entendimiento
> dar luz a mi monarquía.
> —(1.2.1119–1126)

The Portuguese outcast has finally found his "puerto" in the Chinese king, who does not merely promise to protect him from "presagios," "desconsuelos," and "desventuras" but who also is able to appreciate his "valentía," "valor," and "entendimiento." The monarch, gratified with Fernán's loyalty and accomplishments, assures the Portuguese vassal that he is now in safe hands (1.2.1115) because he intends to advance Fernán with all his power:

> Del oficio que te he dado
> te pretendo aventajar
> tanto que venga a igualar
> mi poder a mi cuidado.
> —(1.2.1127–1130)

The character's wish to find a supreme monarch who is appreciative of his talents appears to be fulfilled. At this stage of the play Fernán's fortune is soaring. Once again, he uses a nautical metaphor, comparing his political bliss with downwind sailing: "La fortuna va en popa" (1.2.1609). This maritime metaphor reflects the inward nature of his journey: the fair wind and, subsequently, the implicit calm sea thus symbolize the political euphoria that Fernán is experiencing.

Sudden changes, however, are the rule of Fernán's life. The hero's rising good fortune is transitory, as his life is destined to take a turn for the worse. As it turns out, the king of Tartary is in love with Princess Pantalisa and wishes to be betrothed to her. The princess's father, nevertheless, publicly objects to and derides his daughter's marriage to the Tartar. Seeking vengeance, the humiliated suitor arrives incognito in Beijing in the second act. He sneaks into the Chinese king's chamber and kills him with a knife. The Tartar then flees China, leaving everyone to believe Fernán is responsible for the murder. In act 3 Fernán is imprisoned, put on trial, found guilty of regicide, and condemned to the gallows. He complains bitterly about his "desdichada vida," how it is racked with

> desventuras, males, daños,
> tormentos, persecuciones,
> desdichas, suertes, naufragios.
> —(1.3.2270–2272)

Here again the character's situation takes the form of a maritime analogy: the constant and unpredictable crises and disasters that he endures are portrayed as destructive forces such as "suertes" and "naufragios,"[7] along with other turmoil and crises (*desventuras, tormentos, persecuciones*, etc.). Maritime terrors, in other words, manifested in *suertes* and shipwrecks serve here as metaphors to evoke Fernán's misfortunes and turbulent emotional state.[8] In the face of this "divine holocaust," he, so insignificant and as helpless as "un grano en las arenas" (1.3.2165–2166), invokes divine mercy to alleviate his sufferings by granting him martyrdom: "daré el alma en el martirio, / cesando tantos trabajos" (1.3.2267–2268). Only death can relieve him from his incessant chaos and perils. At this point, the king of Tartary, suddenly feeling concerned about his personal honor, returns to China and confesses the murder. The playwright does not really tackle what has gone through the young Tartar's mind between his ignoble murder of the old emperor of China in the ending scene of act 2 and his sudden change of heart. But it is clear that—ironically, thanks to his confusing sense of honor[9]—Fernán is able to escape death. Part 1 ends with the Tartar declaring his love for Pantalisa and Fernán expressing his gratitude.

Fernán's life in China in part 2 is subject to a similar pattern of sudden changes of fortune as those in part 1, and again the dramatist resorts to the maritime imagery to describe the sharp vicissitudes of the character's life. In the opening scene of part 2, Pantalisa (now queen) and the king of Tartary celebrate their union, and Fernán is triumphant: he is now the tutor of the Tartarian king's nephew, Alcidamante; and the king—now the consort regent of Pantalisa—promotes him to viceroy of Tartary. The hero has now risen to the heights of *privanza*, as both monarchs enthusiastically embrace Fernán's accomplishments. Queen Pantalisa likens him to the "Alcides" of China and states that they owe him their "imperio, honor y vida" (2.2.108). The Tartarian king, on the other hand, uses the epithet "el poderoso Atlante" to praise Fernán's strength and pivotal role in their empire building. It is clear that the sovereigns are both appreciative of the hero's great valor (2.2.106). Not only are they quick and generous to reward the "valiente lusitano" (2.1.109) with the honor he deserves, but they are also emphatic about their support: "Próspera la verás, y nunca errante / sobre el cóncavo de la luna" (2.2.115–116). From this point forward, the king reassures

him, Fernán's fortune shall be prosperous and on solid grounds. It will no longer stray into "the concave of the moon." In Enríquez Gómez's time, the "cóncavo de la luna," which was extensively explored by students of iconography
(including Jesuit Luis del Alcázar and Francisco Pacheco), was the term for the
side of the moon that is not illuminated by the sun.[10] In the play, the image implies
something dark and gloomy and is used as a metaphor to evoke the idea of
despair and misfortune. The Chinese regents' assurance that Fernán's life will
never again go off course into the dark concave of the moon means that they are
both his guide and goal, for they vow to "fijar" Fortune's "rueda varia" (2.2.135)
and assure him of a "próspera bonanza" (2.2.481).

The king's favoritism has unleashed the evil instincts of the villains Pinol and
Tirain. As Fernán appears to be finally achieving his political ambitions, his life
is once again thrown into turmoil. The character's success in the opening scene
of part 2 proves ephemeral as it soon provides Pinol and Tirain with an opportunity to indulge their resentment, hatred, and pure malice. The two evil courtiers, raging at the monarch's favoritism toward the Portuguese *valido*, discuss
how they are going to manage the king:

> Pues, ¿qué podemos trazar?
> Ponerle mal con el rey,
> decirle que es un traidor,
> que aunque es tanto su valor,
> de un extranjero la ley,
> llevará mal de su parte
> la llaneza y la lealtad.
> —(2.2.168–174)

Fearing Fernán will become "el potentado mayor que tengan estos estados"
(2.2.145–146), Pinol and Tirain reveal themselves as violently envious and hungry for power. They contrive Fernán's fall from the king's favor by alleging that
he is a "traitor:"

> Fernando, al rey de Brana,
> quiere entregar esta tierra
> por casarse con la infanta.
> —(2.2.609–611)

Their accusation claims that Fernán has been secretly conspiring with the king
of Burma ("Brana" in the play) to overthrow the king of China so that he can
marry the princess of Burma. In order to further substantiate their allegation,
Pinol also has an ally (Miracol) forge Fernán's handwriting in a letter to the king
of Burma detailing a plan to murder the Chinese king. The king of Tartary immediately becomes suspicious of Fernán's loyalty:

De un estranjero
nunca se pudo aguardar,
sino el suceso que veo.
—(2.2.742–744).

He is quick to believe the evidence that Pinol and Tirain have presented and quickly concurs that one should never trust a "stranger." The Tartar then hastens to order the execution of the disgraced *privado*.

In this way the malevolence of Pinol and Tirain marks the beginning of Fernán's fall from favor. It throws his life into disarray. In a conversation with another character while awaiting his execution in part 2, act 2, the intense political upheaval that Fernán experiences is described in an analogy of a maritime disaster:

Me venía
tan desasida tormenta,
en mi próspera bonanza.
—(2.2.479–481)

The evil courtiers responsible for such "desasida tormenta" are dehumanized and transformed into "idras de sangriento mal" (2.2.912). Contemporary lexicographer Sebastián de Covarrubias explains in his *Tesoro de la lengua castellana* (1611) that Hydra, the multiheaded serpent slain by Hercules, can be associated with heretics "por esta serpiente hidra, entiendo yo la heregía y los hereges por los viboreznos; deben ser consumidos con fuego antes que destruyan la tierra."[11] Covarrubias thus uses the many-headed water serpent as a metaphor to stress the heretic's destructive malevolence and treacherousness. In *Fernán Méndez Pinto*, Enríquez Gómez metaphorically transforms Pinol and Tirain into "idras de sangriento mal" that "veneno escupe de envidia" (2.2.503) to emphasize their inhumanity and cataclysmic sway. The brutality and malevolence of their false accusations assail Fernán's "prosperous bonanza" (2.2.481) and plunge him into a "desasida tormenta" (2.1.480). Nautical and marine metaphors (*bonanza, desasida tormenta,* and *idras*) thus embody the unpredictability and ferocity of a natural and manmade disaster in the *valido*'s life. These images also reflect the hero's inner turmoil, standing not only for the sudden, uncontrolled adversities (*desasida tormenta* and *idras*) that threaten the bonanza of his sailing (*privanza*) in the sea of politics, but also for the inner space whence such a perilous journey has come.

The victim of Pinol and Tirain's evil, Fernán falls from "el cielo de mi privanza" into a violent storm. In order to further convey the powerful impact of his rivals' "envidia venenosa" (2.3.2484), he employs the image of tremendous tumult in "todo el ser del universo" (2.1.758), because of which the whole of life is violent and chaotic, and he—a *triste*—is at the center of the turmoil:

Ir contra un triste
todo el ser del universo:
llover las nubes diluvios,
sembrar la región del fuego
abismos, girar el aire,
arrancando de su centro
las tierras, quebrar el mar
aquel marítimo freno
de arena, bramar su escollo.
                —(2.2.757–765)

Here the Portuguese hero describes the destructive impact of his enemies'
"envidia venenosa" in terms of maritime perils: clouds pouring out deluges of
rain, the burning region spreading abysses, the wind dislodging the earth from
its center, the surging seas crashing on sandy banks, and its reef bellowing. Evil,
translated here into the violent forces of cataclysms (deluges, blazes, abysses,
wind, and surging seas), easily destroys his bonanza and continuously threat-
ens to obliterate him. Stylistically the alliteration that is contained in the verb
arrancando and the enjambment that runs over several verses of this passage—
as if the romance itself were subject to the tempest and were fragmented by its
fury—both reflect the pattern of the play as a whole, in which the violent forces
(deluges, fire, abysses, violent wind, storm surge, and howling reef) that are
unleashed seek to destroy and obliterate the character.[12] Fernán, in other words,
a defenseless "sad being," is suddenly assaulted by the powerful forces of the
whole universe—forces that exist on a scale far vaster than man—that threaten
to destroy him. He says that Pinol and Tirain's evil takes the form of "arrancando
de su centro las tierras" (2.2.762–763). The image suggests the violent destruction
of the order of nature: an evil force that has been unleashed is tearing apart the
earth, destroying any notion of a secure and ordered world. The effect is that the
envious courtiers' actions are not just a matter of misleading the king but of a
violent destruction of the entire natural order of things, from order in the realm
of justice and truth to order in the natural world.

Fortunately, after many intricate twists and turns, Fernán is finally given an
opportunity to refute the false allegations made by Pinol and Tirain. In his final
long speech to the king of Tartary in the ending scene of the play, Fernán defends
himself against the "veneno" that his enemies serve as "un antídoto" (2.2.770)
and reminds the monarch of his unwavering loyalty and sacrifice: "Me llamaste
amigo, siendo / yo en tu defensa una roca" (2.3.2717–2718). Fernán reminds the
Tartar of a recent past when the king cherished him as a friend, for he was and
has been the monarch's most indefatigable defender. He also reminds the for-
getful king of how he has always been a loyal sentinel serving the monarch and
the country, and that it was he who risked his own life by rescuing the king from

"las bocas de las bóvedas de fuego" (2.3.2738). The character's speech also stresses how he has completely devoted himself to serving the king and has gone out of his way to relieve the monarch of the burden of government:

> Te llevé tan a mi costa,
> que porque no te enfadasen
> las pardas y negras sombras.
>   —(2.3.2740–2742)

All of Fernán's devotion and sacrifice prove to be to no avail, as the king has turned a deaf ear to all of his appeals:

> Mis palabras
> no satisfacen . . .
> tantos insultos nacidos
> de la envidia venenosa.
>   —(2.3.2481–2484)

Confiding in Pantalisa and Alcidamante, the Tartar is too worried about safeguarding his throne—"la probanza está de forma, / que si no le dan la muerte / corre riesgo mi corona" (2.2.1274–1276)—so he has decided to ignore "la verdad y la lealtad" (2.3.2797). These words show what a tangled web there is in the country. All individuals act for themselves, even double-crossing their friends. The Tartar, as the sovereign both of China and Tartary, ought to be on the side of justice rather than adding to the wrongdoing. In light of this development, Fernán finally sees the futility of all his efforts. He has gone to the trouble of protecting and watching over the king, gaining honor in the country, yet there is no "nobleza y piedad" to protect "una luz de la justicia" (2.3.2399–2401) in this world. In a manner that reminds us of Fray Luis de Leon's poem "Descanso después de la tempestad," the Portuguese *privado* now realizes that all of his endeavors to gain the king's recognition and his aspirations to achieve his "pasiones" (1.1.401) are nothing but a "vivir loco."[13] Fernán's sentiments of disillusionment thus echo the comments made by Jesuit Juan de Mariana in his "Pro editione Vulgata" (1609) that outline a similar situation at the beginning of the seventeenth century in which betrayals, malicious accusations, and continuous external attacks are part of the reality of everyday life for some Spaniards: "La mayor de las locuras es esforzarse en vano, y cansarse para no conseguir sino odios. Quienes participaban de las opiniones vulgares, seguían haciéndolo con más gusto, y fomentaban las ideas que agradaban, en las que había menor peligro, pero no mayor preocupación por la verdad."[14] Mariana's phrasing, as Américo Castro puts it, voices "la más íntima y valerosa confesión de la agonía intelectual de ciertos españoles de mente clara y nueva."[15] One certainly wonders the extent to which Enríquez Gómez projects his personal experience onto the representation of the play's character. While I do not argue that the playwright intends to simply equate the representation of the hero's life with the conversos' abortive attempts to gain validations and success in contemporary Spain, the analogue between the two is conspicuous. In Mariana's Spain and in Enríquez Gómez's *Fernán Méndez Pinto*, it is foolish and dangerous to even try to be honorable or virtuous, as all endeavors will prove to be in vain.

Furthermore, the complaint also reveals a significant change in Fernán: if the character enters the play as a hopeful wanderer looking for a "sublime monarch" to change his fortune, at the end he finds no princes who are immune to flattery and the evil tongue of envious courtiers. Instead he discovers that pestiferous envy and poisonous malice have blotted out all his hard work and sacrifices. In light of such realization, Fernán's concluding remarks reveal how much his view on the initial quest for "un emperador supremo" has changed. The hero concludes by reiterating that "ni la envidia rigurosa, / ni la traición declarada," and "ni la ingratitud soberbia" could annihilate his "verdad," his "inocencia ofendida," and his "lealtad generosa" (2.2.2751–2762). Clearly Fernán's speech at the end of part 2 serves not only to evoke our sympathy but also to voice a sense of humanity's plight in a chaotic world and an awakening to disillusionment. Perhaps because the journey's end goal is so far removed from this point where Fernán presently finds himself, the disappearance of his aspirations does not seem to produce moments of extreme crisis, and therefore this situation serves as a figure to communicate disillusion rather than crisis. Fallen into disgrace, Fernán is finally forced to reexamine his understanding both of the world and of himself. It is this facing up to the world and to his own position in it that most clearly identifies the change in Fernán.

With this speech Fernán is able to clear his honor in the ending scene of the play. The king of Tartary once again reacts hastily. He immediately believes the "verdad notoria" (2.3.2764) in the aggrieved Fernán's defense and is ready to compensate him for all the toil and indignities he has suffered: "Pide a mi persona heroica / nuevos cargos y favores" (2.3.2786–2787). The remorse prompts the Tartar to attempt to set things right for Fernán. The king's change of mind in the final scene of the play should not come as a surprise, as it is consistent with his previous actions. It appears that the king lacks the personality necessary to live up to what is expected and required of him. His immediate sentence of execution in part 2, act 1 might reflect a king who is acting decisively to protect his country, but the Tartar's confusing sense of honor at the end of part 1, his hasty order of sentence without further verification of the allegation, and his quick change of mind now all seem to indicate that he is impulsive and weak and that things are unstable under his rule. I do not suggest that Enríquez Gómez writes with the intention of providing answers to Fernán's political problems. Instead the dramatist is examining the reality of how people behave. Because of the king's imprudence and lack of leadership, Pinol and Tirain are not only able to mislead him but also destroy the principles of truth and justice in politics. The king's actions undermine the principle of justice he is supposed to represent. He has allowed "tiranía y lisonja" to be the "luz, siendo sombra" (2.3.2472) in his palaces; he has closed the door to mercy and justice, as his "orejas sordas" now gain a reputation as tyrants (2.3.2476–2479); and he is easily swayed by others. In this way Fernán's denunciation conveys a sense of justice and government that is refreshingly secular and seems to be based on "un modelo de justicia y de toleran-cia que escapa de cualquier dogmatismo, ya sea romano o sinagogal."[16] At the end, Fernán finally realizes he can no longer trust the king to be a safe haven that shelters him from the evil and malicious envy that are manifested in del-uges, abysses, hurricanes, and storm surges.

Fernán's experiences in China have made him realize that no matter how far he travels and no matter where he goes, he is destined to live in a world of end-less tempests and catastrophes. He, like a frail craft, is destined to be tossed about by untamed squalls and constantly cast down into dark abysses, as there are no safe harbors to be found, not even in China. It is at this point that Fernán accepts the inevitability of fate and the futility of attempting to evade it, as in this imper-fect world "no siempre estuvo en popa / la verdad y la lealtad" (2.3.2796–2797). Here again the character uses a nautical metaphor to communicate his recogni-tion that "truth and loyalty" do not guarantee a safe voyage. The end of the play maintains certain ambiguity: the current threat of envious courtiers is elim-inated, but Fernán's future remains uncertain. Although he is able to clear himself of any wrongdoings, his decision to return to Spain insinuates more adversities to come rather than a restful retirement. The idea of good fortune remains a remote ideal, as Fernán is forced to accept that such qualities as "truth and loyalty" alone cannot survive in the world given people's capacity for evil and envy. Envy, the "verdugo de la verdad" (2.2.910), can "deslucir la lealtad," mak-ing loyalty appear to be a destructive trait rather than a noble one (2.2.779–781). The success, if there is one, quickly becomes lost, and the *extranjero* must stumble along as best he can through his perilous quest. He is aware that, for someone like him—destined to adverse fortune—death is his only rest (2.3.2491).

One wonders to what extent Enríquez Gómez's converso background comes into play in this work. As Constance Rose notes, Enríquez Gómez finds in the Portuguese hero "a kindred spirit: here was a man persecuted by Fortune from birth."[17] Indeed, the story of drastic vicissitudes endured by a drifter, an exile, is a recurrent theme in the work of many sixteenth- and seventeenth-century New Christian authors.[18] Like so many early modern converso authors, Enríquez Gómez was a New Christian of "mixed" parentage from Cuenca.[19] Born in 1600, the same year as Pedro Calderón de la Barca, the merchant writer led a peripa-tetic kind of life and was persecuted by the Inquisition.[20] Known as Enrique Enríquez de Paz in Madrid between 1624 and 1635, the author fled to France (Bor-deaux and Rouen) toward the end of 1635 or early 1636, probably because of his problem with the Inquisition. He remained in France until 1649, when he decided to return to Spain. He settled in Seville, where he devoted himself exclusively to the theater under the pseudonym Fernando de Zárate y Castronovo, before his imprisonment in the secret jail of the Inquisition in Triana, where he died in 1663.

This quick perusal of his life reveals the story of a drifter, a "figura entrañable . . . marcada por un destino muy triste, a la vez espíritu en lucha contra la tiranía y hombre de fe destruido por la máquina inquisitorial."[21] Like Enríquez Gómez, the Portuguese character is defined as a castaway, a drifter, and an "estrangero." Throughout the entire play, references to Fernán as a stranger abound. In the opening scene of part 1, for instance, the king of China, upon seeing him being rescued from a deep hole, exclaims, "Estranjero es este joven" (1.1.119). On a different occasion, Duarte, the *criado*, warns Fernán of the dangers of an "estranjero" wanting to be "de los reyes privanza" (1.2.1929–1930). Another example can be found in the Tartarian king's quick suspicion of Fernán: "De un estranjero / nunca se pudo aguardar" (2.2.742–743).[22] Just like in his panegyric *Luis dado de Dios a Luis y Ana* (1645) and the first part of the *Política angélica* (1645), an "anti-Inquisitional tract,"[23] being a stranger implies not just being a foreigner but also being someone of a different faith.[24] As I have demonstrated, Fernán Méndez Pinto, *triste* and *desdichado* by birth, never manages to fully integrate into the world in which he finds himself and is continuously forced to live out his life in a situation of alienation. Thus the story of Fernán is driven very much by the personal experience of its author.

In addition, the peripatetic pattern of Fernán's existence also evokes the author's life experience. Enríquez Gómez's own "peregrinación," as he confesses in the prologue to his *Academias morales de las musas* (1642), is also caused by some individuals who "infeccionando la república, recíprocamente falsos, venden por antídoto el veneno a los que militan debajo del solio."[25] Speaking directly to the heavens, the Portuguese character claims that he, as "el que nació desdichado" (2.3.2495), no longer believes that he could ever achieve the

> bien nunca esperado de su estado;
> . . . pues viviendo muero,
> ni vida aguardo, ni esperanza quiero.
> —(2.2.853–855).

Fernán's reference to live dying as a way of expressing disenchantment with life in this world is one of the main themes propounded in St. Teresa of Avila's famous *letrilla* "Muero porque no muero." Clearly the ascetic theme of death to worldly concerns as a way of cultivating love and affective union with God in the Teresian poem is used here to assert a change in Fernán: the character no longer awaits life, nor does he want hope. There is a growing sense of total disillusionment in part 2, act 2. Fernán can only console himself with the conscience of his truth, that he is innocent and loyal. In this light, *Fernán Méndez Pinto* is a vehicle for expressing the dramatist's own situation.

Except for Miguel de Cervantes's and Lope de Vega's dramatic adaptations of Ludovico Ariosto's familiar theme of Princess Angelica of Cathay, none of which takes place in the land of the Chinese,[26] *Fernán Méndez Pinto* may be the first and only drama written during this period that situates its action in the Middle Kingdom. As one may also find in other contemporary Spanish *comedias* about the Far East (Japan or the Spice Islands), there is nothing particularly Chinese about the characters that take part in the play or about the place where the action occurs. There is no mention of problems in communication or cultural misunderstanding. In fact, Fernán seems perfectly capable of fitting in with the Chinese from the very beginning; he and the Chinese are able to communicate with each other without the assistance of a translator. Although staged in China instead of Hungary or Poland (the stock locations for seventeenth-century Spanish political plays),[27] the play belongs to the genre of the so-called *comedia palatina* (drama of palace intrigue), which addresses the highs and lows of royal favorites and princes.[28] As Michael McGaha and Milagros Rodríguez-Cáceres assert, the play not only dramatizes the vicissitudes of Fernán as the *valido* at the court of the Chinese prince but probably also evokes contemporary Spain's political situation—specifically the Count-Duke of Olivares's *privanza*—which is cautiously translated as distant China.[29]

Enríquez Gómez, like many other Spanish authors writing about China at the time, was also inspired by Asian-Iberian encounters. *Fernán Méndez Pinto*, along with a handful of seventeenth-century Spanish *comedias* that stage their actions in the Far East,[30] does not really provide us with insights as to how the Chinese are imagined and defined by the Spanish; rather, it turns China into a space and a vehicle for self-reflection. Yet the playwright's representation of the Asian land departs significantly from the idealization that one normally finds in contemporary historical narratives like Juan González de Mendoza's *Historia de la China* (1585), in which the Chinese court proves similar to Spanish society. Here the Chinese courtiers also live with burdens, quarreling, judges, and malevolent rivals. Far from being the antithesis of corruption or the idyllic picture through which authors such as González de Mendoza express their deep dissatisfaction with Spanish society (and, by implication, criticize it), Enríquez Gómez's Chinese society does not differ from the Spanish one. Rather than writing to provide information about the Middle Kingdom, he uses China as no more than a backdrop against which the perennially nomadic life of a wanderer is dutifully projected. The play is a grim reminder that no matter where he goes or how far he travels, he lives in "a tightrope world of vertical danger in which a life of precaution and prudence could be undone in one moment of carelessness."[31] In this hazardous world, power and justice are easily manipulated and turned against the innocent. At any time, things can lapse into uncontrolled violence.

Enríquez Gómez portrays China in a much more complex light, deviating from the stock image of that nation as an embodiment of virtue and justice.[32] In

fact, his portrayal of it, which is characterized by constant conflict and dis-
agreement, problematizes the conventional notion of China as a paragon of the
well-ordered country. The chaos and mishaps created by jealous stool pigeons
(*malsines*) in Enríquez Gómez's China have striking analogues with some aspects
of seventeenth-century Spain as depicted by such writers as Baltasar Gracián or
Francisco de Quevedo. In fact, although Fernán Méndez is able to regain his
innocence and reaffirm the idea that truth and loyalty always prevail in China,
the constant and abrupt reversals of fortune that he has to endure reveal that
loyalty and truth do not shield him from misfortune, and they can easily be oblit-
erated by dark emotions and desires (2.3.2796–2797). Moreover, in the hierar-
chical society of González de Mendoza's China, this would be a society in which
the king carries out his duties carefully and responsibly, with his subjects respect-
ing and serving their king. Such an orderly state of affairs is, however, not what
we find in *Fernán Méndez Pinto*. The dramatist's representation of the king of
Tartary is a clear contrast to the recurrent idealized image of the Chinese prince
who values personal talents, loyalty, and merits above all else. The play also challenges the notions of China as a place where one's religion, ancestry, and national
origin are not discriminated against and where its people are governed with
justice, charity, and mercy.

    Fernán Méndez Pinto proves to be fundamentally different from most con-
temporary Iberian works on Asia and China. In no part of the work is there a
suggestion of hope to convert the Chinese, nor are there any hints of Christian
superiority. Unlike what one normally would expect from a seventeenth-century
Catholic Spanish author, Fernán never openly expresses any intent to convert
the Chinese or the Tartars. Although the comments that he makes about the land
of the Chinese on one occasion reveal a clear sense of Christian superiority, these
comments appear right after a conversation in which the Portuguese hero briefly
surveys some of the main political institutions (*consejos*), clothing, and universi-
ties in Spain. Thus, despite the undertone of Christian superiority, the remarks—
rather than a statement of firm resolve to convert the Chinese—might actually
be conveying one of the few stereotypical praises for China's political and social
achievements:

> Sólo le falta a este imperio
> aquella luz soberana
> del evangelio divino.
>   —(1.2.1785–1787)

It is clear that the religion of the Chinese does not seem to be a relevant factor
in the playwright's imagination of the Middle Kingdom; their spiritual beliefs
are suggested in passing without being discredited as idolatry.

    Using an almost contemporary Portuguese travelogue, and inspired by Ibe-
rians' historico-imaginative engagement with transoceanic expansion and with

China, Enríquez Gómez dramatizes the story of a fellow wanderer in order to express his personal situation, the trajectory of a social outcast in flight from his native land and pursued by an adverse fortune wherever he goes. As Rose states, "What appealed to the playwright was not the subject of the Far East *per se* but the story of a wandering man, a Peninsular exile."[33] Indeed, *Fernán Méndez Pinto* shows how China becomes both a space and a vehicle for self-reflection. The China where Fernán desperately tries to achieve his ambitions proves to be a place similar to seventeenth-century Spain, where the reversals of fortune are routine for an *estranjero* like himself. Such identification of adverse fortune with continuous aggression from without, as Stephen Gilman discerns, is in profound accord with one aspect of the converso experience. Violent storms and shipwrecks are the recurrent metaphors used to describe the relentless trials and tribulations to which the character is repeatedly subject. These images offer a pessimistic perspective of Fernán's life that is an analogue of the experience of the conversos that "grew used to existing in a vertical circumstance, in which to fall is a routine event rather than a biographical climax."[34] Moreover, in setting the action of the play in a Far Eastern country, Enríquez Gómez does not simply mirror the familiar, conventional notion of the Middle Kingdom as the embodiment of justice and virtue; rather, he reshapes it and portrays China as a kindred image of seventeenth-century Spain, where conversos are often accused of disloyalty and of working against the best interests of their native land. Finally, the story of a peripatetic hero such as Fernán Méndez becomes an effective means of expression to convey the author's own personal experience of a wanderer in flight from his homeland, an exile pursued by the Inquisition.

NOTES

I would like to express my gratitude to the Carolina Asia Center, the Carolina Center for Jewish Studies, the Center for Initiatives, and the Department of Romance Studies at the University of North Carolina in Chapel Hill for their generosity. This chapter is the fruit of their generous support, which made research travel to Spain's Biblioteca Nacional in the summer of 2018 possible.

1. Antonio Enríquez Gómez, *Fernán Méndez Pinto: Comedia famosa en dos partes*, ed. Louise G. Cohen, Francis M. Rogers, and Constance H. Rose (Cambridge, MA: Harvard University Press, 1974). Unless otherwise specified, all quotations are from this edition and will be cited parenthetically in the text, with part, act, and line numbers and with modernized spelling. See also Constance H. Rose, "Antonio Enríquez Gómez and the Literature of Exile," *Romanische Forschungen* 85 (1973): 63–77; and Antonio Márquez, "Dos procesos singulares: Los de Fray Luis de León y Antonio Enríquez Gómez," *Nueva revista de filología hispánica* 30, no. 2 (1981): 526–533.

2. See C. R. Boxer, *Fidalgos in the Far East, 1550–1770* (Hong Kong: Oxford University Press, 1968), 3. Fernão Mendes Pinto wrote his travelogue between 1569 and 1570, but the work was not published until 1614, three decades after the death of its author. Mendes Pinto's account in Portuguese was not a publishing success in the seventeenth century, as no second edition appeared until 1678. What is most extraordinary, as Francis M. Rogers, "Fernão Mendes Pinto, His *Peregrinaçam*, and the Spanish Play," in Enríquez Gómez,

Fernán Méndez Pinto, 13, points out, is that between the first and second Portuguese editions at least eleven translations (in Dutch, English, French, German, and Spanish) made their appearance. The Spanish translation, by Francisco de Herrera Maldonado, was issued in Madrid as early as 1620. Mendes Pinto's "Información" was first published in *Cartas de las Indias Orientales* (1555) in Coimbra; a Spanish translation of the letter was inserted at the end of Francisco Alvarez's 1561 edition of his *Historia de las cosas de Ethiopía* (Zaragoza, Spain: Agostín Millán, 1561), fols. 76r–77v, and Carlos Sanz published a facsimile edition of Alvarez's Spanish translation. See also María Rosa Alvarez Sellers, "Caminos portugueses hacia Oriente de la *Peregrinação* de Fernão Mendes Pinto a la comedia *Fernán Méndez Pinto* de Enríquez Gómez," in *Actas del VIII Congreso Internacional de Caminería Hispánica* (Madrid: Ministerio de Fomento, 2008): 1–14; and Luisa Trías Folch, "La traducción española de la Peregrinação y la comedia española *Fernán Méndez Pinto*," in *Literatura portuguesa y literatura española: Influencias y relaciones*, ed. María Rosa Alvarez Sellers (Valencia, Spain: Universitat de València, 1999), 37–53.

   3. Ricardo Padrón, "Shipwrecked Ambitions," in *The Indies of the Setting Sun: How Early Modern Spain Mapped the Far East as the Transpacific West* (Chicago: University of Chicago Press, 2020), 107–138.

   4. Part 1 of the play was staged in Madrid on May 18, 1633, by the company of Manuel Vallejo; see Hugo A. Rennert, "Notes on the Chronology of Spanish Drama," *Modern Language Review* 2 (1907): 340; and Israël Salvator Révah, *Antonio Enríquez Gómez, un écrivain marrane (v. 1600–1663)*, ed. Carsten L. Wilke (Paris: Chandeigne, 2003), 654. See also N. D. Shergold and J. E. Varey, "Some Palace Performances of Seventeenth-Century Plays," *Bulletin of Hispanic Studies* 40 (1963): 226. Regarding the composition date of part 2, Felipe B. Pedraza Jiménez, "La fascinación de *El médico de su honra*: Sus ecos en la obra de Enríquez Gómez," in *Doctos libros juntos: Homenaje al profesor Ignacio Arellano Ayuso*, ed. Ignacio Arellano, Victoriano Roncero López, and Juan Manuel Escudero (Frankfurt: Iberoamericana, 2018), 419–420, argues that Enríquez Gómez probably wrote it during 1633–1635, right after the successful reception of part 1 and immediately before his self-exile in France toward the end of 1635 or beginning of 1637. Shortly after having been performed, the two parts, undated, were printed in separate chapbooks (*pliegos sueltos*). They were both incorporated into the second volume of Enríquez Gómez's *La Torre de Babilonia* in 1670.

   5. Pattani is "Patanay" in the play. In addition to Pattani, Louise G. Cohen, Francis M. Rogers, and Constance H. Rose, in an endnote to Enríquez Gómez, *Fernán Méndez Pinto*, 164, suggests that "Patanay" could also be "a fusion of Mendes Pinto's Patane and his Pão, Herrera Maldonado's Paon and Paom, which are places the Portuguese explorer visited on his first trip northeastward of Malacca."

   6. Real Academia Española, "Fortuna," in *Diccionario de autoridades*, vol. 2 (Madrid: Editorial Gredos, 1984), 784a.

   7. The 1974 edition has transcribed *fuerte* when clearly it should be *suerte* as it appears in the early seventeenth-century edition, currently held in Spain's Biblioteca Nacional. In the context of Enríquez Gómez's play, *suerte* means "acaso, accidente o fortuna"; Real Academia Española, "Suerte," in *Diccionario de autoridades*, vol. 3 (Madrid: Editorial Gredos, 1984), 178a.

   8. For an examination of the literary representation of the character's life as a voyage across the seas of uncertainty and of the representation of the sea as a reflection of inner emotions, see the study by Carrie L. Ruiz, chapter 1 in the present volume.

   9. Glen Dille, *Antonio Enríquez Gómez* (Boston: Twayne, 1988), 26.

   10. Luis del Alcázar, *Vestigatio arcani sensus in Apocalypsi* (Antwerp: Joannem Keebergium, 1614), 616; Francisco Pacheco, *Arte de la pintura: Su antigüedad y grandezas* (Sevilla, Spain: Simón Fajardo, 1649), 483. See also Reyes Escalera Pérez, "Iconografía y el arte religioso del barroco," in *Escultura barroca española: Nuevas lecturas desde los siglos de oro a*

la sociedad del conocimiento, vol. 1, ed. Antonio Rafael Fernández Paradas (Antequera, Spain: Exlibric, 2016), 59–85.

11. Sebastián de Covarrubias, *Tesoro de la lengua castellana* (Barcelona: Editorial Alta Fulla, 1993), 686a.

12. In chapter 3 of the present volume, Elena Rodríguez-Guridi further explores this symbiosis between the calamities experienced by the castaway and the textual features of the *silva.*

13. Fray Luis de León, *Poesía completa,* ed. Guillermo Serés (Madrid: Taurus, 1990), 98. According to Félix García, "Fray Luis de León, poeta del mar," in *San Juan de la Cruz y otros ensayos* (Madrid: Religión y Cultura, 1950), 201–205, although Fray Luis "no vio nunca el mar," the poet in several of his poems employs the sea imagery as an effective symbol to describe the world in which he lives. See also Guillermo Araya, "Fray Luis de León: La vida como naufragio," in *De Garcilaso a García Lorca (ocho estudios sobre letras españolas)* (Amsterdam: Rodopi, 1983), 179–190.

14. Juan de Mariana, "Pro editione Vulgata," quoted and translated by Américo Castro, in Américo Castro, *De la edad conflictiva* (Madrid: Taurus, 1961), 170. For the original text in Latin, see Juan de Mariana, *Tractatus VII* (Coloniae Agrippinæ: Anton Hierat, 1609), 34a–34b.

15. Castro, *De la edad conflictiva,* 170. See also Stephen Gilman, "Fortune and Space in *La Celestina," Romanische Forschungen* 66, no. 3 (1955): 358.

16. Rafael Carrasco, "Antonio Enríquez Gómez, un escritor judeoconverso frente a la Inquisición," in *Academias morales de las musas,* vol. 1, ed. Milagros Rodríguez Cáceres and Felipe B. Pedraza Jiménez (Cuenca, Spain: Ediciones de la Universidad de Castilla–La Mancha, 2015), 54.

17. Rose, "Antonio Enríquez Gómez and the Literature of Exile," 70.

18. Matthew Warshawsky, "Las múltiples expresiones de identidad judeo-conversa en tres obras poéticas de Antonio Enríquez Gómez," *Calíope* 17, no. 1 (2011): 97–124; Ruth Fine, "Una lectura de Sansón Nazareno de Enríquez Gómez en el contexto de la literatura de conversos," in *Antonio Enríquez Gómez: Un poeta entre santos y judaizantes,* ed. J. Ignacio Díez and Carsten Wilke (Kassel, Germany: Reichenberger, 2015), 96–114; Timothy Oelman, "Tres poetas marranos," *Nueva revista de filología hispánica* 30 (1981): 184–206.

19. For more about Enríquez Gómez's life, see Révah, *Antonio Enríquez Gómez;* Carrasco, "Antonio Enríquez Gómez," 19–54; Carsten L. Wilke, *Jüdisch-christliches Doppelleben in Barock: Zur Biographie des Kaufmanns und Dichters Antonio Enríquez Gómez* (Frankfurt: Peter Lang, 1994); and Jaime Galbarro García, "Antonio Enríquez Gómez: Vida y contexto histórico," in *"El triumpho lusitano" de Antonio Enríquez Gómez,* ed. Jaime Galbarro García (Sevilla, Spain: Universidad de Sevilla, 2015), 13–63.

20. Révah, *Antonio Enríquez Gómez,* 238–245; Carrasco, "Antonio Enríquez Gómez," 30–33.

21. Carrasco, "Antonio Enríquez Gómez," 22.

22. See also Enríquez Gómez, *Fernán Méndez Pinto,* 1.3.2157; 2.1.172; 2.1.648; 2.2.1257; and 3.3.2297.

23. Constance H. Rose, "Portuguese Diplomacy Plays a Role in the Printing of Some Peninsular Works in Rouen in the Seventeenth Century," *Arquivos do Centro Cultural Portugès* 10 (1976): 539.

24. Antonio Enríquez Gómez, *Luis dado de Dios* (Paris: Rene Baudry, 1645), 125–127, enumerates several virtuous Christian *validos* who although they are "estrangeros" become saviors of the empires in Egypt or Persia by serving loyally and wisely. See also Israël Salvator Révah, "Un pamphlet contre l'Inquisition d'Antonio Enríquez Gómez: La seconde partie de la política angélica (Rouen, 1647)," *Revue des études juives* 121, nos. 1–2 (1961): 137.

25. Antonio Enríquez Gómez, "Prólogo," in *Academias morales de las musas* (Bordeaux, France: Pedro de la Court, 1642), n.p.

26. The theme of Angelica, the princess of Cathay, from Ariosto's *Orlando furioso* prompted the productions of several plays in sixteenth- and seventeenth-century Spain. It inspired Lope de Vega to write *Los celos de Rodamonte* (1588–1589), *El pastoral albergue* (1595–1600), and *Angélica en el Catay* (1617), and it also markedly influenced Miguel de Cervantes's *Casa de los celos* (1581–1588). Although these plays make clear references to the character Angelica, the plot of all of them takes place in Charlemagne's court, not in the faraway Middle Kingdom.

27. G. A. Davies, "Poland, Politics, and *La vida es sueño*," *Bulletin of Hispanic Studies* 70, no. 1 (1993): 147; Concepción Argente del Castillo Ocaña, "Hungría en el teatro de Mira de Amescua," in *La teatralización de la historia en el Siglo de Oro español* (Granada: Universidad de Granada, 2001), 83–100; Adrián J. Sáez, "Las comedias húngaras de Lope de Vega: Una cadena de intertextualidad y reescritura," *Dicenda* 33 (2015): 293–307.

28. Defining the genre of the *comedia palatina*, Milagro Rodríguez-Cáceres, "La sombra del Conde-Duque en el teatro de Enríquez Gómez," in *Estrategias y conflictos de autoridad y poder en el teatro del Siglo de Oro*, ed. Ignacio Arellano and Frederick A. de Armas (New York: Instituto de Estudios Auriseculares, 2017), 106, proposes several key characteristics that include "validos fieles y traidores, reyes absolutos tiránicos y benignos, discusiones sobre los límites del poder." For more on the *comedia palatina*, see Frida Weber de Kurlat, "Hacia una sistematización de los tipos de comedia de Lope de Vega," in *Actas del V Congreso Internacional de Hispanistas*, vol. 2, ed. François Lopez, Joseph Pérez, Noël Salomon, and Maxime Chevalier (Bordeaux, France: Université de Bordeaux, 1977), 867–871; Miguel Zugasti, "Comedia palatina cómica y comedia palatina seria en el siglo de oro," in *El sustento de los discretos: La dramaturgia áulica de Tirso de Molina*, ed. E. Galar and B. Oteiza (Madrid: Instituto de Estudios Tirsianos, 2003), 159–185.

29. Michael McGaha, "Antonio Enríquez Gómez and the Count-Duque of Olivares," in *Texto y espectáculo: Nuevas dimensiones críticas de la comedia*, ed. Arturo Pérez-Pisonero and Ana Semidey (New Brunswick, NJ: SLUSA, 1990), 73–81; Rodríguez-Cáceres, "La sombra del Conde-Duque en el teatro de Enríquez Gómez," 123–137.

30. Some emblematic examples from this corpus are Andrés de Claramonte's *El nuevo rey Gallinato* (1601); Lope de Vega's *Los mártires del Japón* (1617), and Mira de Amescua's *Conquista de las Malucas* (1624–1625). The English dramatist John Fletcher also found inspiration in the Portuguese conquest of the Spice Islands and was the author of *The Island Princess* (1621).

31. Stephen Gilman, "The 'Conversos' and the Fall of Fortune," in *Collected Studies in Honour of Américo Castro's Eightieth Year*, ed. M. P. Hornik (Oxford: Lincombe Lodge Research Library, 1965), 136.

32. On this point, my interpretation of the *comedia* differs from Rose's. Constance H. Rose, "Las comedias políticas de Enríquez Gómez," *La torre* 118 (1982): 191–192, argues that "en el reino de la China donde los monarcas son justos y la justicia prevalece, un extranjero virtuoso puede llegar a ser valido del rey."

33. Constance H. Rose, "Enríquez Gómez and the Literature of Exile," in Enríquez Gómez, *Fernán Méndez Pinto*, 47.

34. Gilman, "The 'Conversos' and the Fall of Fortune," 135.

CHAPTER 7

The Manila Galleon Shipwrecks

WRITING CRISIS AND DECLINE IN THE SPANISH GLOBAL EMPIRE

Ana M. Rodríguez-Rodríguez

In *Manifest Perdition: Shipwreck Narrative and the Disruption of Empire*, Josiah Blackmore states that the shipwreck narrative "exposes and promotes breaches in the expansionist mentality and in the textual culture associated with that mentality." It is "a type of counterhistoriography that troubles the hegemonic vision of empire" and therefore "shipwreck narratives undermine the master historiographic narrative of imperialism in all its cultural, political, and economic valences, upsetting the imperative of order and the unifying paradigms of 'discovery' or 'conquest' textuality."[1] This particular vision of shipwreck narratives is especially enlightening in the case of the Philippines, since the archipelago epitomizes, from the first years of the Spanish presence in the islands, the decline that did not befall other areas of the empire for over a century. Spanish colonial power in the Philippines was fragile, and the islands were an eccentric point of the empire whose communication with the rest of it relied on the unstable and dangerous journey of the so-called Manila galleon. This chapter analyzes two crucial texts in the construction of early modern Filipino historiography, Antonio de Morga's *Sucesos de las islas Filipinas* (1609) and Francisco Colín's *Labor evangélica* (1663), and shows how the theme of shipwreck plays a pivotal role therein—in particular, by creating a discourse about the Philippines as a failed colony, which forecasts the decline of the global Spanish Empire.[2]

M. N. Pearson explains that the prosperity of the Philippines "was necessarily based on trade in the products of the surrounding countries, for the Spanish found almost no Philippine product suitable for them to export."[3] The survival of the Philippines was therefore dependent upon its ability to communicate with a variety of territories: the Asian lands, where merchandise was purchased, and New Spain and the metropolis, where the different Asian products were finally sold. The Manila galleon is the name given to the sailing ships that crossed the Pacific Ocean for 250 years, from the Philippines to Mexico and back, transporting "liquor, drugs, silk, cotton, and porcelain (china) from Manila to Acapulco, and [bringing] back olive oil, European and American cloth, wine, lead, tin, gold, and, above all, American silver."[4] Nicholas Cushner explains that "agriculture, mining, and home industries were almost completely ignored until the latter eighteenth century" and therefore "the galleon trade was the only stable source of income for the colonists."[5]

In addition to food and a variety of products, the Manila galleon also allowed the travel of people, books, and ideas from the 1560s on; the galleon constituted the only channel of communication between the islands and the rest of the Spanish Empire, and, as such, it was a "lifeline of the Spaniards in the Philippines with the rest of the world."[6] The galleon became "the overwhelming raison d'être of the Spanish settlers in Manila."[7] But the galleon route was extremely dangerous and subject to a number of obstacles where life was continuously at risk. According to William Schurz, "In all the seas there was no line of navigation so difficult, so attended with perils and hardships, as that of the Manila galleons."[8] The route was full of dangers due to the difficult geography of the islands and the negative weather conditions so frequent in the archipelago. Here strong winds, severe storms, monsoons, typhoons and hurricanes (*brisas* and *vendavales* in Spanish texts) were common. Ships also could always be attacked by the Dutch, who aimed at controlling commerce in the area and who brought to the Pacific a continuation of the conflicts that were taking place in Europe during the sixteenth and seventeenth centuries.[9] Moreover, as Shirley Fish notes, "the Pacific galleon crossed the ocean unaccompanied by warship galleons. The Philippines-Mexican galleons were instead heavily armed to serve as both merchant and war vessels to protect themselves if need arose." In addition to all of the geographical, natural, and political obstacles, shipwrecks sometimes happened because of human error due to the lack of mastery of the vessel captains, who were not always chosen for their nautical abilities but instead for their connections and network relations in colonial society. Fish explains that "the Spanish governor of the Philippines, assigned to the post by the Spanish king, . . . had the ultimate jurisdiction over the appointment of the commanders of the galleons. For a price, he often appointed an individual to the esteemed position of a galleon's captain-general based on his own personal whims." For example, after the 1638 shipwreck of the *Nuestra Señora de la Concepción*, Governor Sebastián Hurtado de Corcuera was charged with inappropriately appointing his nephew, a young man lacking naval or military experience, as the commander of the vessel, and as part of his punishment for its loss, Corcuera's property was confiscated and he was sent to prison for five years.[10]

All passengers were painfully aware of the danger of the voyage; masses and prayers were said daily, hoping that these religious services would protect them.

Vessels were named after patron saints or important religious sites, which was an added measure of protection in the hopes that divine intervention would ensure a safe journey.[11] According to Efren B. Isorena, in the 250 years that the Manila galleon sailed the Pacific Ocean, there were at least four hundred voyages between Manila and Acapulco, with fifty-nine shipwrecks and thirty-five *arribadas*, or forced returns.[12] These numbers are not particularly overwhelming, but we must take into account the profound impact that any one of these incidents had on the economic and social life of the islands. Entire families could go into bankruptcy in a financial system that was completely dependent on the success of the galleon taking merchandise to be sold in New Spain. Additionally, up to four hundred people traveled in a given ship, and their death was a strong blow to the confidence of Spaniards who lived in the Philippines, a minority among the much more numerous Indigenous and mestizo populations and Chinese immigrants. It is easy to imagine the impact that events like the arrival of a galleon—"with all her goods on board but without a living soul, for the ship's company had been lost"[13]—would have on the morale of the colony.

The difficulty of controlling the vast and dispersed territories that constituted the Philippines, coupled with the limited communication with other Spanish lands and the scarcity of the Spanish population, meant that Spaniards never had real control of the islands; consequently, areas that were apparently secured, like Manila, were dangerously vulnerable to possible attacks by nearby powers and to the rebellion of native and immigrant populations that were immensely superior in numbers to the Spaniards. In Spanish minds, "and even more surely in their maps, the Philippines featured as part of their 'Empire.' Those who lived in the islands knew better."[14] There was never a large number of Spaniards living in the Philippines between 1565 and 1898; at its lowest, the Spanish population was four hundred, and it was estimated to be four thousand in the nineteenth century.[15] As late as 1637, after some eighty years of colonization, Manila only had 150 houses inhabited by Spaniards, even though the city grew through the continuous influx of Chinese immigrants, the increasing mestizo population, and the arrival of Black slaves.[16] For most Spaniards, the main thing discouraging them from traveling to the Philippines was the dangerous journey across the Pacific, followed by the hardships that characterized life in the islands. As Fish points out, for civil authorities, the "only incentive for accepting a position in the Philippines was the reputed opportunity to amass a fortune," as "by investing in the galleon trade . . . a Spaniard could accumulate enough funds to eventually return home to the Americas or Spain and establish a business, purchase an estate or simply retire."[17]

Given the disconcerting geography of the archipelago, its unstable climate, and the difficulties of the journey between Acapulco and Manila, shipwrecks in the Philippines were a much more probable occurrence than in other areas sailed by Spanish ships: "Experience showed that leaving after mid-July meant that the galleon would encounter rough weather in the first three months of its voyage all the way to the latitudes of Japan. This was also a frequent cause of *arribadas* or return to port which were disastrous to both merchants and colonial government."[18] If *arribadas* were catastrophic, losing one of these ships was much worse, as it often meant the immediate bankruptcy of many individuals in the Philippines, as well as in New Spain and on the Iberian Peninsula, without the possibility of an easy recovery after the disaster. The missionaries were also affected by these shipwrecks, which were a strong blow to the overconfidence that characterized religious activities on the islands, the almost unlimited faith in Spanish power and prestige, and the God-given ability to achieve the spiritual unity of humankind.[19] The galleon shipwrecks offer a good picture of the global character of the Spanish Empire and the consciousness of the connections of its different areas, including the most remote and apparently insignificant. These disasters (and especially the writings dealing with them) contribute to the discourse of the Philippines in Spain's symbolic imaginary of its empire. The shipwreck writings are pivotal elements in the elaboration of an isolating and adverse image of the Philippines; they are written under the influence of this predetermined vision of the islands while simultaneously reinforcing it.[20]

In general, shipwrecks in the Philippines were much more than dramatic isolated events, as they attacked the core of the insecurities of the Spanish presence in the islands at a variety of levels: economic, social, and religious. And even though reports "on shipwrecks involving Manila galleons are few, short and dispersed in various Spanish accounts,"[21] the shipwreck event is a constant presence in early modern texts produced in the Philippines, revealing that it was a permanent concern that affected how life was lived in the colony at a variety of levels. The shipwreck accounts disrupt a colonial discourse that is centered on the display of success, as they reveal the multiple weaknesses threatening the Spanish Empire in the Pacific. In the Philippines, the shipwreck narrative does not take the shape of an independent, full narration of a particular isolated event. Instead, mirroring the vision of the destroyed lost ships, it dissolves into small pieces that disintegrate the narration of the colonial experience in the islands and transfer the breakage, disruption, disorientation, and fracture of the shipwreck to the more general discourse of conquest and colonization in the Philippines.

Antonio de Morga's *Sucesos de las islas Filipinas* was first published in Mexico in 1609. Morga, born in Seville, arrived in the Philippines in 1595 to hold the position of lieutenant to the governor of the islands. He changed positions several times, finally leaving the archipelago in 1604 to continue working for the crown in New Spain and Peru. Today the *Sucesos* is still considered to be one of the most complete accounts of Spanish colonialism written during this period, and has even been recognized as the first history of the Philippines. Combining Morga's eyewitness testimony and original documents, this book offers a complex and comprehensive account of the first thirty-some years of the Spanish presence in the Philippines and serves as a model for later texts. Throughout the pages of the *Sucesos*, shipwrecks are a constant appearance and act as a thread that connects all groups participating in the colonial enterprise. Soldiers, administrators, "personas ricas de Manila,"[22] missionaries, and Morga himself are victims of shipwrecks in the Philippines. Shipwreck is the threat that unites all social classes in the islands, creating a sense of common enterprise despite the variety of interests moving these characters. Morga pays special attention to the shipwreck of the galleon *San Felipe*,[23] "que era navío grande y muy cargado de mercaderías y pasajeros . . . y perdió el timón en altura de treinta y siete grados, a seiscientas leguas de las Filipinas y ciento y cincuenta del Xapón." The ship ends up finding refuge in Japan after failing to return to the Philippines, though not without previous "confusión y diversidad de pareceres de la gente que iba en la nao" (71). The Spaniards end up being captives in Japan, since "en cuanto a aderezar el navío y volver a salir con él, se les dio a entender no se podía hacer sin licencia y permiso de Taicosama, señor del Xapón, que estaba en su corte en Miaco" (72). Tensions build when the ship's pilot suggests that Spaniards have infiltrated the territories they want to conquer with missionaries; the Japanese lord thus gives orders to crucify all Spaniards, though in the end only some missionaries are tortured. These last become known as the twenty-six martyrs of Japan: "les cortó las orejas derechas y los paseó por las calles . . . con mucho dolor y sentimiento de todos los cristianos que los vían padecer" (75).[24] Felipe de las Casas, one of the Franciscans traveling on the *San Felipe*, is one such martyr. Morga does not hold back on the description of horrors, creating a scene of death and sacrifice with religious undertones:

> Fueron llevados a Nangasaqui estos sanctos, donde, en una loma que estaba a vista del pueblo y puerto sembrada de trigo . . . fueron todos a la hila sacrificados. Los religiosos en medio y los demás a su lado, de una banda a otra, en cruces altas, con argollas de hierro a las gargantas y a las manos y pies, y con lanzas de hierros largos y agudos atravesados por los costados, de abajo para arriba, cruzados. Con que dieron las almas a su Criador, por quien morían con mucho esfuerzo. . . . Los cuerpos de los mártires . . . fueron quitados a pedazos, especialmente los de los religiosos, de las cruces, por reliquias de los cristianos que allí había, que con mucha veneración se repartieron y están por toda la cristiandad. (76–77)

When the news arrives in Manila, it has a tremendous impact on a society that feels that the economic and religious missions of the colony might be on the verge of collapse: "Los españoles de la nao San Felipe desnudos y desaviados, se embarcaron . . . y fueron a Manila . . . de los cuales se tuvo la primera nueva deste suceso por el mes de mayo del año de noventa y siete, que fue de mucho dolor y tristeza por la muerte de los santos religiosos y turbación que se esperaba en lo de adelante en las costas del Xapón con las Filipinas, por la pérdida del galeón y haciendas que en él iban a la Nueva España, cuyo valor era de más de un millón, con que los españoles quedaban muy necesitados" (78). The shipwreck brings material and personal loss, and it underscores the fragility of Spanish power in the Pacific. This was especially important in the last decades of the sixteenth century, when one of the perceived assets of the Philippines was its potential role as the gate to the evangelization of Asia,[25] with special interest in China and Japan. The events surrounding the martyrs of Japan were a strong reminder of the difficulties that such an enterprise involved, and they surely increased the feelings of isolation and danger that so often prevailed in the archipelago.[26]

Another shipwreck is described and explained at length in the *Sucesos*: one resulting from the confrontation with Dutch vessels under Oliver van Noort's command. The shipwreck of the *San Diego* led also to the partial sinking of Morga's own reputation in the Philippines, since this episode of defeat and destruction took place under his authority. In 1600, Van Noort arrived in the Philippines with the intention of attacking and looting a Spanish galleon. Following an unfortunate accumulation of bad decisions and misunderstandings, the ships *San Bartolomé* and *San Diego*, which were prepared for the defense against the Dutch attack, were separated and, in the middle of the battle's fear and confusion, the Spaniards disengaged the *San Diego* and caused it to sink. Many of them lost their lives on the ship, others tried to get to mainland by swimming, and Morga himself finally reached Fortune Island after swimming for four hours. More than 350 crew members died; there were only twenty-two survivors. As J. S. Cummins explains, Morga's "many enemies seized the opportunity to denigrate him. The loss of 137 Spaniards in the battle was a major disaster for the small embattled community. . . . As a result Morga in shame and grief fell ill, . . . [and] tried to justify himself, collecting evidence in his own defence, but the affair was debated even after he had left the islands." Morga's political career only declined thereafter, as the traumatic shipwreck event and its consequences lingered long after his "exile" to other lands in the Spanish Empire. This caused "a steady decline in his moral character. In the Philippines he had been excellent; in Mexico, more than satisfactory; in Quito, disastrous." It has even been suggested that the writing of *Sucesos de las islas Filipinas* originated as an attempt to explain and apologize for the disaster of the *San Diego*, given that the incident was still being discussed in the Council of the Indies as late as 1608.[27] Regardless of the reason for writing and publishing the *Sucesos*, the shipwreck of the *San Diego* marked life in the Philippines for years; its political, military, personal, and cultural consequences are clear evidence of the impact that shipwrecks had in how life and death were conceived in the islands.[28]

The "crisis sentiment" associated with shipwrecks increases exponentially throughout the *Sucesos* as Morga mentions the numerous galleon shipwrecks related to the Philippines that took place in the relatively short period covered by his text: there were the *Espíritu Santo, Jesús María, Nuestra Señora de los Remedios, San Antonio, San Antonio de Sebú* (later *San Diego*), *San Gerónimo, San Juanillo, Santa Margarita, Santiago, Santiago el Menor,* and *Santo Tomás.* Sometimes a ship "se perdió en la mar y jamás della se tuvo nueva" (23); others were swallowed by the sea (197) or sank so quickly that only a few people could be saved (145); some were lost after the crew and travelers were saved or "muerto el general y la mayor parte de la gente . . . los naturales que llegaron a bordo y vieron la nave tan sola y destrozada, entraron dentro y se apoderaron della, y de la ropa y hacienda que la nao tenía. Y la poca gente que en ella iba viva la llevaron consigo a sua poblazones, y algunos mataron" (151). Through the description and constant mention of these events, Morga creates a portrait of the conquest and colonization of the Philippines that is characterized by continuous difficulty, economic and religious instability, and the fragility of a system that unmasks the weakness of the Spanish Empire in Asia and beyond. The frequency of the shipwrecks and the subsequent incapacity to keep constant and fluid communication with the rest of the empire and the metropolis increase the perception of isolation and abandonment shared by many of the colonists. Morga himself tried, with no success, to leave the islands very soon after his initial arrival. He had been in the Philippines for about a year when he wrote to King Phillip II asking to go back to Spain—a petition he would repeat numerous times, explaining his inability to adjust to the climate of the islands and the general corruption and lack of morality of the colonizers.[29]

With a realist approach to the actual situation of the islands, Morga constantly denounces the problems he perceives; further, his perspective allows him to detect the threat of the decline of the Spanish colonial enterprise if drastic changes are not implemented with urgency. In his *Relación sobre el estado de las islas Filipinas* (sent to Madrid in 1598 and published as an appendix to his *Sucesos*), Morga crafts a poignant review of the main problems that devastate the islands, most of which could very easily be extended to other imperial lands, such as the American colonies. He finds serious problems in relation to the preaching of doctrine, the administration of Indigenous labor, the management of war, the administration of justice, the royal treasury, the secular government, and navigation. Morga points out that the navigation issues originate in the corruption and lack of skills of many of the Spaniards who participate in the management of the Manila galleon; he thus concludes that the shipwrecks themselves are not a coincidence or a punishment by God but the result of the crisis in the colonial enterprise.[30] The implication of the report is that the shipwreck of the Spanish Empire in the Pacific, the decline of its mission and objectives, is already a reality and will not improve unless the captain of the empire takes over the helm and steers it in the right direction (324).

Morga's text offers the perspective of the secular government authorities in the Philippines, but many texts produced in the islands were written by missionaries

of several religious orders who arrived in the islands soon after Miguel López
de Legazpi's expedition of 1565. This same year the Augustinians started their
evangelization efforts, followed by the Franciscans (1578), the Jesuits (1581), the
Dominicans (1587), and the Augustinian Recollects (1606). Missionaries had
enormous prestige and power, controlling a great amount of property and out-
numbering the rest of the Spanish population.[31] In the Philippines, as Pearson
puts it, "the glory of God seemed to have taken first place over the glory of Spain
or of the King. It was the influence of the Orders which prevented the abandonment of the Philippines, despite the fact that about 15 *percent* of Spain's total profits from the Indies were, in the seventeenth century, spent on maintaining the
islands."[32] Jesuits, in particular, assumed a prominent role in the conversion
of Indigenous populations following the *Constituciones* (1539), written by Ignatius
of Loyola, which strongly encouraged the mobility of Jesuits to "provecho de las
almas o la propagación de la fe,"[33] even if this implied going "a cualquier parte
a donde nos quiera enviar, o a los turcos, o a los nuevos mundos, o entre lutera-
nos, o a cualesquiera otras tierras de fieles o infieles."[34] Jesuits also encouraged
writing about the missionary enterprise as a way to construct their own historical memory, starting especially with the mandate of Cardinal Acquaviva. With
these writings, Jesuits "invented" the Spanish Empire in the Pacific, as well as
the possibility of controlling that empire.[35] Jesuits also used these texts as a propaganda machine to circulate their achievements and create the image of the
Jesuit order as the true engine of the Spanish Empire in numerous territories—
and particularly the Philippines.

During the sixteenth and seventeenth centuries, Pedro Chirino and Francisco
Colín were the main representatives of this propaganda effort,[36] but many other
Jesuits wrote texts that are crucial for our understanding of what happened in
the Philippines during this period and, in particular, of how this reality was written by a variety of colonial agents with very different approaches and objectives.
Colín's text, *Labor evangélica*,[37] is particularly interesting, as it follows the model
of the chronicle in order to create a history of the Society of Jesus in the Philippines; further, it has a significant political tone, as it was directed at King Phillip IV, who had requested information of Jesuit activities in this part of the
empire. The description of shipwrecks plays a very significant role in Colín's text,
and it is connected to some of the main goals of the book—for example, the cele-
bration of Jesuit successes and their prominent place in the islands. The heroes
of Colín's book are Jesuit priests, as can be found in other writings produced by
the Jesuit order in the Philippines, such as Pedro Chirino's *Relación* (1604) and
Francisco de Combés's *Historia de Mindanao y Joló* (1667).[38] The work of the Jesuits is rescued from the periphery of the empire, and their evangelizing mission is placed at the forefront of the colonial enterprise—this in contrast to the
authorities and merchants who privileged the economic exploitation of the islands
and its intermediary role in the commerce between Asia and Europe. It is not

uncommon that these texts include the portrayal of miracles or quasi-miraculous events carried out by the Jesuit missionaries, as in Colín's book, and particularly in relation to the shipwrecks described among Jesuits' trials. In his text, shipwrecks are sublimated as one more obstacle that the missionaries must overcome in order to perform their duties in the islands; indeed, they are examples of the missionaries' capacity to sacrifice their lives and to simultaneously bring together many different kinds of people under the same mission. For example, in 1608, Father Antonio Pereira survives a shipwreck that has been caused by the overload of slaves on the ship, and the civil authorities kill all slave women and children and throw their bodies overboard for fear of sinking;[39] Pereira protests, risking his own life and putting himself in the precarious position of confronting the Spaniards in the defense of Indigenous peoples. Pedro de Montes, traveling to Mexico from Manila on a boat with over four hundred people, organizes communal confession and repentance sessions when death seems imminent in the middle of a powerful storm. Father Alonso Sánchez, one of the main leaders among the Jesuits in the Philippines, suffers a shipwreck in 1583, and survivors are robbed once they reach the mainland. An image of Saint Ignatius allegedly saves a ship bound for Silan on which Father Pedro de Segura is traveling. In 1600 the galleon *San Gerónimo*, which travels with the *Santa Margarita*, is lost and Father Pedro López de la Parra dies: "Les terciaron los tiempos tan furiosos, que las desaparejaron, y obligaron a arribar, y dar al traves entrambas. La nao Santa Margarita en los Ladrones, donde en ella hicieron su oficio, apoderandose de las haziendas, que las personas iban ya tan rendidas, las que auian escapado del mar, y de su furia, que tuuieron por suma felicidad ser tomados de los bárbaros por esclavos . . . solos los que llevaban alguna apariencia de salud, porque a los enfermos a palos los mataron y entre ellos a gente bien nacida." The *San Gerónimo* arrives in Japan, where "los mismos vientos terrales, allí más furiosos que en el mar, no solo no les dexaron dar fondo, pero les abatieron la primera cubierta y maltrataron mucho la nao . . . dieron en Catanduanes con solas siete personas, y la una era mujer, a cabo de ocho meses de puros naufragios." Father Parra "aunque enfermo y trabajado del mal tratamiento, hambres, sed, y congojas, ayudó a los demás en sus muertes."[40]

Shipwreck is also linked to captivity on several occasions—for example, in Andrés Pereira's and Pedro de Montes's stories—thus adding drama and sacrifice to the narrated events and connecting them to the martyrologies, so popular in the Middle Ages, that were experiencing a revival in the sixteenth century. More works were written in this genre in the 1500s than in all the time that had passed since the appearance of the first martyrologies in the fourth century. In addition to the *Flos sanctorum* (1599–1601) by Pedro de Rivadeneyra and the *Acta martyrum* (1594) by Antonio Gallonio, some of the most popular hagiographic texts at the end of the sixteenth century were the Jesuit martyrologies, which reveals how important this type of discourse was in the propagandistic effort of the Jesuit Society. The connection of the shipwreck motive to captivity, and therefore to the possibility of dying at the hands of heretics or infidels while defending the Catholic faith, sublimated the failed naval enterprise and gave it a renewed resonance for the advertisement of the Jesuit work in Asia in general, and in the Philippines in particular:

> Echaron mano con furia del Padre, desnudáronle de toda su ropa; amanazáronle con la muerte si no llamaba a los demás, y obligaba a entregarse con el batel . . . y estos viendose ya dueños de tan honrados cautivos, . . . porque no se les huyesen en las barcas, sacaban a los miserables cautivos a una isleta donde en la dura tierra, el sereno, al viento, al agua, y sin abrigo ninguno contra los crueles enjambres de mosquitos, que cubren los lugares pantanosos en estas regiones cálidas, tomaban el reposo que podían. Allí todas las noches antes de dormir se consolaba el buen padre Pereira con sus concautivos, animándoles con su ejemplo a llevar con paciencia y ofrecer a Dios aquellos trabajos.[41]

It was not only books focusing specifically on martyrdom that played a role in the dissemination of the many sacrifices of Jesuits on behalf of their faith and their king; a number of *relaciones de sucesos* also served as instruments in the cultural creation of the Philippines as a depiction of Jesuit glorification.[42] It is no mere coincidence that, together with the *relaciones* that focused on the martyrdom of priests, the accounts describing disasters such as the shipwrecks surrounding the islands reached the greatest popularity on the Iberian Peninsula and in New Spain.[43] Shipwrecks, hurricanes, and earthquakes were introduced as part of the trials that Jesuits must endure in order to fulfill their heroic mission, which was to bring religious harmony and peace to the new lands while contributing to the greater success of the king's empire. Yet the Philippines were, in reality, an appendix to the empire, positioned as they were literally and symbolically at the margin of the crown's interests. In contrast with the American colonies, it was necessary to "sell" the presence of Spaniards in the Philippines to representatives in the metropolis and New Spain, and therefore any opportunity to give value to the Asian enterprise was to be taken advantage of. The lack of actual riches in the islands, as well as their marginal location and the difficulty of maintaining effective communications with them, unconsciously caused an association of the Philippines with danger, failure, and alienation. The narration of shipwrecks in Colín's text thus resonated with these negative associations and linked the Philippine experience to concepts that anticipated the collapse of the Spanish imperial project, which was felt first in the isolated corners of the empire.

The Philippines were colonized when the original enthusiasm of the Renaissance was already gone. We can look at it as a baroque colonization characterized by disillusion, instability, and rupture of the harmony with the natural world. The colonial mood in the Philippines was one of disappointment rather than wonder, and it left a deep mark on the way the colonization was lived, reflected on, and written about. Even the overflowing enthusiasm of the Jesuits was not able to overcome the baroque melancholy that defined the colonization of the Spanish Empire in the Pacific. Beginning in the last years of the sixteenth century, the negative "colonial mood" in the Philippines was an accurate forecast of the general decline of the empire; as the British and French increased their power conservatism and resistance to progress prevailed in Spain. As Pearson notes, "A good example of this conservatism was seen in the Northerly route taken by the galleons from Manila. The galleons always sailed South from Manila, East through an extremely dangerous passage, and then North up the East coast of Luzon. Had the galleons gone North from Manila up the West coast much time could have been saved and danger avoided. Yet even such an obvious reform as this was never undertaken in the seventeenth century."[44] Fernando Rodríguez de la Flor posits a critical question in his essay "On the Notion of a Melancholic Baroque": "Can an epoch or a certain chronological space (or, a geographical one) be *melancholic*?"[45] In terms of Spanish colonization, the Philippines is such a space; here the illusions and hopes of the so-called age of discovery are confronted with the harsh realities of failure and isolation. This colony is the reminder of the possible loss of the empire, given the difficulties involved in keeping all of its territories under control and in maintaining good communication channels with them. The long and dangerous journey to the Philippines from New Spain is a constant and unavoidable wake-up call that puts the Asian colonizing enterprise permanently on edge and makes it subject to the instabilities surrounding the Manila galleon, and the representation of the shipwreck is the epitome of the region's precariousness. The frequency and intensity with which the theme reappears in a variety of texts on the Philippines, written by different authors with diverse approaches and objectives, reveals a shared perception of radical melancholy that is caused by fear of destruction and anxiety of annihilation—both figurative and literal—in this corner of the Spanish Empire.

NOTES

1. Josiah Blackmore, *Manifest Perdition: Shipwreck Narrative and the Disruption of Empire* (Minneapolis: University of Minnesota Press, 2002), xxi.

2. In chapter 8 of the present volume, Noemí Martín Santo also examines the challenges to the Spanish Empire in East Asia through an analysis of the missionary texts on Japan.

3. M. N. Pearson, "Spain and Spanish Trade in Southeast Asia," in *European Entry into the Pacific: Spain and the Acapulco-Manila Galleons*, ed. Dennis O. Flynn, Arturo Giráldez, and James Sobredo (Burlington, VT: Ashgate, 2001), 118.

4. Hugh Thomas, *World without End: Spain, Philip II, and the First Global Empire* (New York: Random House, 2014), 255.

5. Nicholas Cushner, *Spain in the Philippines: From Conquest to Revolution* (Quezon City, Philippines: Ateneo de Manila University, 1971), 130.

6. Pedro Picornell, "The Anatomy of the Manila Galleon," in *The Manila Galleon: Traversing the Pacific*, ed. Edgardo J. Angara and Sonia Pinto Ner (Manila: Read Foundation, 2012), 41.

7. Thomas, *World without End*, 256.

8. William Schurz, *The Manila Galleon* (New York: E. P. Dutton, 1959), 253.

9. This is what happened to the galleon *San Diego* in 1600, in a confrontation with the Dutch under Admiral van Noort. Antonio de Morga, judge of the Real Audiencia and the vice governor general of the Philippines, was in command of the *San Diego* while the *San Bartolomé*, the *almiranta* or admiral's ship, was under the command of Juan de Alcega. See Marya Svetlana T. Camacho, "Eastward Crossing: The Galleon Voyage from Manila to Acapulco," in Angara and Pinto Ner, eds., *The Manila Galleon*, 69.

10. Shirley Fish, *The Manila-Acapulco Galleons: The Treasure Ships of the Pacific* (Central Milton Keynes, UK: AuthorHouse, 2011), 30, 5, 14.

11. Fish, *The Manila-Acapulco Galleons*, 2, 185.

12. Efren B. Isorena, "Maritime Disasters in Spanish Philippines: The Manila-Acapulco Galleons, 1565–1815," *International Journal of Asia Pacific Studies* 11, no. 1 (2015): 53–83. For an annotated list of the transpacific Galleons, see Fish, *The Manila-Acapulco Galleons*, 492–523.

13. Thomas, *World without End*, 255.

14. Henry Kamen, *Empire: How Spain Became a World Power, 1492–1763* (New York: HarperCollins, 2003), 204.

15. Fish, *The Manila-Acapulco Galleons*, 72.

16. Kamen, *Empire*, 208–209.

17. Fish, *The Manila-Acapulco Galleons*, 72–73.

18. Camacho, "Eastward Crossing," 83.

19. John Leddy Phelan, *The Hispanization of the Philippines: Spanish Aims and Filipino Responses, 1565–1700* (Madison: University of Wisconsin Press, 1959), 4–5.

20. For a complete analysis of the role of the Pacific in general, and of the Philippines in particular, in the Spanish geopolitical imaginary, see Ricardo Padrón, *The Indies of the Setting Sun: How Early Modern Spain Mapped the Far East as the Transpacific West* (Chicago: University of Chicago Press, 2020), especially chaps. 4 and 5. The Philippines were, Padrón notes, the "central node of the geopolitical imagination of everyone who mapped the Spanish Pacific after 1565" (12).

21. Isorena, "Maritime Disasters in Spanish Philippines," 53.

22. Antonio de Morga, *Sucesos de las islas Filipinas*, ed. Francisca Perujo (Mexico City: Fondo de Cultura Económica, 2007), 196; hereafter, page numbers will be cited parenthetically in the text.

23. Fray Juan Pobre de Zamora, *Historia de la pérdida y descubrimiento del galeón "San Felipe"* (Avila, Spain: Diputación de Avila, 1997), which was written sometime between the end of the sixteenth century and the beginning of the seventeenth, narrates the events that unraveled after the *San Felipe*'s shipwreck.

24. For an in-depth study of the shipwreck of the *San Felipe* galleon and the martyrdom of the Spanish missionaries, see Martín Santo, chapter 8 in the present volume.

25. Kamen, *Empire*, 233.

26. For further information about the relations with Japan, including the *San Felipe* incident, see Arturo Giraldez, *The Age of Trade: The Manila Galleons and the Dawn of the Global Economy* (New York: Rowman and Littlefield, 2015), 102–110.

27. J. S. Cummins, "Editor's Introduction," in Antonio de Morga, *Sucesos de las Islas Filipinas*, ed. and trans. J. S. Cummins (Cambridge: Hakluyt Society, 1971), 9, 13, 18.

28. The remains of the *San Diego* were located in 1991, and divers were able to recover many of the objects that were on the ship when it sank in 1600, including eight hundred large ceramic jars from Burma, twelve hundred pieces of porcelain from the Ming dynasty,

and an ivory chess set. See Robert Marx and Jenifer Marx, *Treasure Lost at Sea: Diving to the World's Great Shipwrecks* (Buffalo, NY: Firefly Books, 2004), 103.

29. Francisca Perujo, "Estudio preliminar," in Morga, *Sucesos*, xxix.

30. Superstitions of all kinds abounded around the galleon shipwrecks. The Pacific island Doña María de la Jara was said to cause death since supposedly a desperate woman by that name had thrown herself into the sea. And several irrational beliefs were popular among the sailors: that shipwrecks were divine punishment for those who blasphemed or committed sins at sea or for the exploitation of native labor, greed of the traders, and corruption. Some even thought that they were the result of the construction of ships on Sundays. See Camacho, "Eastward Crossing," 103.

31. Michael O. Mastura, "Administrative Policies towards the Muslims in the Philippines: A Study in Historical Continuity and Trends," *Mindanao Journal* 3, no. 1 (1976): 104.

32. Pearson, "Spain and Spanish Trade in Southeast Asia," 134.

33. Jesús Corella and Ignacio Iglesias, "Fórmula del Instituto," in *Constituciones de la Compañía de Jesús: Introducción y notas para su lectura*, ed. Santiago Arzubialde, Jesús Corella, and Juan Manuel García-Lomas (Bilbao, Spain: Mensajero, 1993), 33.

34. Jean Lacouture, *Jesuitas*, vol. 1, *Los Conquistadores* (Barcelona: Paidós, 1993), 142–143.

35. The Jesuit writings during the sixteenth and seventeenth centuries were the main source of information about the Philippines, and they had a pivotal role in the perception of the islands in Spain, where the main decisions about them were made. Without these writings, it would not have been possible to have a comprehensive understanding of the Philippines and their role in the wider context of the Spanish empire.

36. Even if *Labor evangélica* is not completely original, since it is based on Pedro Chirino's *Relación de las islas Filipinas*, Father Francisco Colín is recognized as the main figure in the dissemination and circulation of Jesuit history in the Philippines in the first two centuries of Spanish presence in the colony.

37. Francisco Colín, *Labor evangélica: Ministerios apostólicos de los obreros de la Compañía de Jesús* (Madrid: José Fernández de Buendía, 1663). The next (expanded) edition was published by Father Pablo Pastells in 1900–1902.

38. For an analysis of Francisco de Combes's *Historia de Mindanao y Joló* and its role in the Jesuit approach to the Southern islands of the Philippines, which were mostly inhabited by Muslims, see Ana M. Rodríguez-Rodríguez, "Old Enemies, New Contexts: Early Modern Spanish (Re)-Writing of Islam in the Philippines," in *Coloniality, Religion, and the Law in the Early Iberian World*, ed. Santa Arias and Raúl Marrero (Nashville: Vanderbilt University Press, 2013), 137–157.

39. For the role of the galleon in human trafficking, see Kristyl N. Obispado, "The Plight of Filipino Seamen and Slaves in the 17th Century Nueva España," in Angara and Pinto Ner, eds., *The Manila Galleon*, 185–195.

40. Colín, *Labor evangélica*, 401–411.

41. Colín, *Labor evangélica*, 634.

42. For other examples of how missionary accounts serve to glorify the Christian enterprise in Asia, see Martín Santo, chapter 8 in the present volume.

43. To execute a search of *relaciones* on a variety of topics and periods, see the Catálogo y Biblioteca Digital de Relaciones de Sucesos database, coordinated by Nieves Pena Sueiro and Sagrario López Poza, https://www.bidiso.es/CBDRS/.

44. Pearson, "Spain and Spanish Trade in Southeast Asia," 137. See also Schurz, *The Manila Galleon*, 224–226.

45. Fernando Rodríguez de la Flor, "On the Notion of a Melancholic Baroque," in *Hispanic Baroques: Reading Cultures in Context*, ed. Nicholas Spadaccini and Luis Martín-Estudillo (Nashville: Vanderbilt University Press, 2005), 3.

CHAPTER 8

The Shipwreck of the Manila Galleon *San Felipe* in Seventeenth-Century Histories and Accounts on Japan

Noemí Martín Santo

The relationship between Iberia and Japan in the sixteenth and seventeenth centuries is one of the most interesting cases of cultural, religious, and commercial encounters between East Asian and European civilizations. With the arrival of the Portuguese *naos*, Nagasaki and other Japanese ports flourished and became transoceanic emporiums and contact zones. Several Japanese *daimyō* welcomed the missionary Francis Xavier and his fellows in 1549 and converted to Christianity.[1] Members of the Society of Jesus expressed in their writings the fascination with this East Asian society, categorized as equal or even superior to European ones. Nevertheless, the Spanish and Portuguese presence in Japan lasted only around one hundred years. After the country's unification during the rule of the powerful Tokugawa family, the government transitioned into an autocracy. In 1614 all Christian missionaries were banned from the archipelago, and in 1639 an edict of isolation ended all relations with Iberians.

This chapter focuses on rhetorical devices used in several works narrating an event that is considered to be the turning point in the relationship between Japan and Spain: the shipwreck of the Spanish galleon *San Felipe* on the Japanese island of Shikoku on October 19, 1596, and the crucifixion of six Franciscan missionaries and twenty Japanese Christians.[2] I propose that the choice of expressions and figures of pathos intertwine with the legal language of the *relaciones* in these texts in order to fulfill two objectives: first, to sustain the idea that divine providence wanted the intervention of Spain in the Japanese evangelization; and second, to warn the ecclesiastical and imperial authorities for whom the texts were written about the perils that Japan represented as an adversary.

The texts discussed here are *Historia de la pérdida y descubrimiento del galeón "San Felipe"* (1598–1603), by the Franciscan Juan Pobre de Zamora; the "Relación del viaje del galeón San Felipe de su majestad, arribada que hizo al Japón" (c. 1597), by the notary of the galleon, Andrés de Zuazola (or Çuaçola); and the *Relación del reino del Nipón a que llaman corruptamente Japón* (1615–1619), by the Spanish merchant and notary Bernardino de Avila. I have chosen these writers because the first two were on board the galleon and the third witnessed the crucifixions. Furthermore, their different backgrounds reflect the dialogues they establish with their respective readers: the Congregation of Rites, the Council of Indies, and the governor of Manila.

Pobre de Zamora was a soldier who participated in the battles of Flanders during the Eighty Years' Wars (1568–1648) and became a missionary. He wrote his *Historia* for the Congregation of Rites and the Spanish crown. Zuazola was the notary of the galleon who had the duty of annotating the events that happened on board. Avila was a merchant in Nagasaki who may have acted as a spy under the orders of the governor of Manila, Francisco Tello;[3] he did not travel aboard the *San Felipe* but was a witness to the martyrdoms and helped some of the castaways return to Manila after the crucifixions (*RRN*, 332).

The historian Charles Boxer, whose book *The Christian Century in Japan 1549–1650* contextualizes the arrival and presence of Iberians in the archipelago, asserts that the purpose of Pobre de Zamora's *Historia* is "to give an eyewitness account of the events leading to the martyrdom . . . with the aim of securing their beatification and, in due course, their canonization."[4] I propose that the beatification was part of a wider project of commercial and territorial expansion of the Spanish Empire and that the importance of the readers dictated the style of these writings. I therefore place these *historias* and *relaciones* in the field of the *historias verdaderas* written in the sixteenth and seventeenth centuries for the imperial or ecclesiastical authorities. These texts are among the works reserved for privileged readers and not intended to reach a wider public; they were printed and published publicly only at the end of the twentieth century. As Lara Vilà asserts in her analysis of chronicles from the Orient in the Spanish Golden Age, they can be compared with the Portuguese documents that were kept unpublished and secret in the Casa da India in Lisbon as part of the "política do sigilo nacional," which restricted access to writings related to commercial and strategic routes in East Asia.[5]

The origins of works such as these are, as Enrique Pupo-Walker defines them in his characterization of Alvar Núñez Cabeza de Vaca's *Naufragios*, "documentos severos que resumían las comunicaciones oficiales entre funcionarios e instituciones de la Corona."[6] They follow, in part, the structure and contents stated by the *Ordenanzas de descubrimientos, nueva población y pacificación de las Indias* of 1573, a report or general compilation of news and information on new lands based on a questionnaire.[7] They do not, however, correspond to the strict model of the *Ordenanzas*, which requires simple answers to each of the parts of the questionnaire. Their content and style depend on each case, as Walter Mignolo explains in his foundational article, "Cartas, crónicas y relaciones del descubrimiento y la conquista."[8] Merchants, ambassadors, and missionaries would adapt the genre to their respective duties, as happens with the mandatory accounts sent by the Dominican friars from Japan and the Philippines from 1609 onward. They were created in legal and notarial jargon and reflect the importance of small details: the authors carefully annotate the days, even the hours, when events occurred and include formulas that reinforce the presence of their authors as witnesses of the events and the assurance that they are telling the truth, such as "soy testigo de vista" (*RRN*, 125) and "que me hallé presente" (*HP*, 191).

The use of these expressions in the narration of facts and events is also part of the narrative of shipwreck, as Sarissa Carneiro explains in her work on persuasion, enjoyment, and exemplarity, *Retórica del infortunio*. Composing "un discurso que pretendía también acusar o defender, disuadir o aconsejar, tareas propias de los géneros jurídico y deliberativo" is an important part of shipwreck narrative that seeks to inspire emotions in the readers while attempting to convince the relevant authorities of the veracity of their reports.[9] In order to achieve both purposes—to inform and to convince—the works discussed employ techniques and expressions intended to emotionally impact the reader: hyperbolic depictions of supernatural phenomena, enumeration of the negative qualities of the Japanese, use of biblical terms to describe scenes, and the like. Otherwise these three writings differ in length, content, and structure. Pobre de Zamora (whose *Historia* follows a model more related to the *relaciones* than what would have been considered a book of history during his lifetime) includes chapters in praise of each martyr.[10] The account by Zuazola includes praise for the actions of Pobre de Zamora, which would not have been considered obligatory in the content of an account of travel. Avila's *Relación* is divided into three parts: observation of Japanese customs, a history of Japan, and accounts of martyrdoms. The merchant was part of the public that gathered around the crosses and presents himself as a direct witness to martyrdom. What these works have in common is their adherence to the model of shipwreck narrative as defined by Josiah Blackmore in his seminal work, *Manifest Perdition*: "a practice of prose writing, defined not solely by the thematic presence of shipwreck in a text but by a relationship between calamity and writing, where a certain kind of experience generates a certain kind of text."[11] The shipwreck and martyrdom that these three writers relate are the same, but their personal experiences were different and thus, therefore, are their narrations.

Blackmore asserts that shipwreck narrative "exposes and promotes breaches in the expansionist mentality and in the textual culture associated with that mentality."[12] Although he focuses on Portuguese texts, I argue that his definition can be applied to the writings selected for this chapter for two reasons. First, the expansion of Christianity is what the Spanish Empire used for justifying conquests. Second, works on East Asia circulated widely between both Iberian kingdoms, and, in many cases, the Spanish documents were translations of or contained materials taken from Portuguese editions;[13] thus, many accounts on the Spanish Pacific were adapted from narrations in Portuguese. With these Spanish texts, the authors reflect the interest in the *propaganda fide* and the expansion of commercial routes in East Asia, but their narratives reveal the fragility with which the Spanish Empire held its colonies in the eastern Pacific region.[14] In the case of Japan, the sixteenth-century writings were mostly in Portuguese, as the archipelago was part of the *padroado*, or the crown's patronage of the church.[15]

At the time of the *San Felipe* affair, Japan was still in the sphere of the *padroado*, the agreement between Portugal and the Holy See that granted Portugal the administration of ecclesiastical posts overseas. The Japanese people were still considered "the best that have as yet been discovered," as the Jesuit Francis Xavier states in the letter to his companions in Goa in 1549. In the same letter he assures them that the Japanese (and the Chinese) are "informed and intelligent" and "more subject to reason than any other pagan race that I have ever seen,"[16] to the point that the Jesuits established seminars for young Japanese to become priests. Indeed, the Japanese mission was the most important for the Jesuits at that time, and Japan was perceived as "the utopian counterexample to a morally degraded Europe," as Ricardo Padrón notes in his study on Lope de Vega's account of Japanese Christians.[17] That "utopia" was exclusive to the Society of Jesus and guaranteed by the brief *Ex pastorali officio* of Pope Gregory XIII. Times had changed, however, since the first letters of Francis Xavier. In his final years, Toyotomi Hideyoshi, known as Taikō,[18] had nearly unified all of Japan. Still, things were not easy for him, and the *nanbanjin*, or southern barbarians (that is to say, the Portuguese and other Europeans), were allowed to stay in Japan as long as they were not perceived as a threat to the balance of power. In 1587 Hideyoshi forbade Christianity and expelled the Jesuits. Most of them remained in Japan and were respected, provided that they did not celebrate Mass in public. This fragile situation worsened when an embassy of Franciscans arrived in 1592 and started preaching, disobeying both Rome and the Japanese ruler.

Pobre de Zamora had visited these Franciscans in 1596 and was traveling to New Spain on the *San Felipe*. The route, dictated by the weather, convinced him that divine providence wanted him to return to Japan, so in his account he insists on the divine design of the travel. In his conversation with other travelers and the pilot of the galleon, Francisco de Olandia, he states that God wants them in Japan instead of New Spain:

> —Mas ¿si quiere Dios que vayamos al Japón?
> Esto vino a entender el Piloto, el cual muy enfadado dijo en altas voces:
> —Pues aunque peses a los vientos y a los elementos no tengo de ir al Japón.
> Hallose allí Fray Juan el simple y dijo:
> —Eso será como Dios quisiere.
>
> —(*HP*, 191)

Pobre de Zamora writes "simple," although his actions contradict the deprecating tone that he uses to characterize himself. His strong personality was shaped by his time as a soldier in Flanders. As Boxer relates, Philip III was so impressed by "the restless zeal of this much-travelled friar" that he commissioned a portrait for his gallery.[19] Pobre de Zamora is not as timid as he claims to be, yet because he is writing an account for his superiors, he also avoids any sentiment of self-importance. Another example of his calculated narrative of humility appears in the depiction of his encounter with the governor of Manila, Luis Dasmariñas, when Pobre de Zamora advises the governor to lighten the ship's load: "Señor, mire vuesa señoría que este navío se cargó con mal término y se sobrecargó con muchas ofensas de Dios y con más de cuatrocientas o quinientas piezas de más de las que puede llevar" (*HP*, 191).

As Blackmore asserts, "the departure is the inaugural action of unaccomplishment."[20] Pobre de Zamora shows that, before leaving the Philippines, the voyage was tainted by the sin of avarice and that this would be the first cause of failure. Furthermore, his humble tone in addressing the governor reveals to the Council of Indies how the Manila galleon was managed in the Philippines while demonstrating to the Franciscan authorities in Madrid and Rome that the Catholic Church and its envoys were not as respected in the Philippines as they were in other areas of the Spanish Empire.

Dasmariñas ignores Pobre de Zamora's apprehension, while the pilot and dockworkers mock him: "Como el Padre no tiene hijos, qué poco se le da que se alije" (*HP*, 191). This oxymoron (a father without sons) clashes with the Christian role of Pobre de Zamora, discredited in his position as a father of believers. He has equal or more experience with travel than the *manileños*, but is relegated to a simple *fraile* and considered merely part of the cargo, a nuisance. The Franciscan does not retort, but, in the conversation with his reader, he announces the retribution, "No tardará mucho que él se burle de todos," anticipating that the ship, "cargado con tantas ofensas a Dios," would meet a bad end (*HP*, 191). His prudent advice is received with taunts, and he cannot prevent the ship from being excessively loaded.

Once at sea, someone took the friar's words seriously. Zuazola states that the ship was overloaded and that they had sailed hastily and too late in the season:

"Salimos del puerto de Cavite en el dicho galeón 233 personas, españoles, negros, indios, a doce de julio del dicho año. . . . Salió el galeón sobrecargado y con mal avío y muy tarde; y así por lo uno como por lo otro, y haberse perdido algunos tiempos de vendavales, siempre temimos algún mal suceso; y también por la poca conformidad y muchas pasiones que, desde luego que comenzamos el viaje, unos con otros tuvimos" (*RV*, 105). Zuazola begins his account with information about the date and the people on the galleon, as was expected in a *relación* in which all information was to appear clearly and concisely. Yet he immediately diverts the narration and relates the unwise decisions regarding the journey: the galleon was overloaded, it departed late in the season, and relations between the people on board were poor. "Siempre temimos algún mal suceso" is not the response to any part of a questionnaire but states the opinion of Zuazola as an experienced traveler in commercial enterprises. The prolepsis of the negative events demonstrates that Zuazola respected and trusted Pobre de Zamora's opinion more than that of the others on the passage and demonstrates the positive relationship between the notary and the Franciscan. Both were engaged in parallel missions: the evangelization of Japan and the economic gain that the galleon would provide. Zuazola acts beyond his duties as notary by describing not only facts (as expected in an account addressed to an authority) but his own feelings, based on Pobre de Zamora's dreams: "Este sancto varón nos descubrió un sueño ocho días antes de que nos diese la primera tormenta y, con mucho sentimiento, se llegó a algunos de nosotros y nos dijo . . . «estamos condenados a muerte todos» . . . con que todos los que lo oímos quedamos admirados y temerosos" (*RV*, 110). Upon Pobre de Zamora's announcement, Zuazola depicts his feelings as Carneiro explains them: the anticipation and certainty of death provoke bewilderment, regret, and ultimately fear. The apprehension that Zuazola expresses about the future is typical in the discourse of misfortune,[21] with the difference that fortune is not mentioned in the accounts: rather, all supernatural actions are part of a divine design. In this passage Zuazola assigns Pobre de Zamora a holy status: the Franciscan is a *santo* whose visions will prove true. He is not only a saint but a prophet, whose predictions must be inspired by God. In Zuazola's account, Pobre de Zamora recovers his authority as a member of the church, the only intermediary between earth and heaven, who would be in charge of saving souls.

If Zuazola portrays him as a prophet, Pobre de Zamora characterizes himself as a protector of the vulnerable. The Franciscan's tone remains humble and pious, but his actions are brave as he defies the authority of the pilot and crew who mock him. He does not tolerate the mistreatment of the subalterns onboard: "Los indios, por tener el natural muy pacífico, cuyas oraciones nos ayudaron" to save the ship from sinking, and they are the only ones who do not engage in arguments or fights. Pobre de Zamora takes charge of their protection from the abuses of the sailors: "Si no los tomara Fray Juan Pobre debajo de su amparo, y se pusiera a la defensa de ellos fueran muy mal tratados" (*HP*, 191). In writing about himself in the third person he creates a heroic, epic characterization of a defender of those in need while fulfilling one of the main duties of a missionary abroad: the protection of the former heathens converted to Christianity.

In Zuazola's account, it is not the natives who help to save the ship, but the friars: "Fue de mucha importancia para con Dios Nuestro Señor las oraciones de siete benditos padres que allí venían" (*RV*, 107). In these lines, Zuazola shows the union between church and empire in contemporary Spanish ideology: the clergy saves the ship and, by extension, the cargo—the money of Spain. Both narrations reveal yet another dimension of the travel: the ship—which, according to Blackmore, is a symbol of the "body of nation, order, and authority"[22]—turns over the natural order and is not saved by the officials in charge but by missionaries and natives. This subversion of authority transforms Pobre de Zamora into a divinely favored hero who is guided by God when his predictions are materialized upon seeing two comets.[23]

Zuazola mentions the awe that this phenomenon caused: "La misma noche vimos, a las nueve de ella, una cometa que a todos nos causó admiración" (*RV*, 105), confirming the dreams of the Franciscan. They annotate the day and time: nine o'clock in Zuazola (*RV*, 105) and "entre las seis y siete de la tarde" in Pobre de Zamora (*HP*, 189). Zuazola fulfills his duty as notary by registering the exact hour in which they saw the comet but also expresses his amazement. While the details in the chronological sequence form part of the typical narrative of a *relación*, the *thaumasmus* (a rhetorical device in which the writer marvels at something rather than describing it neutrally) does not. In this sense, the notary uses the sense of wonder to remind the reader of the travelers' solitude and fear as they cross strange seas dominated by the Portuguese, not the Spanish.

Pobre de Zamora offers a different interpretation of the event. For him, the direction of the comet suggests a change in Spain's Asian enterprises. The comet menaced "no solo a Portugal, como todos decían, mas pasaba a Africa y se extendía por las Indias Occidentales y aun creo llegó hasta el Japón que, por lo que vi el año de 96 y principio de 97, aún creo que dura el rastro que dejó, y como era el Japón lo último hasta donde se extendía Portugal, hasta allí parece se extendía la cola de la cometa" (*HP*, 131). The imaginary line drawn by the comet reveals the Franciscan's (and his order's) desire to diminish Portugal's influence and ultimately that of the Society of Jesus in Japan, which was the only order allowed to evangelize in the archipelago. It also reveals a specific geographical area, one that Pobre de Zamora would use in his work *Carta apologética*, with which, according to Boxer, he tried successfully "to prove that Japan, China, and Siam did not lie within the Portuguese sphere of demarcation" that divided the world according to the Treaty of Tordesillas.[24] The *Carta* would be one of the documents that would convince Pope Paul V to end the exclusivity of the Jesuits in the Japanese mission in 1608.[25]

The shape of the comet would change to "una cruz en el cielo blanca y después tornó color de sangre" (*HP*, 379). Zuazola's depiction adds more detail: "Vimos en el cielo un celaje, naturalmente como una cruz de esta hechura, el cual estuvo como un cuarto de hora muy blanca y resplandeciente y, al cabo de esto, se puso color de sangre; y duraría este color otro tanto de tiempo, y después quedó hecho una nube muy negra, que nos causó grandísima admiración, y más nos admiró cuando el fin de nuestros trabajos fue cruz y sangre, como adelante se dirá" (*RV*, 108). Zuazola's prolepsis associates the light and color of the comet with the travelers' suffering, but this passage functions as a metaphor of crosses and the blood of the martyrs. The images of "cruz y sangre" in the sky would be reflected in the crucifixion. This strange phenomenon is followed by an "huracán . . . que duró cinco días, del cual no creímos salir con vida" (*RV*, 108). The anticipation of destruction would not materialize for the passengers aboard the galleon, but it foreshadows death—if not for the narrators, then for the Christians who would be crucified (although the Franciscan Felipe de las Casas o de Jesús would be one of the martyrs).

In the following months, Pobre de Zamora learned that, on land, there was an earthquake followed by strange phenomena: rain made of "tierra color de sangre y ceniza y arena y en algunas partes, dicen, caían revueltos gusanos" (*HP*, 186). He writes also that "tembló toda la tierra de Japón; abriéronse las piedras, salió la mar de su acostumbrado curso con pérdida de pueblos que se anegaron y otras muchas señales que sucedieron, y avisos que Dios enviaba" (*HP*, 188).

These strange incidents allegedly occurred in the cities where the martyrs were exposed to public humiliation. Blood, ashes, sand, and worms are omens of the decay of the bodies after the crucifixion. One of the martyrs, Martín de la Ascensión, would claim before being crucified, "Consideraos después de muertos . . . írseos cayendo las entrañas y carne a pedazos, llena de gusanos y tan hedionda" (*RV*, 132). Moreover, for Pobre de Zamora, the fissures that appeared within the earth represent the result of the separation of the orders (Franciscans and Jesuits) preaching in Japan. He asserts his belief that God sent these signs to warn against the rivalry between religious orders that should be working together in faraway lands. As Blanca López de Mariscal explains, catastrophes can be interpreted as divine punishments or as warnings to change the behavior of the earth's inhabitants.[26] The Franciscan, engaged in the mission of obtaining permission for his order to evangelize in Japan, implies that the *avisos* sent by God are for the Jesuits. As he would later ask, "¿No somos todos de un Dios y de un Rey?" (*HP*, 206). He implies that the Jesuits did not think the same.

On land, Bernardino de Avila does not interpret the earthquake as a sign of God, but he does suggest that there is something marvelous about the fact that, in the midst of the disaster, only a Franciscan church remained standing: "En este subceso se vio una no pequeña maravilla, y fue que habiendo caído tantos palacios, templos y casas fuertes, quedase en pie la iglesia de san Francisco,

dormitorio de los padres, y hospitales de los pobres, y sin recibir daño notable"
(*RRN*, 296).

While Avila considers the event marvelous rather than miraculous, the church
that remained standing was indeed Franciscan, not Jesuit. His discretion is a sign
of the independence he wanted to maintain. He was a merchant unattached to
any particular order, but the mendicants (Franciscans and, later, Augustinians
and Dominicans) would make him a notary of relics. The friars would invest him
with authority and provide him with work; considering his relations with Manila
(where he lived for several years), he would be more interested in maintaining
alliances with the Spaniards rather than the Portuguese. The intention of this
passage, the description of a humble church remaining while the opulent build-
ings of the capital fall, was to indicate the strength of Christianity over paganism and of the Franciscan order over the Society of Jesus.

On board, Pobre de Zamora would not know that the house of his brothers on
land was safe; the travelers were busy trying to remain afloat: "Era tanta la agua
que andaba por lo alto y bajo del navío, que sin caer ninguna del cielo, todos
andábamos hechos un diluvio" (*HP*, 193). The use of a term referring to the biblical
flood does not seem chosen at random, as they were attempting to placate what
they believed to be the wrath of God. They prayed and threw pieces of the cargo
into the sea, which, together with the wind, took it "que parece que decía: Dadlo
acá, que por esto venimos" (*HP*, 193). The prosopopeia attributes avarice to the sea
and the wind and mirrors the greed of the crew, the merchants, and the Japanese.
Pobre de Zamora, noticing that his companions accepted to lose their treasures in
order to save their lives, observes that the objects served as alms: "Acabada de
pedir y de mandar la limosna, sosegó la gran furia de la tormenta" (*HP*, 195).

Nevertheless, their efforts were futile. The poor weather resumed, convincing the Franciscan and Zuazola that God wanted them to end up in Japan. As
the notary writes, "Conocimos claro que Nuestro Señor quería que arribáramos
a Japón porque, aunque hicimos muchas diligencias para hacer bordo a la mar,
no podíamos; antes, parecía que la nao estaba amarrada con muchas anclas y
cables, porque las corrientes nos tenían . . . y la nao, sin timón ni tocar cabo,
gobernó más de diez horas la vuelta de la tierra del Japón" (*RV*, 109). Zuazola
generalizes the feelings of the travelers by stating that "we" understood clearly
the intentions of God. He omits the earlier discussions between Pobre de Zamora
and the pilot of the galleon (in which Olandia declared that he would not go to
Japan), even though his duty is to record the events that occur on the ship, not
to interpret God's designs. The sense of predestination aroused by the Franciscan affects Zuazola and his writing.

In the eyes of the Christians onboard, divine providence brought the *San
Felipe* to the shores of Tosa with the rudder and mast destroyed. As the crew and
passengers strove to reach the mainland, the galleon was surrounded by Japanese ships. People from the neighboring areas and the soldiers of the *daimyō*

seized its valuable cargo (*HP*, 199). Zuazola was confident that they would be well received, since Japan was under the rule of Taikō, who was "rey de cuatro reinos adquiridos y sujetados por pura prudencia y valor, que de su nacimiento es hijo de padres humildes y bajos, y el que tuvo por oficio leñador, aunque hombre de grandísima astucia y valor" (*RV*, 110).

The meritocratic system that enabled Hideyoshi's rise to power had provoked admiration in the Iberian writers because they were acquainted with this powerful warrior. They would write with deep respect of a leader who, in his earlier years, was more concerned with defeating his enemies than paying attention to strange foreigners. After he ordered the expulsion of the Jesuits in 1587, however, that respect turned to fear. In his last years, Hideyoshi would be portrayed as a tyrant in the European accounts. Pobre de Zamora, who had visited Japan in 1596 and was convinced that the nation's conversion to Christianity was "la mejor del mundo" (*HP*, 115) and that its ruler was "another great Tamerlane" (*HP*, 133), would realize that his earlier interpretation was wrong. In his words, Hideyoshi becomes a traitor: "Rompió Taico Sama con la palabra que tenía dada de paz, rompió con la seguridad que tenían en sus reinos los de Luzón, que rompió también con las loables costumbres del Japón" (*HP*, 197). The peace and security he mentions here refers to the friendship that Hideyoshi and the Philippines had formed in 1593, when Hideyoshi promised to protect the envoys from the Spanish colony.[27] Although both archipelagoes had been on good terms since 1592, the Taikō would then menacingly send a letter stating, "Soy tan poderoso que tengo gentes que vayan a conquistar cualquier reino," threatening to send his army to the Spanish colony "a sujetarla, con copia de gente, de suerte que se arrepienta esa tierra."[28] Governor Gómez Pérez, concerned about these threats, sent a diplomatic mission formed by Franciscans to conciliate. Hideyoshi accepted his good faith, which led the Spanish mendicants to believe that they would be able to start a mission in Japan. Ironically, these ambassadors would be the ones crucified in 1597.

When the *San Felipe* arrived at Tosa, Japan and the Philippines were still on amicable terms. Nevertheless, the notion that Japan was an unpredictable neighbor remained ever present in the minds of the *manileños*, who feared that its invasion of Korea (1592–1598) might be followed by an invasion of the Philippines. With the description of Hideyoshi's treason, Pobre de Zamora confirms these concerns. When crew and passengers were forced to disembark and taken as prisoners, his narration evinces his disillusionment depicting the humiliations they were made to endure: "Con tanta seguridad íbamos todos muy seguros, pareciéndonos que íbamos a nuestras casas: mas sucedió muy al contrario de lo que pensábamos" (*HP*, 197). He anticipates the harm they would suffer as captives of the Japanese. Only one year earlier, Pobre de Zamora had been acquainted with the Japanese and was certain that their lives would be spared. He expressed doubts, however, about the cargo: "De la hacienda no sé yo que será, mas las vidas las tenemos seguras, porque aunque estos japones tienen malas costumbres, tienen una muy buena, y es no matar jamás a gente extranjera" (*HP*, 200).

Pobre de Zamora reveals to the reader that Hideyoshi was not as amiable as the Manila authorities believed, and he announces that the cargo would be lost. The Franciscan believed that the Japanese were unpredictable in some ways; nevertheless, he trusted in some of their virtues. His trust soon changed to bewilderment when he saw a new side of the people who were once praised as superior to Europeans: their alleged greed and cruelty. The Japanese confiscated the cargo and apprehended the passengers and crew. Pobre de Zamora and his companions were separated and held in different locations and thus unable to determine their situation, comfort each other, or reorganize the hierarchies established on board. They were imprisoned and isolated with no way of communicating with one another, knowing who had survived, or making decisions as a group. This may explain the mistakes and poor decisions that they would later make. The Franciscan's writing reflects the desperation of the Spaniards as they see how the *yakunin* (magistrate or governor) opened the crates and exposed everything. The haul was, as the Franciscan depicts, very valuable: "Encontraron con algunos cajones, escritorios, escribanías, en que venían Cristos de marfil, niños Jesúses y otras imágenes y gran multitud de cruces de ébano, unas labradas, otras con reliquias, y otras cosas de marfil de gran valor. Yo vi una pieza de estas que valía quinientos pesos, por estar guarnecida de oro" (*HP*, 218). These are not only treasures made of precious metal, wood, and ivory but also instruments of the lettered European culture, such as the desks (*escritorios* and *escribanías*) used to compose and write histories, poetry, pious narrations, and the like. Pobre de Zamora watched as objects of liturgical value—that is, figures of Christ and crosses—lost their sacred significance and power in the hands of the Japanese, who wanted them only for their monetary worth. The passage functions also as an inventory—a list of the objects that the missionary had advised not be loaded onto the galleon. By stating the prices of some of the items, Pobre de Zamora notes both the sacrilege and the economic loss.[29] But more than money and dignity were lost once the Japanese opened the crates containing the travelers' documents. Pobre de Zamora exclaims, "¡Oh santo Dios, y quién viera allí llegar a los religiosos y a los pasajeros y marineros, por ver si encontraban con sus papeles!" (*HP*, 219). Alliances, debts, contracts, and secrets were exposed to all. Having nothing in his possession and nothing to hide, Pobre de Zamora is the only one who remains calm. He narrates this scene with ironic rejoicing, as it confirms his predictions: he would deride the ones who laughed at his concerns back in the Philippines.

Divine providence protected the objects of real value from the purported greed of the Japanese: "Cierto, aquí se mostró un gran juicio de Dios, que fue: todo lo profano y fingido guardado, y todo lo divino y sagrado hollado; por aquel suelo, porque como vieron tanta multitud de cruces y Cristos e imágenes, arrojabanlas por aquel suelo" (*HP*, 218). The humble symbols of faith are on the ground but not stolen, unlike the objects made of rich metals and gems—those with empty significance for authentic Christians. The image of the most sacred images of Christianity scattered, amplified by their humble nature, intends to provoke outrage in the reader. The liturgical objects are violated, victims of the supposed heathens who desecrate them, while the crew and passengers of the *San Felipe* worry only about money. Pobre de Zamora situates himself in the middle of a pandemonium in which greed makes equals of the Spaniards and the Japanese. Nevertheless, he is aware that the Congregation of Rites is judging not only the actions of his companions but also his own. He thus includes in his narrative his confrontation with the other captives, in which he urges them to save at least the crosses: "De esto que yo veo es de lo que tengo gran lástima, y vosotros no hacéis caso de ello, metidos en vuestras haciendas, donde tenéis metidos vuestros corazones. ¿No veis lo que pasa por aquel suelo? ¿No veis como estos tiranos huellan nuestras insignias?" (*HP*, 219).

His admonishment to the men who are not doing enough to save the divine icons serves to reunite the group and create a dichotomy of *them* versus *us*: the tyrants insulting *our* insignia, the most cherished representations of *our* identity as Spaniards and Christians. His accusation of avarice designates him once again as the lone hero, surrounded by cruel heathens and cowardly Christians. Ironically, his attempt to save the most modest objects has the opposite effect when the Japanese realize the importance of the religious figures. The image of apostates destroying symbols of Catholicism would inspire indignation among the readers, but it would also reinforce the idea that the Japanese mission was not well established: "Viendo los gentiles con la instancia que les pedían las imágenes y cruces, vieron a entender por algunos cristianos, que debían de ser los que habían dejado la fe, que eran nuestros dioses aquellos, y algunos los guardaban y otros los hollaban y delante de nuestros ojos los pisaban" (*HP*, 219).

The depiction of the destruction of the galleon cargo is directed at three different readers: the Franciscan authorities and the Congregation of Rites (who would each read how Pobre de Zamora was the only one concerned about the symbols of faith), and the Council of Indies (who would record the amount of losses and look for those who were responsible for the misadventure). This passage adds more information: the Japanese, who had apostatized, understand the importance of the Christian symbols and commit sacrilege. The fact that there were apostates among the Japanese is something that Rome would notice—perhaps interpreting it, as Pobre de Zamora expected, as a sign that the evangelization the Jesuits were conducting was not enough for the total conversion of Japan to Christianity.

The poor relations between the Franciscans and the Society of Jesus are evident in Pobre de Zamora's writing: in conversation with the missionary Pedro Bautista, he learns that the bishop of Japan had commanded all of the Franciscans in Japan to leave the country and come back to the Philippines. Thus, the Franciscans had found two enemies: the Japanese, who wanted the contents of the galleon, and the Jesuits, who would do little to help them. In the meantime, however, the lives of the shipwrecked were spared, and they were eventually allowed to reunite. They met the Franciscans who were already in Nagasaki and decided to appease Hideyoshi by sending presents. To have a true chance of success, the shipwrecked party needed intermediaries, those acquainted with the region and its customs. Pobre de Zamora would find help in the missionaries of his order, the Franciscans Pedro Bautista and Gonzalo García, who had been in Japan since 1592. They accompanied Pobre de Zamora and his companions to Miyako (Kyoto) in order to fulfill two missions: the first was to keep the cargo and request permission to continue on with their voyage to New Spain, and the second was to demonstrate to the Roman authorities that the Franciscans were suited to remain in Japan to solve problems and, ultimately, evangelize.

Once in Miyako, they were received as ambassadors, they sent the presents to the court, and they waited for a favorable answer. They thought they would be favored, but this prediction proved incorrect. The day after their arrival to the capital, they received bad news: "A Taico sama le han informado mal." Pobre de Zamora took this brief statement as "a muy mala señal." He does not reveal immediately the cause of his apprehension but feared "alguna traición" (*HP*, 204). He had already noted the treacherous nature of Hideyoshi, as well as the enmity of the Jesuits. He makes his antipathy against the members of the Society of Jesus evident in a conversation with another Franciscan, who tells him that the Jesuits had offered to act as intermediaries and that Hideyoshi would probably take a third of the cargo. Expressing his surprise, Pobre de Zamora writes, "¿Por ventura, hermano, no somos todos de un Dios y de un Rey? Pues bien podrían los Padres remediarlo ahora, si quisieren mirar en la grande aflicción que estarán aquellos pobres españoles. . . . Mas, ¡ay, hermano, que creo que no andan por ayudarnos!" (*HP*, 206). With this paragraph he achieves several objectives. First, he criticizes the Jesuits' intention of a negotiation that would benefit Hideyoshi at the expense of the Spanish crown's treasury. Second, he asserts that the Jesuits clearly do not think themselves subjects of the Spanish Empire (Francis Xavier, Morejón, and other important Jesuits were Spaniards), or even believers in the same God. Finally, he demonstrates that the Jesuits do not want to help the Franciscans or the other travelers retain possession of cargo belonging to the crown. By asking questions, or by using a verb that expresses doubt (*creo*), Pobre de Zamora avoids making these statements directly and leaves the reader to answer. His narration becomes bitter and the accusations against the Jesuits more explicit: "Se echó de ver el gran odio con que el Obispo venía a echarlos del Japón" (*HP*, 211). By narrating the conflict in a crescendo, Pobre de Zamora develops a narrative in which the Society of Jesus are portrayed as antagonists that are more dangerous than the Japanese.

Zuazola does not write such direct accusations, but nonetheless suggests the same enemies in a different way. In his account, "algunas personas y tres portugueses" had informed Hideyoshi that "éramos ladrones corsarios que veníamos a comarcar la tierra para tomarla, como lo habíamos hecho en el Perú y en Nueva España y Filipinas, enviando primero a los padres de San Francisco para que predicaran la ley de Nambal" (*RV*, 117). In this passage Spaniards are degraded as simple thieves and pirates who only want to seize the land of Japan, as they did that of the Americas. The heteroglossia of the term *nambal* (*nanban*) in a text in Spanish implies that this opinion is shared by both the Japanese and the Portuguese.[30]

The blame for this imagined plan was placed on Pedro Bautista, who had acted as ambassador for the ones who, in the eyes of Hideyoshi, had come to Japan to conquer it. Pedro Bautista and five Franciscans (among them Felipe de las Casas or de Jesús, one of the shipwrecked) were accused of preaching Christianity against the explicit orders of the Taikō; they were arrested and condemned to die in Nagasaki. First, however, they had to have their own *via crucis* from Miyako in the cold Japanese winter. They were forced to walk until they arrived in Nagasaki, where they were crucified along with twenty Japanese men, three of them educated by the Jesuits. Avila, who was a witness to the martyrdom, translates the reason given by Hideyoshi: "Por cuanto estos hombres de Luzón vinieron a mi reino con título de embajadores, y se quedaron en él predicando y enseñando la ley de los cristianos que yo había prohibido regurosamente los años pasados, mando que por el caso referido sean llevados a Nangasaqui, donde sean crucificados con los japones que hubieran convertido" (*RRN*, 315). With this statement Avila demonstrates that Hideyoshi was the one who decided to execute the missionaries and relates the reason for his actions: evangelization in Japan was forbidden, regardless of which order practiced it. The warning to the Philippines was clear: the Taikō was a dangerous ally and not someone to be trusted.

As only one of the travelers who had been aboard the *San Felipe* died (Felipe de las Casas) in the three narrations, the messengers of peace are the ones who suffer martyrdom, whereas the survivors of the shipwreck are saved. Juan Bautista and his fellow Franciscans had endeavored to help the group of stranded Spaniards who had the misfortune of arriving in hostile lands, and the result was their gruesome sacrifice. As Carneiro explains, "La muerte misma no conmueve tanto como, por ejemplo, la muerte del que se ofrecía como mensajero para la paz."[31] In Rome the members of the Congregation of Rites would read how six Franciscans had died for the promotion of the Christian faith. In Madrid, the Spanish crown would read how they had tried to save the Spanish possessions.

The image of six missionaries on their crosses, together with the Japanese Christians, was a fruitful way to convince Rome of the need for more clergy in Japan. But the narration of their death was not enough; the dead had to be illustrated as worthy of canonization, which would make the petition of the Franciscans stronger. The crucifixion of the twenty-six Christians needed to be represented not as a punishment but as a martyrdom. It needed to be narrated not as torment and execution but as a scene of Christian triumph, "the ultimate *imitatio christi*," according to Padrón.[32] The representation of the scene was ideal. The martyrs were secured to the crosses planted in the ground, such that they were elevated above the heads of the common people, who were already worshipping them: "El primero que pareció en el aire fue el sancto fray Pedro, como capitán valeroso. Y quedó en aquella cruz con una majestad que admiraba" (*RRN*, 327–328). In this depiction of the scene, the public comprises Nagasaki's Christians: "Fue tanto el estruendo de voces, lloros, sollozos y gemidos de todos los presentes, que retumbaban muy lejos de allí . . . había tanta gente, hombres y mujeres, que era un copioso número. Y de la ciudad estaban mirando desde los tejados otras infinitas gentes . . . cuyos alaridos subían al cielo y retumbaban los ecos por todas aquellas calles, montes y cañadas, encontrándose las unas a las otras, y todo era un doloroso grito" (*RRN*, 327). The reference to the noise assures the reader that the martyrdom did not go unnoticed: the number of believers was so large that it became uncountable, "infinite"; the Japanese Christians' cries were so loud that they reached heaven. The reaction of the Japanese Christians appeals to the reader more than the references to the relics and the miracles (which would be declared nonexistent afterward). Avila, Pobre de Zamora, and Zuazola vividly represent the disorganization of the scene, the pain of the Christians, the cruelty of the executioners, and, above all, the reminiscence of the death of Jesus Christ. Coincidentally, "la muerte más afrentosa que se da en el Japón" (*RV*, 123), which consists of crucifying the convict, is one of the greatest symbols of Christianity. The portrayal of this punishment enables Avila to reinterpret the process in terms that will enhance the religious value of the execution. These Christians from a distant culture were arrested, tortured, and made to walk a long way; they then died in a manner very similar to that of Jesus Christ. The event had all the elements of a tragedy: *via crucis* and crucifixion. Even the differences in time and space between this execution and that of Christ were interpreted as symbols of the universality of Christianity: after exposing the prisoners on the crosses, they speared them, "atravesando el cuerpo de modo que, entrando la lanza por el costado siniestro, salía al hombro derecho, dejando hecha en cada uno una cruz en lo interior del pecho" (*RRN*, 328). With this scene of "dramatic, extraordinary and gory details," which are part of the narrative of shipwreck,[33] the bodies are glorified not with one cross but with two: one on the outside of the body, the other inside.

In the eyes of the Christian readers, Nagasaki becomes the "segundo Calvario, primero de Japón" (*RRN*, 327). Avila uses a trope well known to the European reader in order to feature the sense of distance: even a crucifixion in the most distant place that European Christians can imagine occurs on a cross, the same symbol that they adore and wear. As Carneiro illustrates, images such as this one achieve "una supuesta identificación entre el ser de los personajes en acción de los textos y la emoción de los lectores."[34] The image of Franciscans being executed for expanding the faith transforms them into symbols of essential Christian values. Nevertheless, the authors of these texts have the specific objective of convincing Rome to end the Jesuit exclusivity. The appeal to commiseration is not enough, so the writers add further proof in order to guarantee the canonization: relics and miracles.

Several days after the crucifixion, Pobre de Zamora returned to the place of the execution in order to examine the remains of the dead. He depicts the decay and deterioration of the corpses as miraculous. In his account, even though the bodies are dismembered, they remain intact. The scavengers, he writes, did not touch them: "Nunca ave les tocó habiendo tantas, que luego en siendo crucificados o muerto alguno le sacan los ojos y comen la carne, y habiendo tanta abundancia de cuervos o de otras aves en Nangasaque, nunca comieron sus carnes, aunque algunas aves se posaban en las cruces; y nunca jamás olieron mal en todo el tiempo que estuvieron en ellas" (*HP*, 380). Likewise, Avila, who also visited the crosses, considered the bodies uncorrupted. He states that, sixty-two days after the martyrdom, "Estaba el sancto comisario con el rostro muy hermoso y como si estuviera durmiendo . . . y de color tan hermoso, que no parecía sino un rosicler" (*RRN*, 335). In mentioning other people who were present, he reinforces his own role as witness. Zuazola repeats the same, also using notarial prose: "*Nos asegura la certeza* de sus milagros . . . *odo consta por información* que se hizo para enviar al Sumo Pontífice" (*RV*, 135; emphasis added).[35] He does not state who wrote the *información* or report, but by using this jargon he intends to assure the reader that the phenomena were actual miracles. He disregards the report of the Japanese Christians: "Todos los viernes después que los crucificaron se aparecen sobre las cruces ciertas lumbres y luminarias, y esto no está muy clarificado porque no lo han visto si no es japones" (*RV*, 134). That the testimony of the Japanese is less reliable than that of the Iberians indicates that the only authority entitled to determine if there were miracles lies in Europe.

Pobre de Zamora considers the Japanese and Portuguese valid witnesses. He affirms that they saw fire columns in the area of the crosses as well as "grandes centellas a manera de cometas" in the house of the Society of Jesus (*HP*, 381). With this statement he attempts to erode the authority of the Jesuits by using their allies (the Portuguese) as attestants. He does not hide his resentfulness toward the Jesuits, but the mention of the comets recalls the phenomena that he and his companions witnessed on board the *San Felipe*—the signs that God wanted them to arrive in Japan.

After the martyrdom, Pobre de Zamora, Zuazola, and the other survivors of the galleon were separated again and forced to embark to Macao and Manila. Avila, who was still living in Japan, remained there. In recounting the rest of the story, he depicts the arrival of the diplomats sent by the new governor of Manila, Francisco Tello de Guzmán, and how they tried to recover the bodies of the crucified Franciscans. Yet, according to Avila, when the Spaniards arrived in Nagasaki there was not much left of the martyrs. The Christians had taken their clothes, blood, and bones as relics. Some days later, "ni aun las cruces" were left (*RRN*, 349). Avila himself received a drop of blood and brought it with him on a journey to India, where he gave it to a friend, perhaps with the intention of spreading the legend of the martyrs.

Ultimately, the martyrdom did help the Franciscan cause. Pobre de Zamora fulfilled his mission and the pope allowed Augustinians, Dominicans, and Franciscans to establish missions in several areas of Japan. Nevertheless, their efforts to convert Japan to Christianity failed. Japan was "the land of the gods," as the new ruler Tokugawa Ieyasu stated in a letter to the Manila governor in 1603. In 1614 all the missionaries were expelled, and those who remained had to preach furtively. Some of them were discovered and put to death, while others simply disappeared. The only Europeans allowed to access the Japanese territory were the Dutch, on the artificial island of Dejima. The principal condition for this exchange was clear: no religion could be implied, and only commerce would be allowed.

In the history of European cultural colonialism, Japan is probably the most famous case of failure, as the nation forced the Europeans to accept relations on its own terms. While the legend of the martyrs of Nagasaki (and many more who died afterward) became a written example for the Christians, no one stood as strong in the face of European powers, and one of the world's most invasive religions, as Japan did.

In this chapter I have attempted to demonstrate how a selection of texts relating a shipwreck develop into accounts narrating the European's failed cultural and commercial colonization of Japan. These writings demonstrate that the breaches in the expansionist mentality occur at many levels: enmity between religious orders, frustration of commercial enterprises, and defeat of cultural expansionism. I propose that scholars of Hispanic literatures expand their borders of study to include not only the geographical area of the eastern Pacific but also the extant writings of notaries, merchants, and less-studied authors of marginalized texts who manifest in a more nuanced way the fragilities, fissures, and ultimate decline of the Spanish Empire.

NOTES

1. The term *daimyō*—literally, "great name"—is the equivalent of "feudal lord."

2. Juan Pobre de Zamora, *Historia de la pérdida*, ed. Jesús Martínez Pérez (Avila, Spain: Diputación Provincial de Avila, 1997; hereafter, passages will be cited parenthetically in the text as *HP*; Andrés de Zuazola, "Relación del viaje," in *Libro de maravillas del oriente lejano*, ed. Emilio Sola (Madrid: Editora Nacional, 1980), 105–138 (hereafter, passages will be cited parenthetically in the text as *RV*); Bernardino de Avila Girón, *Relación del reino*

del Nipón, ed. Noemí Martín Santo (Madrid: Clásicos Hispánicos, 2019; hereafter, passages will be cited parenthetically in the text as *RRN*).

3. Reinier Hesselink, *The Dream of Christian Nagasaki: World Trade and the Clash of Cultures, 1560–1640* (Jefferson, NC: McFarland, 2015), 105.

4. Charles Boxer, "Fray Juan Pobre de Zamora and His Lost and Found 'Ystoria' of 1598–1603 (Lily MS.BM 717)," *Indiana University Bookman* 10 (1969): 33.

5. Lara Vilà, "La historia del gran reino de la China de Juan González de Mendoza: Hacia un estudio de las crónicas de Oriente en la España del Siglo de Oro," *Boletín hispánico helvé-tico* 21 (2013): 73.

6. Enrique Pupo-Walker, "Notas para la caracterización de un texto seminal: Los *Naufra-gios* de Alvar Núñez Cabeza de Vaca," *Nueva revista de filología hispánica* 38, no. 1 (1990): 168.

7. See "Instrucción para la descripción de las Indias," Diversos-Colecciones, 25, N.49, 1r–4v, Archivo Histórico Nacional, Portal de Archivos Españoles (PARES), accessed January 3, 2021, http://pares.mcu.es/ParesBusquedas20/catalogo/description/1339466.

8. Walter Mignolo, "Cartas, crónicas y relaciones del descubrimiento y la conquista," in *Historia de la literatura hispanoamericana*, ed. Luis Iñigo Madrigal (Madrid: Cátedra 1992), 75.

9. Sarissa Carneiro, *Retórica del infortunio: Persuasión, deleite y ejemplaridad en el siglo XVI* (Madrid: Vervuert, 2015), 39.

10. Pobre de Zamora adds also an account of his time in the Mariana Islands, which is not included in this chapter's discussion.

11. Josiah Blackmore, *Manifest Perdition: Shipwreck Narrative and the Disruption of Empire* (Minneapolis: University of Minnesota Press, 2002), xxi.

12. Blackmore, *Manifest Perdition*, xxi.

13. Vilà, "La Historia del Gran Reino de la China," 72–73.

14. For further examination of the precariousness of the colonial enterprise in East Asia and the Spanish presence in the Philippines, see the study by Ana M. Rodríguez-Rodríguez, chapter 7 in the present volume.

15. Boxer, "Fray Juan Pobre de Zamora," 28.

16. Francis Xavier, "To His Companions Living in Goa," in *The Letters and Instructions of Francis Xavier*, trans. M. Joseph Costelloe (St. Louis: Institute of Jesuit Sources, 1992), 297, 382, 334.

17. Ricardo Padrón, "The Blood of the Martyrs Is the Seed of the Monarchy: Empire, Uto-pia, and the Faith in Lope's *Triunfo de la fee en los reynos del Japón*," *Journal of Medieval and Early Modern Studies* 36, no. 3 (2006): 520.

18. Hideyoshi had several names and titles during his life. In the European accounts, he appears as Taicosama, for the title Taikō (retired regent) or Cambaco, for Kanpaku (impe-rial regent). Sometimes the suffix -*sama*, which denotes profound respect, is added to the title.

19. Boxer, "Fray Juan Pobre de Zamora," 25, 29.

20. Blackmore, *Manifest Perdition*, 67.

21. Carneiro, *Retórica del infortunio*, 111, 78.

22. Blackmore, *Manifest Perdition*, 69.

23. In this sense, this narration becomes a sublimated account of a failed enterprise. For further elaboration of this concept see Rodríguez-Rodríguez, chapter 7 in the present volume.

24. For more on the mapping of the Pacific and on the role of the missionaries in the controversial lines of demarcation between Portugal and Spain, see Ricardo Padrón, *The Indies of the Setting Sun: How Early Modern Spain Mapped the Far East as the Transpacific West* (Chicago: University of Chicago Press, 2020).

25. Boxer, "Fray Juan Pobre de Zamora," 28. As Boxer notes, "The papal brief *Sedis Apos-tolicae providentia* (11th of June of 1608) formally abrogated the Jesuit's monopoly" (28).

26. Blanca López de Mariscal, "Terremotos, tormentas y castátrofes en las crónicas y los relatos de viaje al Nuevo Mundo," in *Historia de la literatura hispanoamericana*, ed. Luis Iñigo Madrigal (Madrid: Cátedra, 1992), 64.

27. Ubaldo Iaccarino, "El papel del Galeón de Manila en el Japón de Tokugawa Ieyasu (1598–1616)," in *Un océano de seda y plata: El universo económico del galeón de Manila*, ed. Salvador Bernabeu and Carlos Martínez Shaw (Sevilla, Spain: Consejo Superior de Investigaciones Científicas, 2013), 134.

28. Gómez Pérez Dasmariñas, "Carta de Dasmariñas al rey, de 11/6/1592," in *Libro de las maravillas del Oriente lejano*, ed. Emilio Sola (Madrid: Editora Nacional, 1980), 51.

29. The economic losses of the ship were valued at more than 1.5 million silver pesos. See Shirley Fish, *The Manila-Acapulco Galleons: The Treasure Ships of the Pacific* (Central Milton Keynes, UK: AuthorHouse, 2011), 497.

30. *Nambal* is a transliteration of *nanban*, which as *nanbanjin* means "southern barbarian."

31. Carneiro, *Retórica del infortunio*, 59.

32. Padrón, *The Indies of the Setting Sun*, 219.

33. Blackmore, *Manifest perdition*, xx.

34. Carneiro, *Retórica del infortunio*, 129.

35. The investigation of these events was completed on February 3, 1599, with the final verdict being that no miracles had occurred, that the preservation of the bodies of the twenty-six martyrs was due to the cold weather, and that the Japanese guards protected the bodies of the martyrs from scavenging birds. See Michael Cooper, *Rodrigues, o intérprete* (Lisbon: Quetzal Editores, 2003), 177–178.

Bibliography

Acosta, José de. *Historia natural y moral de las Indias.* Edited by José Alcina Franch. Madrid: Dastin, 2002.

Adorno, Rolena. "New Perspectives in Colonial Spanish American Literary Studies." *Journal of the Southwest* 32, no. 2 (1990): 173–191.

———. *The Polemics of Possession in Spanish American Narrative.* New Haven, CT: Yale University Press, 2007.

Adorno, Rolena, and Patrick Charles Pautz. *Alvar Núñez Cabeza de Vaca: His Account, His Life, and the Expedition of Pánfilo de Narváez.* 3 vols. Lincoln: University of Nebraska Press, 1999.

Alcázar, Luis del. *Vestigatio arcani sensus in Apocalypsi.* Antwerp: Joannem Keebergium, 1614.

Alciato, Andrea. *Emblemas.* Edited by Manuel Montero and Mario Soria. Madrid: Nacional, 1975.

———. *Los emblemas de Alciato traducidos en rimas españolas.* Edited by Rafael Zafra. Barcelona: J. J. Olañeta, 2003.

Alighieri, Dante. *Purgatorio.* Project Gutenberg, 1997. http://www.gutenberg.org/files/1010/1010-h/1010-h.htm.

Alvarez, Francisco. *Historia de las cosas de Ethiopia.* Zaragoza, Spain: Agostín Millán, 1561.

Alvarez Sellers, María Rosa. "Caminos portugueses hacia Oriente de la *Peregrinação* de Fernão Mendes Pinto a la comedia *Fernán Méndez Pinto* de Enríquez Gómez." In *Actas del VIII Congreso Internacional de Caminería Hispánica*, 1–14. Madrid: Ministerio de Fomento, 2008.

Araya, Guillermo. "Fray Luis de León: La vida como naufragio." In *De Garcilaso a García Lorca (ocho estudios sobre letras españolas)*, 179–190. Amsterdam: Rodopi, 1983.

Argente del Castillo Ocaña, Concepción. "Hungría en el teatro de Mira de Amescua." In *La teatralización de la historia en el Siglo de Oro español*, 83–100. Granada: Universidad de Granada, 2001.

Arzubialde, Santiago, Jesús Corella, and Juan Manuel García-Lomas, eds. *Constituciones de la Compañía de Jesús: introducción y notas para su lectura.* Bilbao, Spain: Mensajero, 1993.

"Asiento y capitulación hecho por el Capitán Hernando de Soto con el Emperador Carlos V para la conquista y población de la provincia de la Florida, y encomienda de la gobernación de la isla de Cuba." In *Colección de varios documentos para la historia de la Florida y tierras adyacentes*, edited by Buckingham Smith, 140–146. London: Trübner, 1857.

Avila Girón, Bernardino de. *Relación del reino del Nipón a que llaman corruptamente Japón*. Edited by Noemí Martín Santo. Madrid: Clásicos Hispánicos, 2019.

Baena, Julio. *Discordancias cervantinas*. Newark, DE: Juan de la Cuesta, 2003.

———. *Quehaceres con Góngora*. Newark, DE: Juan de la Cuesta, 2011.

Bataillon, Marcel. *Erasmo y España*. Mexico City: Fondo de Cultura Económica, 1979.

Bauer, Ralph. *The Cultural Geography of Colonial American Literatures: Empire, Travel, Modernity*. Cambridge: Cambridge University Press, 2003.

Bennassar, Bartolomé. *Valladolid en el Siglo de Oro*. Valladolid, Spain: Maxtor, 2015.

Beverley, John. *Aspects of Góngora's "Soledades."* Purdue University Monographs in Romance Languages. Amsterdam: John Benjamins, 1980.

———. "Soledad Primera, Lines 1–61." *MLN* 88 (1973): 233–248.

Biblia: Antigua versión de Casiodoro de Reina (1569). Sociedades Bíblicas Unidas, 1960.

Blackmore, Josiah. "Foreword." In *The Tragic History of the Sea*, edited and translated by C. R. Boxer, vii–xv. Minneapolis: University of Minnesota Press, 2001.

———. *Manifest Perdition: Shipwreck Narrative and the Disruption of Empire*. Minneapolis: University of Minnesota Press, 2002.

———. "The Sunken Voice: Depth and Submersion in Two Early Modern Portuguese Accounts of Maritime Peril." In *Shipwreck in Art and Literature: Images and Interpretations from Antiquity to the Present Day*, edited by Carl Thompson, 60–76. New York: Routledge, 2014.

Blanco, Mercedes. *Góngora heroico: "Las Soledades" y la tradición épica*. Madrid: Centro de Estudios Europa Hispánica, 2012.

Blumenberg, Hans. *Shipwreck with Spectator: Paradigm of a Metaphor for Existence*. Translated by Steven Rendall. Cambridge, MA: MIT Press, 1997.

Boncan, Celestina P. "The Westbound Galleon Trade Route from Acapulco: The Return to Manila." In *The Manila Galleon: Traversing the Pacific*, edited by Edgardo J. Angara and Sonia Pinto Ner, 95–103. Manila: Read Foundation, 2012.

Boruchoff, David A. "The Poetry of History." *Colonial Latin American Review* 13, no. 2 (2004): 275–282.

Boxer, Charles R. *Fidalgos in the Far East, 1550–1770*. Hong Kong: Oxford University Press, 1968.

———. "Fray Juan Pobre de Zamora and His Lost and Found 'Ystoria' of 1598–1603 (Lily MS. BM 717)." *Indiana University Bookman* 10 (1969): 24–46.

Brownlee, Marina S. "Postmodernism and the Baroque in María de Zayas." In *Cultural Authority in Golden Age Spain*, edited by Marina S. Brownlee and Hans Ulrich Gumbrecht, 107–127. Baltimore: Johns Hopkins University Press, 1995.

Cabeza de Vaca, Alvar Núñez. *La relación que dio Alvar Núñez Cabeça de Vaca de lo acaescido en las Indias en la armada donde yva por governador Pá[n]philo de Narbáez, desde el año de veynte y siete hasta el año d[e] treynta y seys que bolvió a Sevilla con tres de su compañía*. Zamora, Spain: Agustín de Paz y Juan Picardo, 1542.

———. *Naufragios*. Edited by Juan Francisco Maura. Madrid: Cátedra, 1989.

———. *Naufragios y comentarios*. Edited by Roberto Ferrando. Madrid: Historia 16, 1984.

———. *Relación*. In *Alvar Núñez Cabeza de Vaca: His Account, His Life, and the Expedition of Pánfilo de Narváez*, vol. 1, edited by Rolena Adorno and Patrick Charles Pautz, 14–279. Lincoln: University of Nebraska Press, 1999.

———. *Relación y comentarios del gobernador Alvar Núñez Cabeça de Vaca, de lo acaescido en las dos jornadas que hizo a las Indias*. Valladolid, Spain: Francisco Fernández de Córdova, 1555.

Calderón Calderón, Manuel. "Autoridad, poder y razón de estado en el teatro de Antonio Enríquez Gómez." *Revista de literatura* 79, no. 157 (2017): 95–120.

Camacho, Marya Svetlana T. "Eastward Crossing: The Galleon Voyage from Manila to Acapulco." In *The Manila Galleon: Traversing the Pacific*, edited by Edgardo J. Angara and Sonia Pinto Ner, 79–93. Manila: Read Foundation, 2012.

Camamis, George. *Estudios sobre el cautiverio en el Siglo de Oro*. Madrid: Gredos, 1977.

Camões, Luís de. *Os Lusíadas*. Edited by Emanuel Paulo Ramos. Porto, Portugal: Porto Editora, n.d.

Cancelliere, Enrica. "Las rutas para las Indias y la imaginación poética de Góngora." In *Actas del XIV Congreso de la Asociación Internacional de Hispanistas*, vol. 2, edited by Isaías Lerner, Roberto Nival, and Alejandro Alonso, 73–88. Newark, DE: Juan de la Cuesta, 2004.

Cañedo, Jesús. "El curriculum vitae del pícaro." *Revista de Filología Española* 49, nos. 1–4 (1966): 125–180.

Carneiro, Sarissa. *Retórica del infortunio: Persuasión, deleite y ejemplaridad en el siglo XVI*. Madrid: Vervuert, 2015.

Carrasco, Rafael. "Antonio Enríquez Gómez, un escritor judeoconverso frente a la Inquisición." In *Academias morales de las musas*, vol. 1, edited by Milagros Rodríguez Cáceres and Felipe B. Pedraza Jiménez, 19–54. Cuenca, Spain: Ediciones de la Universidad de Castilla-La Mancha, 2015.

Castro, Américo. *De la edad conflictiva*. Madrid: Taurus, 1961.

Cavillac, Michel. *Gueux et marchands and le "Guzmán de Alfarache" (1599–1604): Roman picaresque et mentalité bourgeoise dans l'Espagne du Siècle d'Or*. Bordeaux, France: Institut d'Etudes Ibériques et Ibéro-Américaines de l'Université de Bordeaux, 1983.

———. "*L'hidalgo-mercader* dans la littérature du siècle d'or." In *Hidalgos & hidalguía dans l'Espagne des XVIe–XVIIIe siècles: Théories, pratiques et représentations*. Paris: Centre National de la Recherche Scientifique, 1989.

Cervantes, Miguel de. *El ingenioso hidalgo don Quijote de la Mancha*. Edited by Francisco Rico. Edición del Instituto Cervantes. 2 vols. with CD. Madrid: Crítica, 1998.

———. *El ingenioso hidalgo don Quijote de la Mancha*. Edited by Thomas Lathrop. Newark, DE: Juan de la Cuesta, 2000.

———. *Los trabajos de Persiles y Sigismunda: Historia septentrional*. Edited by Juan Bautista Avalle-Arce. Madrid: Castalia, 1969.

———. *Novelas ejemplares*. Edited by Harry Sieber. 2 vols. Madrid: Cátedra, 1981.

Chambers, Ian. "Maritime Criticism and Theoretical Shipwrecks." *PMLA* 125, no. 3 (2010): 678–685.

Chemris, Crystal Anne. *Góngora's "Soledades" and the Problem of Modernity*. Woodbridge, UK: Támesis, 2008.

Chevalier, Maxime. *Lectura y lectores en la España de los siglos XVI y XVII*. Madrid: Turner, 1976.

Clamurro, William H. "Ideological Contradiction and Imperial Decline: Toward a Reading of Zayas's *Desengaños amorosos*." *South Central Review* 5, no. 2 (1988): 43–50.

——. "Madness and Narrative Form in *Estragos que causa el vicio*." In *María de Zayas: The Dynamics of Discourse*, edited by Amy R. Williamsen and Judith A. Whitenack, 219–233. Madison, NJ: Fairleigh Dickinson University Press, 1995.

Colín, Francisco. *Labor evangélica: Ministerios apostólicos de los obreros de la Compañía de Jesús*. Madrid: José Fernández de Buendía, 1663.

Collins, Marsha S. *The "Soledades," Góngora's Masque of the Imagination*. Columbia: University of Missouri Press, 2002.

Connery, Christopher. "Sea Power." *PMLA* 125, no. 3 (2010): 685–692.

Cooper, Michael. *Rodrigues, o intérprete*. Lisbon: Quetzal Editores, 2003.

Covarrubias Orozco, Sebastián de. *Emblemas morales*. Madrid: Luis Sánchez, 1610. Accessed January 3, 2021. https://archive.org/details/emblemasmoralesd00covar.

——. *Tesoro de la lengua castellana*. Barcelona: Editorial Alta Fulla, 1993.

Cristóbal, Vicente. "Ovid in Medieval Spain." In *Ovid in the Middle Ages*, edited by James G. Clark, Frank T. Coulson, and Kathryn L. McKinley, 231–256. New York: Cambridge University Press, 2011.

Cruz, Anne. *Discourses of Poverty: Social Reform and the Picaresque Novel in Early Modern Spain*. Toronto: University of Toronto Press, 1999.

Curtius, Ernst R. *Literatura europea y edad media latina*. 2 vols. Mexico City: Fondo de Cultura Económica, 1998.

Cushner, Nicholas P. *Spain in the Philippines: From Conquest to Revolution*. Quezon City, Philippines: Ateneo de Manila University, 1971.

Darnis, Pierre. "Génesis de la picaresca, absolutismo e individuo en las *Vidas* de Lázaro de Tormes y Guzmán de Alfarache." *Creneida* 2 (2014): 316–348.

Davies, Gareth A. "Poland, Politics, and *La vida es sueño*." *Bulletin of Hispanic Studies* 70, no. 1 (1993): 147–163.

Deleuze, Gilles, and Félix Guattari. *A Thousand Plateaus: Capitalism and Schizophrenia*. Translated by Brian Massumi. Minneapolis: University of Minnesota Press, 1987.

Díaz de Rivas, Pedro. *Discursos apologéticos por el estylo del "Polyphemo" y "Soledades."* In *Documentos apologéticos de Pedro Díaz de Rivas; el antídoto de Juan de Jáuregui*, edited by Eunice Joiner Gates, 31–67. Mexico City: Colegio de México, 1960.

——. *Discursos apologéticos por el estilo del "Polifemo" y "Soledades."* In *La batalla en torno a Góngora (selección de textos)*, edited by Ana Martínez Arancón, 127–154. Barcelona: Antoni Bosch, 1978.

Díaz del Castillo, Bernal. *Historia verdadera de la conquista de la Nueva España*. Madrid: Espasa-Calpe, 1982.

Dille, Glen. *Antonio Enríquez Gómez*. Boston: Twayne, 1988.

Docter, Mary. "Enriched by Otherness: The Transformational Journey of Cabeza de Vaca." *Christianity and Literature* 58, no. 1 (2008): 3–27.

Domínguez, Frank. "Laberintos, *mappae mundi* y geografías en el *Laberinto de Fortuna* de Juan de Mena y en la edición de las *Trezientas* de Hernán Núñez." *La Corónica* 40, no. 1 (2011): 149–182.

Dunsch, Boris. "'*Describe nunc tempestatem*': Sea Storm and Shipwreck Type Scenes in Ancient Literature." In *Shipwreck in Art and Literature: Images and Interpretations from Antiquity to the Present Day*, edited by Carl Thompson, 42–59. New York: Routledge, 2013.

Eco, Umberto. "On the Impossibility of Drawing a Map of the Empire on a Scale of 1 to 1." In *How to Travel with a Salmon and Other Essays*, translated by William Weaver, 95–106. New York: Harcourt Brace, 1995.

Egginton, William. *The Theater of Truth: The Ideology of (Neo)Baroque Aesthetics*. Stanford, CA: Stanford University Press, 2010.

El libro de Job. Translated by Fray Luis de León. Lima: Pontificia Universidad Católica del Perú, 2007.

Enríquez Gómez, Antonio. *Academias morales de las musas*. Bordeaux, France: Pedro de la Court, 1642.

———. *Fernán Méndez Pinto: Comedia famosa en dos partes*. Edited by Louise G. Cohen, Francis M. Rogers, and Constance H. Rose. Cambridge, MA: Harvard University Press, 1974.

———. *Luis dado de Dios*. Paris: Rene Baudry, 1645.

Erasmus of Rotterdam. *Coloquios*. Edited by Ignacio Anzoátegui. Buenos Aires: Espasa Calpe, 1947.

Escalera Pérez, Reyes. "Iconografía y el arte religioso del barroco." In *Escultura barroca española: Nuevas lecturas desde los siglos de oro a la sociedad del conocimiento*, vol. 1, edited by Antonio Rafael Fernández Paradas, 59–85. Antequera, Spain: Exlibric, 2016.

Ferguson, William. "Visión y movimiento en las *Soledades* de Góngora." *Hispanófila* 86 (1986): 15–18.

Fernández de Oviedo, Gonzalo. *Historia general y natural de las Indias*. 5 vols. Edited by Juan Pérez de Tudela Bueso. Madrid: Atlas, 1959.

Fine, Ruth. "Una lectura de *Sansón Nazareno* de Enríquez Gómez en el contexto de la literatura de conversos." In *Antonio Enríquez Gómez: Un poeta entre santos y judaizantes*, edited by J. Ignacio Díez and Carsten Wilke, 96–114. Kassel, Germany: Reichenberger, 2015.

Fish, Shirley. *The Manila-Acapulco Galleons: The Treasure Ships of the Pacific*. Central Milton Keynes, UK: AuthorHouse, 2011.

Francis Xavier. "To His Companions Living in Goa." In *The Letters and Instructions of Francis Xavier*, translated by M. Joseph Costelloe, 292–312. St. Louis: Institute of Jesuit Sources, 1992.

Galbarro García, Jaime. "Antonio Enríquez Gómez: Vida y contexto histórico." In *"El Triumpho lusitano" de Antonio Enríquez Gómez*, edited by Jaime Galbarro García, 13–63. Sevilla, Spain: Universidad de Sevilla, 2015.

García, Félix. "Fray Luis de León, poeta del mar." In *San Juan de la Cruz y otros ensayos*, 201–205. Madrid: Religión y Cultura, 1950.

García Calvo, Agustín. *Contra el tiempo*. 2nd ed. Zamora, Spain: Lucina, 2001.

Garcilaso de la Vega, Inca. *Historia general del Perú*. Edited by Angel Rosenblat. 3 vols. Buenos Aires: Emecé, 1944.

———. *La Florida del Inca*. Edited by Sylvia L. Hilton. Madrid: Historia 16, 1986.

———. *La Florida del Inca*. Edited by Emma Susana Speratti Piñero. Mexico City: Fondo de Cultura Económica, 1956.

Gilman, Stephen. "The 'Conversos' and the Fall of Fortune." In *Collected Studies in Honour of Américo Castro's Eightieth Year*, edited by M. P. Hornik, 127–136. Oxford: Lincombe Lodge Research Library, 1965.

———. "Fortune and Space in *La Celestina*." *Romanische Forschungen* 66, no. 3 (1955): 342–360.

Giraldez, Arturo. *The Age of Trade: The Manila Galleons and the Dawn of the Global Economy*. New York: Rowman and Littlefield, 2015.

Glantz, Margo. "El cuerpo inscrito y el texto escrito o la desnudez como naufragio: Alvar Núñez Cabeza de Vaca." In *Obras Reunidas*, vol. 1, *Ensayos sobre literatura colonial*, 86–116. Mexico City: Fondo de Cultura Económica, 2006.

Goedde, Lawrence Otto. *Tempest and Shipwreck in Dutch and Flemish Art: Convention, Rhetoric, and Interpretation*. University Park: Penn State University Press, 1989.

Góngora, Luis de. *Fábula de Polifemo y Galatea*. In *Góngora y el "Polifemo,"* vol. 3, edited by Dámaso Alonso, 529–889. Madrid: Gredos, 1985.

———. *Soledades*. Edited by John Beverley. Madrid: Cátedra, 1989.

González Echevarría, Roberto. *Myth and Archive: A Theory of Latin American Narrative*. New York: Cambridge University Press, 1990.

Goodman, Nan. "Mercantilism and Cultural Difference in Cabeza de Vaca's *Relación*." *Early American Literature* 40, no. 2 (2005): 229–250.

Goodwin, Robert T. C. "Alvar Núñez Cabeza de Vaca and the Textual Travels of an American Miracle." *Journal of Iberian and Latin American Studies* 14, no. 1 (2008): 1–12.

Guillén, Claudio. "Toward a Definition of the Picaresque." In *Literature as System*, 71–106. Princeton, NJ: Princeton University Press, 1971.

Hegel, Georg Wilhelm Friedrich. *The Philosophy of History*. Translated by J. Sibree. New York: Willey, 1944.

Hernáez, Francisco Javier. *Colección de bulas, breves y otros documentos relativos a la iglesia de América y Filipinas*. 2 vols. Vaduz, Liechtenstein: Kraus, 1964.

Herrero, Miguel. "Renaissance Poverty and Lazarillo's Family: The Birth of the Picaresque Genre." *PMLA* 94, no. 5 (1979): 876–886.

Hesselink, Reinier. *The Dream of Christian Nagasaki: World Trade and the Clash of Cultures, 1560–1640*. Jefferson, NC: McFarland, 2015.

Horkheimer, Max, and Theodor W. Adorno. *Dialectic of Enlightenment*. Translated by John Cumming. New York: Seabury, 1972.

Hulme, Peter. "The Cannibal Scene." In *Cannibalism and the Colonial World*, edited by Francis Barker, Peter Hulme, and Margaret Iversen, 1–38. Cambridge: Cambridge University Press, 1998.

Iaccarino, Ubaldo. "El papel del Galeón de Manila en el Japón de Tokugawa Ieyasu (1598–1616)." In *Un océano de seda y plata: El universo económico del galeón de Manila*, edited by Salvador Bernabeu and Carlos Martínez Shaw, 133–153. Sevilla, Spain: Consejo Superior de Investigaciones Científicas, 2013.

"Instrucción para la descripción de las Indias." Diversos-Colecciones, 25, N.49, 1r–4v, Archivo Histórico Nacional, Portal de Archivos Españoles (PARES). Accessed January 3, 2021. http://pares.mcu.es/ParesBusquedas20/catalogo/description/1339466.

Isorena, Efren B. "Maritime Disasters in Spanish Philippines: The Manila-Acapulco Galleons, 1565–1815." *International Journal of Asia Pacific Studies* 11, no. 1 (2015): 53–83.

Jáuregui, Carlos A. "Cabeza de Vaca, Mala Cosa y las vicisitudes de la extrañeza." *Revista de estudios hispánicos* 48, no. 3 (2014): 421–447.

———. "Going Native, Going Home: Ethnographic Empathy and the Artifice of Return in Cabeza de Vaca's *Relación*." *Colonial Latin American Review* 25, no. 2 (2016): 175–199.

Jáuregui, Juan de. *Antídoto contra la pestilente poesía de las "Soledades."* In *La batalla en torno a Góngora (selección de textos)*, edited by Ana Martínez Arancón, 156–190. Barcelona: Antoni Bosch, 1978.

Johnson, Christopher D. "'El Homero español': Translation and Shipwreck." *Translation and Literature* 20, no. 2 (2011): 157–174.

Jones, Alexander, ed. *The Jerusalem Bible.* Garden City, NY: Doubleday, 1966.

Juan-Navarro, Santiago. "Constructing Cultural Myths: Cabeza de Vaca in Contemporary Hispanic Criticism, Theater, and Film." In *A Twice-Told Tale: Reinventing the Encounter in Iberian / Iberian American Literature and Film*, edited by Santiago Juan-Navarro and Theodore Robert Young, 69–79. Newark: University of Delaware Press, 2001.

Kamen, Henry. *Empire: How Spain Became a World Power, 1492–1763.* New York: HarperCollins, 2003.

Krieger, Alex D. *We Came Naked and Barefoot: The Journey of Cabeza de Vaca across North America.* Edited by Margery H. Krieger. Austin: University of Texas Press, 2002.

Kristeva, Julia. "La armada documenta 1580 naufragios de buques en aguas españolas o de nacionalidad española desde el siglo XIII." *Europa Press*, January 31, 2013. https://www.europapress.es/murcia/noticia-armada-documenta-1580-naufragios-buques-aguas-espanolas-nacionalidad-espanola-siglo-xiii-20130131112741.html.

———. *Revolution in Poetic Language.* Translated by Margaret Waller. New York: Columbia University Press, 1984.

Lacouture, Jean. *Jesuitas.* Vol. 1, *Los Conquistadores.* Barcelona: Paidós, 1993.

Lafaye, Jacques. "Los 'milagros' de Alvar Núñez Cabeza de Vaca (1527–1536)." In *Notas y comentarios sobre Alvar Núñez Cabeza de Vaca*, edited by Margo Glantz, 24–25. Mexico City: Grijalbo, 1993.

Lagmanovich, David. "Los naufragios de Alvar Núñez como construcción narrativa." *Kentucky Romance Quarterly* 25, no. 2 (1978): 27–37.

Las Casas, Bartolomé de. *Apologética historia sumaria.* 2 vols. Edited by Edmundo O'Gorman. Mexico City: Universidad Nacional Autónoma de México, 1967.

Lazarillo de Tormes. Edited by Francisco Rico. Madrid: Cátedra, 2000.

Lee, A. G. "Ovid's 'Lucretia.'" *Greece & Rome* 22, no. 66 (1953): 107–118.

León, Fray Luis de. *Poesía completa.* Edited by Guillermo Serés. Madrid: Taurus, 1990.

Lewis, Robert E. "Los *Naufragios* de Alvar Núñez: Historia y Ficción." *Revista iberoamericana* 48, nos. 120–121 (1982): 681–694.

Lida de Malkiel, María Rosa. "Dido y su defensa en la literatura española." *Revista de filología hispánica* 4 (1942): 367–373.

López de Gómara, Francisco. *Historia general de las Indias.* Edited by Jorge Gurría Lacroix. Caracas: Biblioteca Ayacucho, 1979.

López de Mariscal, Blanca. "Terremotos, tormentas y catástrofes en las crónicas y los relatos de viaje al Nuevo Mundo." *Historia de la literatura hispanoamericana.* Edited by Luis Iñigo Madrigal. Madrid: Cátedra, 1992.

López Martín, Francisco Javier. *Representaciones del tiempo y construcción de la identidad entre España y América.* Huelva, Spain: Servicio de Publicaciones de la Universidad de Huelva, 2012.

López Pinciano, Alonso. *Filosofía antigua poética.* 3 vols. Edited by Alfredo Carballo Picazo. Madrid: Consejo Superior de Investigaciones Científicas, 1973.

Maravall, José Antonio. *La literatura picaresca desde la historia social (siglos XVI y XVII).* Madrid: Taurus, 1986.

Mariana, Juan de. *Tractatus VII.* Coloniae Agrippinæ: Anton Hierat, 1609.

Márquez, Antonio. "Dos procesos singulares: Los de Fray Luis de León y Antonio Enríquez Gómez." *Nueva revista de filología hispánica* 30, no. 2 (1981): 513–533.

Marx, Robert, and Jenifer Marx. *Treasure Lost at Sea: Diving to the World's Great Shipwrecks.* Buffalo, NY: Firefly Books, 2004.

Mastura, Michael O. "Administrative Policies towards the Muslims in the Philippines: A Study in Historical Continuity and Trends." *Mindanao Journal* 3, no. 1 (1976): 98–115.

Maura, Juan Francisco. *El gran burlador de América: Alvar Núñez Cabeza de Vaca.* Valencia, Spain: Universidad de Valencia, 2008.

———. "Introducción," in Alvar Núñez Cabeza de Vaca, *Naufragios,* edited by Juan Francisco Maura, 9–72. Madrid: Cátedra, 1989.

———. "Veracidad en los *Naufragios*: La técnica narrativa de Alvar Núñez Cabeza de Vaca." *Revista iberoamericana* 61, nos. 170–171 (1995): 187–195.

McGaha, Michael. "Antonio Enríquez Gómez and the Count-Duke of Olivares." In *Texto y espectáculo: Nuevas dimensiones críticas de la comedia,* edited by Arturo Pérez-Pisonero and Ana Semidey, 73–81. New Brunswick, NJ: SLUSA, 1990.

Mentz, Steve. *Shipwreck Modernity: Ecologies of Globalization, 1550–1719.* Minneapolis: University of Minnesota Press, 2015.

Mignolo, Walter D. "Cartas, crónicas y relaciones del descubrimiento y la conquista." In *Historia de la literatura hispanoamericana: Epoca colonial,* vol. 1, edited by Iñigo Madrigal, 57–116. Madrid: Cátedra, 1982.

Morga, Antonio de. *Sucesos de las islas Filipinas.* Edited and translated by J. S. Cummins. Cambridge: Hakluyt Society, 1971.

———. *Sucesos de las islas Filipinas.* Edited by Francisca Perujo. Mexico City: Fondo de Cultura Económica, 2007.

Morrison, James V. *Shipwrecked: Disaster and Transformation in Homer, Shakespeare, Defoe, and the Modern World.* Ann Arbor: University of Michigan Press, 2014.

Motolinía, Juan Toribio de. *Memoriales.* Edited by Nancy Joe Dyer. Mexico City: El Colegio de México, 1996.

Muñoz Martínez, Ana Belén. "Pobreza, enfermedad y exclusión en la iconografía bíblica románica." In *Relegados al margen: Marginalidad y espacios marginados en la cultura medieval.* Madrid: Consejo Superior de Investigaciones Científicas, 2010.

Navia, Bernardo E. "Colón y Cabeza de Vaca: Su encuentro con el Nuevo Mundo." *Hispanófila* 172 (2014): 9–24.

Nelson, Bradley J. "Góngora's *Soledades*: Portrait of the Subject." *Romance Languages Annual* no. 8 (1996): 608–614.

Obispado, Kristyl N. "The Plight of Filipino Seamen and Slaves in the 17th Century Nueva España." In *The Manila Galleon: Traversing the Pacific,* edited by Edgardo J. Angara and Sonia Pinto Ner, 185–197. Manila: Read Foundation, 2012.

Oelman, Timothy. "Tres poetas marranos." *Nueva revista de filología hispánica* 30 (1981): 184–206.

Operé, Fernando. *Historias de la frontera: El cautiverio en la América hispánica.* Mexico City: Fondo de Cultura Económica, 2001.

———, comp. *Relatos de cautivos en las Américas desde Canadá a la Patagonia: Siglos XVI al XX.* Buenos Aires: Corregidor, 2016.

Pacheco, Francisco. *Arte de la pintura: Su antigüedad y grandezas.* Sevilla, Spain: Simón Fajardo, 1649.

Padrón, Ricardo. "The Blood of the Martyrs Is the Seed of the Monarchy: Empire, Utopia, and the Faith in Lope's *Triunfo de la fee en los reynos del Japón.*" *Journal of Medieval and Early Modern Studies* 36, no. 3 (2006): 517–537.

———. *The Indies of the Setting Sun: How Early Modern Spain Mapped the Far East as the Transpacific West.* Chicago: University of Chicago Press, 2020.

Pastor, Beatriz. *Discursos narrativos de la conquista: Mitificación y emergencia.* Hanover, NH: Ediciones del Norte, 1988.

———. *El segundo descubrimiento: La conquista de América narrada por sus coetáneos (1492–1589).* Barcelona: Edhasa, 2008.

Pearson, Michael N. "Spain and Spanish Trade in Southeast Asia." In *European Entry into the Pacific: Spain and the Acapulco-Manila Galleons,* edited by Dennis O. Flynn, Arturo Giráldez, and James Sobredo, 117–137. Burlington, VT: Ashgate, 2001.

Pedraza Jiménez, Felipe B. "La fascinación de *El médico de su honra*: Sus ecos en la obra de Enríquez Gómez." In *Doctos libros juntos: Homenaje al profesor Ignacio Arellano Ayuso,* edited by Ignacio Arellano, Victoriano Roncero López, and Juan Manuel Escudero, 405–429. Frankfurt: Iberoamericana, 2018.

Pérez-Amador Adam, Alberto. *De legitimatione imperii Indiae Occidentalis: La vindicación de la Empresa Americana en el discurso jurídico y teológico de las letras de los Siglos de Oro en España y los virreinatos americanos.* Madrid: Iberoamericana-Vervuert, 2011.

Pérez Dasmariñas, Gómez. "Carta de Dasmariñas al Rey, de 11/6/1592." In *Libro de las maravillas del Oriente lejano,* edited by Emilio Sola, 48–54. Madrid: Editora Nacional, 1980.

Pérez Fernández, Isacio. *El derecho hispano-indiano: Dinámica social de su proceso histórico constituyente.* Salamanca, Spain: San Esteban, 2001.

———. "Hallazgo de un nuevo documento básico de Fray Bartolomé de las Casas: Guión de la redacción de las *Leyes Nuevas.*" *Studium* 32, no. 3 (1992): 459–504.

Phelan, John Leddy. *The Hispanization of the Philippines: Spanish Aims and Filipino Responses, 1565–1700.* Madison: University of Wisconsin Press, 1959.

Phillips, Carla Rahn. "The Organization of Oceanic Empires." In *Seascapes: Maritime Histories, Littoral Cultures, and Transoceanic Exchanges,* edited by Jerry H. Bentley, Renate Bridenthal, and Kären Wigen, 71–86. Honolulu: University of Hawai'i Press, 2007.

Picornell, Pedro. "The Anatomy of the Manila Galleon." In *The Manila Galleon: Traversing the Pacific,* edited by Edgardo J. Angara and Sonia Pinto Ner, 41–63. Manila: Read Foundation, 2012.

Pobre de Zamora, Fray Juan. *Carta apologética, probando que los reinos de China, Japón y Siam pertenecen al rey de España, según la demarcación hecha por S.S.,* MS/Mendel 757, Lilly Library, Indiana University.

———. *Historia de la pérdida y descubrimiento del galeón "San Felipe."* Edited by Jesús Martinez Pérez. Avila, Spain: Institución "Gran duque de Alba," Diputación Provincial de Avila, 1997.

Poema de Mío Cid. Edited by Colin Smith. Madrid: Cátedra, 1998.

Prieto Calixto, Alberto. "Aculturación en las fronteras de América: Cabeza de Vaca, el primer mestizo cultural." *Estudios Fronterizos* 8, no. 16 (2007): 123–143.

Pupo-Walker, Enrique. "Los *Naufragios* de Alvar Núñez Cabeza de Vaca: Notas sobre la relevancia antropológica del texto." *Revista de Indias* 47, no. 181 (1987): 755–776.

————. "Notas para la caracterización de un texto seminal: Los Naufragios de Alvar Núñez Cabeza de Vaca." *Nueva revista de filología hispánica* 38, no. 1 (1990): 163–196.

————. "Pesquisas para una nueva lectura de los *Naufragios*, de Alvar Núñez Cabeza de Vaca." *Revista iberoamericana* 53, no. 140 (1987): 517–539.

Quevedo, Francisco de. "Poderoso caballero es don Dinero." In *Poesía lírica del Siglo de Oro*, edited by Elias L. Rivers, 341–343. Madrid: Cátedra, 1997.

Rabasa, José. "De la *allegoresis* etnográfica en los *Naufragios* de Alvar Núñez Cabeza de Vaca." *Revista iberoamericana* 61, nos. 170–171 (1995): 175–185.

————. *Writing Violence on the Northern Frontier: The Historiography of Sixteenth-Century New Mexico and Florida and the Legacy of Conquest*. Durham, NC: Duke University Press, 2000.

Real Academia Española. *Diccionario de autoridades*. 3 vols. Madrid: Editorial Gredos, 1984.

————. *Diccionario de autoridades*, 1726–1739. https://apps2.rae.es/DA.html

Reff, Daniel T. "Text and Context: Cures, Miracles, and Fear in the *Relación* of Alvar Núñez Cabeza de Vaca." *Journal of the Southwest* 38, no. 2 (1996): 115–138.

Regimiento de navegación. Madrid: Instituto de España, 1964.

Rennert, Hugo A. "Notes on the Chronology of Spanish Drama." *Modern Language Review* 2 (1907): 331–341.

Révah, Israël Salvator. *Antonio Enríquez Gómez, un écrivain marrane (v. 1600–1663)*. Edited by Carsten L. Wilke. Paris: Chandeigne, 2003.

————. "Un pamphlet contre l'Inquisition d'Antonio Enríquez Gómez: La seconde partie de la *Política angélica* (Rouen, 1647)." *Revue des études juives* 121, nos. 1–2 (1961): 81–168.

Rhodes, Elizabeth. *Dressed to Kill: Death and Meaning in Zayas's "Desengaños."* Toronto: University of Toronto Press, 2011.

Rodrigues Vianna Peres, Lygia. "El cautivo, el taumaturgo: Caminos y caminantes en la escena de la vida y de la muerte." In *El cautiverio en la literatura del Nuevo Mundo*, edited by Miguel Donoso, Mariela Insúa, and Carlos Mata, 195–205. Madrid: Iberoamericana/Vervuert, 2011.

Rodríguez-Cáceres, Milagro. "La sombra del Conde-Duque en el teatro de Enríquez Gómez." In *Estrategias y conflictos de autoridad y poder en el teatro del Siglo de Oro*, edited by Ignacio Arellano and Frederick A. de Armas, 123–137. New York: Instituto de Estudios Auriseculares, 2017.

Rodríguez de la Flor, Fernando. "On the Notion of a Melancholic Baroque." In *Hispanic Baroques: Reading Cultures in Context*, edited by Nicholas Spadaccini and Luis Martín-Estudillo, 3–19. Nashville: Vanderbilt University Press, 2005.

Rodríguez-Guridi, Elena. "La orilla del discurso: una topografía del desorden poético en las *Soledades* de Luis de Góngora." *Hispanic Review* 80, no. 1 (2012): 41–61.

Rodríguez-Rodríguez, Ana M. "Old Enemies, New Contexts: Early Modern Spanish (Re)-Writing of Islam in the Philippines." In *Coloniality, Religion, and the Law in the Early Iberian World*, edited by Santa Arias and Raúl Marrero, 137–157. Nashville: Vanderbilt University Press, 2013.

Rose, Constance H. "Antonio Enríquez Gómez and the Literature of Exile." *Romanische Forschungen* 85 (1973): 63–77.

————. "Las comedias políticas de Enríquez Gómez." *La torre* 118 (1982): 183–196.

——. "Portuguese Diplomacy Plays a Role in the Printing of Some Peninsular Works in Rouen in the Seventeenth Century." *Arquivos do Centro Cultural Portugès* 10 (1976): 523–541.

Sáez, Adrián J. "Las comedias húngaras de Lope de Vega: Una cadena de intertextualidad y reescritura." *Dicenda* 33 (2015): 293–307.

San José, Jerónimo de. *Genio de la historia.* Edited by Higinio de Santa Teresa. Vitoria, Spain: Ediciones El Carmen, 1957.

Sánchez Ferlosio, Rafael. *God and Gun: Apuntes de polemología.* Barcelona: Destino, 2008.

——. *Mientras no cambien los dioses, nada ha cambiado.* Madrid: Alianza Editorial, 1986.

Sánchez Robayna, Andrés. *Silva Gongorina.* Madrid: Cátedra, 1993.

Sanfuentes, Olaya. "Morirse de hambre: El hambre del conquistador." In *El cautiverio en la literatura del Nuevo Mundo,* edited by Miguel Donoso, Mariela Insúa, and Carlos Mata, 233–251. Madrid: Iberoamericana/Vervuert, 2011.

Santa Cruz, Alonso de. *Crónica del Emperador Carlos V.* Edited by Antonio Blázquez y Delgado-Aguilera and Ricardo Beltrán y Rózpide. Madrid: Real Academia de la Historia, 1922.

Sasaki, Betty. "Góngora's Sea of Signs: The Manipulation of History in the *Soledades.*" *Calíope* 1, nos. 1–2 (1995): 150–168.

Schurz, William Lytle. *The Manila Galleon.* New York: E. P. Dutton, 1959.

Sepúlveda, Juan Ginés de. *Demócrates segundo o de las justas causas de la guerra contra los Indios.* Edited and translated by Angel Losada. Madrid: Consejo Superior de Investigaciones Científicas, Instituto Francisco de Vitoria, 1984.

Serrano y Sanz, Manuel. "María de Zayas." In *Apuntes para una biblioteca de escritoras españolas desde el año 1401 al 1833,* vol. 2, 583–621. Madrid: Estado español, 1903.

Shepherd, Gregory J. *An Exposition of José de Acosta's "Historia natural y moral de las Indias," 1590: The Emergence of an Anthropological Vision of Colonial Latin America.* Lewiston, NY: Edwin Mellen, 2002.

Shergold, N. D., and J. E. Varey. "Some Palace Performances of Seventeenth-Century Plays." *Bulletin of Hispanic Studies* 40 (1963): 212–244.

Smith, Paul Julian. *Writing in the Margin: Spanish Literature of the Golden Age.* Oxford: Oxford University Press, 1978.

Solórzano Pereira, Juan de. *Emblemas regio-políticos.* Edited by Jesús María González de Zarate. Madrid: Tuero, 1987.

Sousa, Lucio de. "The Jewish Presence in China and Japan in the Early Modern Period: A Social Representation." In *Global History and New Polycentric Approaches: Europe, Asia and the Americas in World Network System,* edited by Manuel Pérez García and Lucio de Sousa, 183–218. Singapore: Palgrave Macmillan, 2017.

Spitta, Silvia. *Between Two Waters: Narratives of Transculturation in Latin America.* Houston: Rice University Press, 1995.

——. "Chamanismo y cristiandad: Una lectura de la lógica intercultural de los *Naufragios* de Cabeza de Vaca." *Revista de crítica literaria latinoamericana* 19, no. 38 (1993): 317–330.

Steinberg, Philip E. *The Social Construction of the Ocean.* New York: Cambridge University Press, 2001.

Suess, Paulo, ed. *La conquista espiritual de la América española: 200 documentos del siglo XVI.* Quito: Abya-Yala, 2002.

Tanabe, Madoka. "Imágenes del mar en Góngora." PhD diss., Universidad de Córdoba, 2016.

Tasso, Torquato. *Opere*, vol. 5, *Apologia in difesa della Gerusalemme liberata*, edited by Bruno Maier. Milan: Rizzoli Editore, 1965.

Tausiet, María. "Taming Madness: Moral Discourse and Allegory in Counter-Reformation Spain." *History* 94, no. 315 (2009): 279–293.

Thomas, Hugh. *World without End: Spain, Philip II, and the First Global Empire*. New York: Random House, 2014.

Thompson, Carl, ed. *Shipwreck in Art and Literature: Images and Interpretations from Antiquity to the Present Day*. New York: Routledge, 2013.

Thompson, Colin. "Myth and the Construction of Meaning in the *Soledades* and the *Polifemo*." *Bulletin of Spanish Studies* 90, no. 1 (2013): 83–105.

Torquemada, Antonio. *Jardín de flores curiosas*. Edited by Giovanni Allegra. Madrid: Castalia, 1982.

Trías Folch, Luisa. "La traducción española de la *Peregrinação* y la comedia española *Fernán Méndez Pinto*." In *Literatura portuguesa y literatura española: Influencias y relaciones*, edited by María Rosa Alvarez Sellers, 37–53. Valencia, Spain: Universitat de València, 1999.

Turner Bushnell, Amy. "A Requiem for Lesser Conquerors: Honor and Oblivion on a Maritime Periphery." In *Beyond Books and Borders: Garcilaso de la Vega and "La Florida del Inca,"* edited by Raquel Chang Rodríguez, 66–74. Lewisburg, PA: Bucknell University Press, 2006.

Vargas, Claret M. "'De muchas y muy bárbaras naciones con quien conversé y viví': Alvar Núñez Cabeza de Vaca's *Naufragios* as a War Tactics Manual." *Hispanic Review* 75, no. 1 (2007): 1–22.

Vilà, Lara. "La historia del gran reino de la China de Juan González de Mendoza: Hacia un estudio de las crónicas de Oriente en la España del Siglo de Oro." *Boletín hispánico helvético* 21 (2013): 71–97.

Vitoria, Francisco de. *Sobre el poder civil. Sobre los indios. Sobre el derecho de la guerra*. Edited by Luis Frayle Delgado and José-Leandro Martínez-Cardós Ruiz. Madrid: Tecnos, 2007.

Voigt, Lisa. *Writing Captivity in the Early Modern Atlantic: Circulations of Knowledge and Authority in the Iberian and English Imperial Worlds*. Chapel Hill: University of North Carolina Press, 2009.

Wardropper, Bruce. "El trastorno de la moral en el *Lazarillo*." *Nueva revista de filología hispánica* 15, nos. 3–4 (1961): 441–447.

Warshawsky, Matthew. "Las múltiples expresiones de identidad judeo-conversa en tres obras poéticas de Antonio Enríquez Gómez." *Calíope* 17, no. 1 (2011): 97–124.

Weber de Kurlat, Frida. "Hacia una sistematización de los tipos de comedia de Lope de Vega." In *Actas del V Congreso Internacional de Hispanistas*, vol. 2, edited by François Lopez, Joseph Pérez, Noël Salomon, and Maxime Chevalier, 867–871. Bordeaux, France: Université de Bordeaux, 1977.

Wilke, Carsten L. *Jüdisch-christliches Doppelleben im Barock: Zur Biographie des Kaufmanns und Dichters Antonio Enríquez Gómez*. Frankfurt: Peter Lang, 1994.

Yllera, Alicia. "Introduction." In María de Zayas y Sotomayor, *Desengaños amorosos*, edited by Alicia Yllera, 9–99. Madrid: Cátedra, 1983.

Zamora, Fray Juan Pobre de. *Historia de la pérdida y descubrimiento del galeón "San Felipe."* Avila, Spain: Excelentísima Diputación de Avila, 1997.

Zayas y Sotomayor, María de. *Desengaños amorosos.* Edited by Alicia Yllera. Madrid: Cátedra, 1983.

Zuazola, Andrés de. "Relación del viaje del galeón San Felipe de su majestad, arribada que hizo al Japón." In *Libro de maravillas del oriente lejano,* edited by Emilio Sola, 105–138. Madrid: Editora Nacional, 1980.

———. "Voyage of the *San Felipe* to Japan, 12th July 1596 to 21st March 1597." *Boxer Mss. II, 1500–1899,* Lilly Library, Indiana University.

Zugasti, Miguel. "Comedia palatina cómica y comedia palatina seria en el siglo de oro." In *El sustento de los discretos: La dramaturgia áulica de Tirso de Molina,* edited by E. Galar and B. Oteiza, 159–185. Madrid: Instituto de Estudios Tirsianos, 2003.

Notes on Contributors

Julio Baena (PhD in Spanish literature, Georgetown University) is a professor of Spanish at the University of Colorado–Boulder. The focus of his work has been critical theory issues resulting from the necessary contradictions and fissures inherent to the birth (pangs) of the modern novel and the modern praxis of poetic language in sixteenth- and seventeenth-century Spain. Among his books are *El círculo y la flecha: Principio y fin, triunfo y fracaso del "Persiles," Discordancias cervantinas*, and *Quehaceres con Góngora*. His most recent book *Dividuals* focuses on the theoretical implications of the attraction/repulsion between the study of love and the study of misery in the Spanish Renaissance. Baena also writes poetry, including the books *Glosas de la naranja entera* and *Compañía de títulos y poemas*, and has penned a quasi-sequel to *Don Quixote* with his novel *Tosilos*.

Carmen Hsu (PhD in romance languages and literatures, Harvard University) is an associate professor of Spanish in the Department of Romance Studies at the University of North Carolina–Chapel Hill. Her main scholarly interests are sixteenth- and seventeenth-century Spanish literature, with particular attention to Hispano-Asian literary and intellectual relations. Hsu is the author of *Courtesans in the Literature of the Spanish Golden Age* and *Cervantes y su tiempo*.

Noemí Martín Santo (PhD in Hispanic language and literatures, Boston University) is an assistant professor of Spanish at Hampden-Sydney College in Virginia whose research focuses on the cultural encounters between early modern Iberia and Asia. She is currently working on a book-length manuscript that examines the images of Asian kings and warlords in Iberian historiography.

NATALIO OHANNA (PhD in Hispanic studies, McGill University) is an associate professor of Spanish at Western Michigan University (WMU) in Kalamazoo and an affiliated faculty member of the WMU Medieval Institute. His research focuses on the intellectual history of the early modern period; the cultural triangle of Africa, the Americas, and Europe in struggle and exchange; the discursive configuration of the East and the New World; Spanish humanism during the Counter-Reformation, and the social and political meanings of cross-cultural plays and narratives of travel and captivity. Ohanna's scholarly work has been published in the *Bulletin of Hispanic Studies*, the *Hispanic Review*, and the *Revista de Estudios Hispánicos*, among other journals. He is the author of *Cautiverio y convivencia en la edad de Cervantes*, and the first critical edition of *Los cautivos de Argel* by Lope de Vega.

ELENA RODRÍGUEZ-GURIDI (PhD in Spanish literature, University of Colorado–Boulder) is an associate professor of Spanish at Le Moyne College in Syracuse, New York. She has published several book chapters and articles on early modern Spanish literature in various journals, including *eHumanista*, the *Hispanic Review*, and *Neophilologus*. Rodríguez-Guridi is the author of *Exégesis del "error": Una reinterpretación de la praxis de escritura en "Libro de la vida," "Novelas ejemplares" y "Desengaños amorosos."*

FERNANDO RODRÍGUEZ MANSILLA (PhD in Spanish philology, Universidad de Navarra) is an associate professor of Spanish at Hobart and William Smith Colleges in Geneva, New York and an associate member of the Grupo de Investigación Siglo de Oro and Proyecto Estudios Indianos. He is the author of *Picaresca femenina de Alonso de Castillo Solórzano, El Inca Garcilaso en su Siglo de Oro*, and several articles on early modern Spanish literature. Rodríguez Mansilla received the Luis Andrés Murillo Award for the best article of 2014 by the Cervantes Society of America.

ANA M. RODRÍGUEZ-RODRÍGUEZ (PhD in Spanish literature, University of Wisconsin–Madison) is an associate professor specializing in early modern Spanish literature at the University of Iowa–Iowa City. She has published articles on a variety of topics, including Christian-Muslim relations in the Mediterranean, women's writing, and the Spanish Empire in Asia. In 2013 Rodríguez-Rodríguez published *Letras liberadas: Cautiverio, escritura y subjetividad de la época imperial española*, which explores Spanish captivity writings during the sixteenth and seventeenth centuries. She is currently writing a monograph about the Philippines during Spanish colonial rule of the archipelago, and is preparing a critical edition of the *Libro de cassos impensados* by Alonso de Salamanca.

CARRIE L. RUIZ (PhD in early modern Spanish literature, University of Colorado–Boulder) is an associate professor of Spanish at Colorado College in Colorado

Springs. She is coeditor of *Transitions: Journal of Franco-Iberian Studies* and has published her work in several edited collections, including *Baroque Projections: Images and Texts in Dialogue with the Early Modern Hispanic Worlds*, and in journals such as *Letras Peninsulares, Neophilologus, Viator: Medieval and Renaissance Studies*, and the *Western Humanities Review*. She is currently preparing an edited volume on the myths and legends of Spain.

Index